# Lecture Notes in Computer Science 8279

Commenced Publication in 1973
Founding and Former Series Editors:
Gerhard Goos, Juris Hartmanis, and Jan van Leeʋ

Shalini R. Urs    Jin-Cheon Na
George Buchanan (Eds.)

# Digital Libraries: Social Media and Community Networks

15th International Conference
on Asia-Pacific Digital Libraries, ICADL 2013
Bangalore, India, December 9-11, 2013
Proceedings

 Springer

Volume Editors

Shalini R. Urs
University of Mysore
International School of Information Management, Mysore, India
E-mail: shalini@isim.ac.in

Jin-Cheon Na
Nanyang Technological University
Wee Kim Wee School of Communication and Information, Singapore
E-mail: tjcna@ntu.edu.sg

George Buchanan
City University London
School of Informatics, London, UK
E-mail: george.buchanan.1@city.ac.uk

ISSN 0302-9743                              e-ISSN 1611-3349
ISBN 978-3-319-03598-7                      e-ISBN 978-3-319-03599-4
DOI 10.1007/978-3-319-03599-4
Springer Cham Heidelberg New York Dordrecht London

Library of Congress Control Number: 2013953392

CR Subject Classification (1998): H.3.7, H.3, H.2, H.5, I.2, H.4, I.7, J.1

LNCS Sublibrary: SL 3 – Information Systems and Application,
incl. Internet/Web and HCI

*Typesetting:* Camera-ready by author, data conversion by Scientific Publishing Services, Chennai, India

Printed on acid-free paper

Springer is part of Springer Science+Business Media (www.springer.com)

# Preface

## Digital Libraries: A Conceptualization

Since its birth in the early 1990s, the field of digital libraries (DL) has evolved and changed its focus and contour from digital repositories to dynamic spaces for user engagement. The DL field has developed and matured significantly since the early successes of the National Science Foundation (NSF), U.S. digital library programs – Digital Library Initiative-1 (DLI-1) and Digital Library Initiative-2 (DLI-2) (http://www.nsf.gov/news/special_reports/cyber/digitallibraries.jsp). The first six major projects funded by the NSF set in motion the popular conceptions of digital libraries. The success stories of the first decade of DL research, include the "Google" which is a spin-off of the research projects at the Stanford University database group, one of the six DLI-1 projects. Some believe that these six projects—though exciting and very successful, were essentially experiments, and did not really resemble libraries. At the end of the first decade of the domain, there were still concerns about the differing disciplinary perspectives on DL and developing a comprehensive definition that encapsulates the richness of the differing perspectives was felt and led to the DELOS manifesto (2007), which laid the framework for a more comprehensive envisioning of a Digital Library as a tool at the centre of intellectual activity having no logical, conceptual, physical, temporal, or personal borders or barriers on information (http://www.dlib.org/dlib/march07/castelli/03castelli.html).

Over the years, the notion of DL has moved from a content-centric system that simply organizes and provides access to particular collections of data and information, to a person-centric system that aims to provide interesting, novel, personalized experiences to users. This new vision of digital library corresponds to the notion of dynamic information spaces inhabited by connected communities and bound by best practices of user interactions and experiences.

## Social Media and Community Networks

One of the challenges that digital libraries faced since inception is the oft-asked question "if we build it, will they come?" "The big challenge is to provide a platform for engagement and conversation" says Bob Schrier and according to him the challenge is much more than at a regular brick-and-mortar library, where one is naturally engaged because you're engaged with the space. In the digital world, it is different and more difficult, especially when compared with Google, Facebook, and other information spaces. (http://www.dlib.org/dlib/july11/schrier/07schrier.html).

Social media offers a platform and enormous opportunities for user engagement. Since its emergence in 2004, social media has become not just a rage but also an integral part of our daily lives and professional activities. Organizations—academic, government, and corporates, are increasingly veering towards social media for not only reaching out to but also to engage with their customers and other stakeholders. Libraries are no exceptions and libraries across the world are using social media to promote services, highlight resources, integrate access, and to listen to the voices of their users. Libraries—the traditional agencies for building local communities of practice, are finding new ways to build virtual communities with the help of the social media and its tools.

The power of the social media—if deployed strategically and tactically, will help digital libraries to move beyond collections and information retrieval systems to be the ultimate democratic information spaces built on the principles of co-creation and crowdsourcing. Social media for building digital libraries is not just a leap of faith or a paradigm change, but essentially a broader epistemological shift.

## The ICADL Series

Following its birth in the mid-1990s, the digital library movement has spread and spawned three significant and vibrant international conferences series—the Joint Conference on Digital Libraries (JCDL, http://www.jcdl.org) in the US, the European Conference on Digital Libraries, now renamed the Theory and Practice of Digital Libraries (TPDL, http://www.tpdl.eu/), and the International Conference on Asian Digital Libraries (ICADL, http://www.icadl.org). The three conferences help create stimulating and collegial forums for reporting significant digital library research and development activities.

ICADL 2013 is the fifteenth in the series of conference series which began in 1998, rotating among the Asia-Pacific countries like Hong Kong, Taiwan, Korea, India, Singapore, Malaysia, China, Thailand, Japan, Vietnam, Indonesia, and Australia and has become one of the premier meetings in digital libraries.

ICADL 2013 received a good response for its call for papers on the theme of "Social Media and Community Networks" from across different countries of the world. True to its origins and characteristics, the papers were authored by a multidisciplinary group of academics and experts. The topics covered by the papers included areas such as ontologies to mining social networks to document classification. We had a total of eighty seven submissions and after the due process of refereeing, fifteen full papers, six short papers, and ten poster presentations have been accepted.

We are happy to present to you this volume comprising of the thirty-one papers, which are essentially contributions of a total of one hundred and one authors.

December 2013

Shalini R. Urs
Jin-Cheon Na
George Buchanan

# Organization

## General Co-chairs

N. Balakrishnan      Indian Institute of Science, India
Shalini R. Urs      University of Mysore, India

## Program Co-chairs

Abhinanda Sarkar      MYRA School of Business, India
Jin-Cheon Na      Nanyang Technological University, Singapore
George Buchanan      City University London, UK

## Workshop and Doctoral Student Consortium Co-chairs

Shigeo Sugimoto      University of Tsukuba, Japan
Gobinda Chowdhury      Northumbria University, UK
Unmil Karadkar      University of Texas, USA
Mandar R. Mutalikdesai      University of Mysore, India

## Publicity Co-chairs

P.Y. Rajendrakumar      Department of Public Libraries, Karnataka
H.S. Siddamallaiah      National Institute of Mental Health and
     Neurosciences, Bangalore, India

## Financial Co-chairs

N.V. Sathyanarayana      Informatics India Ltd., Bangalore, India

## Local Co-chairs

Anand Byrappa      Knowledge Centre, Bangalore, India
B.M. Meera      Raman Research Institute, Bangalore, India

## Program Committee

Sally Jo Cunningham      Waikato University, New Zealand
Ee-Peng Lim      Singapore Management University, Singapore
Edie Rasmussen      University of British Columbia, Canada

# Abstracts of Keynote

# From Crowd-Sourcing to Concept Mining

Ian H. Witten

University of Waikato, New Zealand
ihw@cs.waikato.ac.nz

**Abstract.** The technology of crowd-sourced collaborative editing is gradually shifting the curation of our society's knowledge treasury from academia (who, at least in Europe, seized control from the Church several hundred years ago) to the public sphere – a development that was foreshadowed by the American philosopher CS Pierce 150 years ago.

Enormous repositories of interlinked knowledge in the form of text, epitomized by Wikipedia, constitute comprehensive knowledge bases that promise to revolutionize our techniques for automatic understanding of documents. Researchers in artificial intelligence have long yearned for large, general-purpose, common sense knowledge bases, but they want them to be highly structured, typically as formal ontologies. Can a casual hyperlinking structure (as exemplified by Wikipedia) be used to support better natural language processing?

The answer is yes. This talk will explain how it is possible to automatically produce a semantic representation of any document in terms of the concepts contained in a hyperlinked textual knowledge repository. The process involves associating phrases in the document with concepts in the repository, disambiguating them with respect to the context in which they appear, and selecting a focused set of pertinent concepts that accurately represents the document's content.

Applications are legion, wherever textual documents are processed. They include text search, index term selection, keyphrase extraction, document similarity measures, document clustering and classification, and the production of back-of-the-book indexes.

# Digital Library: The National Library Board of Singapore's Experience

Ping Wah Chan [1] and Lek Choh Ngian [2]

[1] Assistant Chief Executive, Technology and Innovation
[2] Deputy Chief Executive, National Library, Archives and Collections
National Library Board, Singapore
{Pingwah,Lekchoh@nlb.gov.sg}

**Abstract.** The National Library Board (NLB) of Singapore has been providing an online access to its digital resources for nearly 20 years now. Since it became a statutory board in 1995, efforts were intensified to increase the richness and extend the reach of its digital content and services. The first few years were focused on bringing access to internet to its users.

Starting in the early 2000, earnest efforts were made to create more digital content to bring the NLB resources to its users in a more intuitive and convenient manner. One of the first databases created was called Singapore Infopedia which comprises curated articles written by librarians, based on frequently asked questions received on Singapore. Over the years, the NLB learnt valuable lessons in curating and packaging useful content and putting them out in microsites for easier search and find through Internet search engines, itself a learning journey.

The past 5 years saw concerted efforts in digitising valuable Singapore content for digital access, 24 by 7, and using social media to reach out to users who may not come to its physical libraries. In total, some 30 newspapers in the various languages were digitised and complete runs of these were put out to users for online use, from all over the world.

Three years ago, the NLB started a national project called the Singapore Memory Project (SMP) to collect personal memories of anyone who had experience with Singapore to contribute to the library's heritage collection. To date, some one million personal memories have been collected. These complement the documentary heritage materials that the NLB has developed over the years. Social media was used in a big way to publicise the SMP and also to create a buzz, to attract more contributions.

These efforts have brought the NLB results which have been very encouraging, spurring the board to do more to use digital platforms and social media to reach communities beyond its physical libraries, and to build physical and virtual communities to create greater value for its stakeholders.

# Table of Contents

# Collaboration and Communities

# Analysing Social Media and Social Networks

# Mobile Devices and Services

# Metadata and Information Extraction

# Manhattan Based Hybrid Semantic Similarity Algorithm for Geospatial Ontologies

K. Saruladha[1], E. Thirumagal[1], J. Arthi[1], and G. Aghila[2]

[1] Pondicherry Engineering College, Department of Computer Science and Engineering,
Puducherry, India
[2] Pondicherry University, Department of Computer Science and Engineering,
Puducherry, India
charusanthaprasad@yahoo.com,
{tmagaleng,arthighp}@gmail.com, aghila.csc@pondiuni.edu.in

**Abstract.** The interest on the geo-spatial information system is increasing swiftly, which leads to the development of the competent information retrieval system. Among the several semantic similarity models, the existing models such as Geometric Model characterizes the geo-spatial concept using their dimensions (i.e. properties) and the Network Model, using their spatial relations which has yielded less precision. For retrieving the geo-spatial information efficiently, the dimensions and the spatial relations between the geo-spatial concepts must be considered. Hence this paper proposes the Hybrid Model which is the concoction of the Geometric Model's dimensions and the Network Model's relations using the Manhattan distance method for computing semantic distance between geo-spatial query concept and the related geo-spatial concept in the data sources. The results and analysis illustrates that the Hybrid Model using Manhattan distance method could yield better precision, recall and the relevant information retrieval. Further the Manhattan Based Similarity Measure (MBSM) algorithm is proposed which uses the Manhattan Distance Method for computing the semantic similarity among the geo-spatial concepts which yields 10% increase in precision compared to the existing semantic similarity models.

**Keywords:** Geospatial information retrieval, Hybrid Model, Euclidean distance, Manhattan distance, Dimensions, Spatial relations, Conceptual contexts.

## 1 Introduction

Geospatial information system [1] plays a major role to help people to gather and examine the related spatial data. The geo-spatial information system has its application in managing floodplains, land acquisition, agricultural lands, water quality management, etc. Hence the geo-spatial system must be designed in a way to afford sufficient knowledge representations and also the semantic similarity measures. The geo-spatial ontology is used to capture the knowledge about the geo-spatial domain.

The geo-spatial concepts are characterized by the dimensions and the spatial relations. The dimensions [1] are the properties or the characteristics that describe the

S.R. Urs, J.-C. Na, and G. Buchanan (Eds.): ICADL 2013, LNCS 8279, pp. 1–10, 2013.

geo- spatial concept. Some significant examples of dimensions are elevation, gradient and altitude difference. The spatial relation specifies the relationship between the features of two geo-spatial concepts. Some key examples of spatial relations are next to, is a, connected to, adjacent to and in. For retrieving the geo-spatial information efficiently both the dimensions and the spatial relations must be considered.

The various existing semantic similarity models reported in literature are discussed in this paper. Those semantic similarity models consider either the dimensions or the spatial relations which have achieved less precision when used for geo-spatial information retrieval system. Those semantic similarity models which are used for computation of semantic similarity using the existing methods have certain limitations. Hence Schwering [2] proposed the existing Hybrid Model using the Euclidean distance method for computing the semantic similarity [3] between the query concept and the related geo-spatial concepts which does not yield better precision and recall and could not retrieve the information efficiently.

So this paper proposes the Hybrid Model that uses the Manhattan distance method [4] to calculate the semantic similarity between the geo-spatial concepts. Further the Manhattan Based Similarity Measure (MBSM) algorithm has been designed and its detailed design is depicted. This paper further explains the related works and their drawbacks in section II. The existing Hybrid Model and its implementation are described in section III. In section IV, the Proposed Hybrid Model and its sample calculation are explained. In section V, the experimental results and analysis are discussed. In section VI, the conclusions derived and the future enhancements are mentioned.

## 2    Related Works

This section discusses the related semantic similarity models and its drawbacks. The **Geometric Model** considers the dimensions alone for retrieving the related geo-spatial concepts for the given query concept. The Geometric Model uses the Minkowski semantic similarity measure [5] which uses the Euclidean distance method for computing the semantic distance among the geo-spatial concepts. The drawback of this model is that it computes only the semantic distance and the similarity judgment cannot be made i.e. it cannot state whether the retrieved geo-spatial concept is similar to the query concept or not. The **Feature Model** uses the dimensions alone to describe the geo-spatial concept like the Geometric Model. Rodriguez and Egenhofer [6] proposed the Matching Distance Similarity Measure for the Feature Model to compute the semantic distance. Based on the matching features of query and the related geo- spatial concept, the similarity judgment is made. The limitation of this model is that if there are large numbers of features, the matching of the features will not afford better semantic similarity measurement.

The **Network Model** considers the spatial relations for describing the geo-spatial concepts. Rada et al [7] proposed the graph theory and the semantic network for representing the knowledge. The limitation of this model is that the path length between the geo-spatial concepts is considered for computing the semantic distance and the computation of semantic neighborhood is an extra step. The Alignment **Model** considers only the relations for describing the geo-spatial concepts. For this model, Goldstone [8] introduced Similarity, Interactive Activation, and Mapping (SIAM) model for computing the semantic distance between the geo-spatial concepts. The alignable features between the concepts are found and its match values are obtained for computing the semantic   distance. The drawback of this model is that there is a possibility of two concepts can map to the singe concept which leads to inconsistency.

The **Transformational Model** computes semantic similarity by the number of changes that are made in transforming one geo-spatial concept to another geo-spatial concept. Based on the number of changes made the similarity judgment is made. When the number of changes is more, then the geo-spatial concept is said to be less similar. When the number changes made are less, then the geo-spatial concept is said to be more similar. Levenshtein [9] edit distance is the most eminent transformation-al semantic similarity measure which uses three changes or transformations namely deletion of letter in the word, insertion of letter in the word and replacement of letters in the word. The    limitation of this model is that the semantic distance computation alone is made. The image retrieval application [10] is evaluated using five histo-grams namely RGB  histogram [11], Jain and Vailaya's histogram [12] implementa-tion, an HSV-based histogram [13], an HSV-based histogram with soft decision [14] and the histogram used in the QBIC system [15]. For each type of this histogram two distance measures such as Euclidean distance and Manhattan distance are used for image retrieval and from which the Manhattan distance method have yielded good precision. The next section discuss in detail about the existing Hybrid Model.

## 3    Existing Hybrid Model

This section discuss about the existing Hybrid Model [2] which uses the Euclidean distance method for computing the semantic distance which is the mixture of the Ge- ometric Model's dimensional computation and the Network Model's relational com- putation. This model combines the knowledge representation of the Geometric Mod- el's conceptual space and the knowledge representation of the Network Model's semantic network.

**Concept Hulls (CoHu) similarity measure:** This semantic similarity measure pro-poses an approach for comparing two geo-spatial concept hulls [3]. For each dimensional point on the query concept hull one matching dimensional point of the compared geo-spatial concept is chosen. Hence the semantic similarity computation problem is reduced to the semantic distance computation between dimensional points. For each dimensional point $q_i$ of the query concept hull Q 'river' the search is made for obtaining the matching dimensions of related geo-spatial concept C 'lake' with the smallest distance. The semantic similarity distance of the matching dimensional points between the query concept hull Q and the related geo-spatial concept hull is given by $D_i$ as shown in Fig. 1. The Euclidean distance between two dimensions in an n-dimensional space is given by Minkowski Distance Metrics. For the Query concept Q, the dimensions are $a_1, a_2 \ldots a_n$ and the dimensions for the related concepts are $b_1, b_2 \ldots b_n$. For each dimension of the Q and R, the Euclidean distance method is used. For i = 1 to $n$, the semantic distance between the query concept Q and the related concept R is given by equation (1).

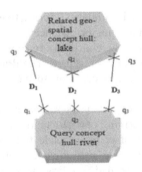

**Fig. 1.** Conceptual Hull

$$\text{Semanticdist} = \{[|a_1 - b_1|^r]^{1/r} + \ldots \ldots \ldots + [|a_n - b_n|^r]^{1/r}\}^{1/r} \tag{1}$$

When the semantic distance between the query concept and the related concept is less, then the concept is said to be more similar and vice versa. The limitations of Hybrid Model using Euclidean distance measure are it could not yield better precision and recall. On keeping these limitations of existing Hybrid model in mind, the new Hybrid Model is proposed using the Manhattan distance method for which the design principles are discussed.

The design principles of the proposed Hybrid model are:

- The Hybrid semantic similarity model combines the advantages of the Geometric Model and the Network Model. The existing Hybrid semantic similarity model uses Euclidean distance method to compute the semantic distance between the query concept and the retrieved related geo-spatial concept which does not yield better precision and recall. Hence this paper proposes the Manhattan distance method for computing the semantic distance between the query concept and the retrieved concept. The sample calculation and result and analysis illustrate the efficiency of the proposed Hybrid Model.

- Manhattan distances when used for image retrieval application have yielded better results. A Hybrid Model with the Manhattan distance has not been attempted for the geo-spatial applications. Hence this paper have attempted to design a Hybrid semantic similarity model with the Manhattan distance method to compute the semantic distance which could improve precision, recall and the retrieval of relevant information. The next section discuss about the geo-spatial ontology and the datasource.

## 4     Proposed Hybrid Model

This section focuses on the design of the proposed Hybrid Model, evaluation metrics and comparison of the existing system with proposed system. The detailed design and algorithm of the proposed model are also discussed. As the Hybrid Model is the combination of the geometric and the feature model, this model enables the concept to be described using the dimensions of the concept as well as the relations of the concept. In the hybrid model the N-dimensional problem is reduced to one dimensional problem. In order to improve the precision and recall of Geo-spatial In- formation systems Manhattan distance method [4], [10] is used to estimate the seman- tic distance between the Geo-spatial concepts. In this proposed Hybrid model, the se- mantic distance is computed by considering the matched query concept and its associated relations and sub relations. The next section discuss about the detailed de- sign of proposed MBSM algorithm.

## 4.1 Detailed Design of MBSM Algorithm

This section discuss about MBSM algorithm. The MBSM algorithm is **Manhattan Based Similarity Measure** algorithm which uses the Manhattan Distance method to increase the precision and recall. For the query given by the user and the Geo - spatial Concept in datasource all the dimensions are obtained. All the matching and non- matching dimensions of the Query given by the user and Geo-spatial Concept in data source are obtained. The Manhattan distance method is used for computing semantic similarity between the Geo-spatial concepts. The general Manhattan distance [10] is given by equation (2).

$$\text{Manhattan distance} = |a_1 - b_1| + |a_2 + b_2| + \ldots + |a_n + b_n| \tag{2}$$

In the general Manhattan distance given by equation (2), $a_1, a_2, \ldots a_n$ and $b_1, b_2, \ldots b_n$ are the points in the N- dimensional space. The MBSM algorithm uses Manhattan distance method to compute semantic distance which could improve the precision , recall and the information retrieval as shown in the Fig.3. For the query concept given, the related geo-spatial concepts are retrieved from the ontology. The quantitative dimensions of the query concept given, the related geo-spatial concepts are obtained from shared vocabulary. With the quantitative dimensions the matching and non-matching relations and dimensions are computed and the semantic distance is computed by considering the dimensions and the relations. The matching dimensions of the query concept and the related datasource geo-spatial concept are computed using Manhattan distance which is given by equation (3).

$$\text{Manhattan distance} = |qd_1 - dd_1| + |qd_2 - dd_2| + \ldots + |qd_n - dd_n| \tag{3}$$

where qd is quantitative query dimensions and dd is quantitative datasource dimensions. If one geo-spatial concept has a particular dimension and the related geo-spatial concept does not have the same dimension, then it is said to be non–matching dimension. The non-matching dimensional values aggregated between two geo-spatial concepts is said to be standardized distance. The non-matching dimensional values between two geo-spatial concepts is said to be standardized distance. The dimensional semantic distance is given by equation (4).

$$\text{Dimensional\_semantic\_distance} = \alpha * \text{Standardised\_distance} + \beta * \text{Manhattan\_distance} \tag{4}$$

Likewise for the relations, the relational semantic distance is computed which is given by equation (5).

$$\text{Relational\_semantic\_distance} = \alpha * \text{Standardised\_distance} + \beta * \text{Manhattan\_distance}. \tag{5}$$

The ratio α is chosen for the non-matching dimensions of the geo-spatial concepts and the ratio β is chosen for the matching dimensions. The α and β values ranges from 0 to 1. The experiments are conducted by considering various values of α and β. It is found that the values of 0.8 and 0.2 of α and β yields better result. The semantic distances among the geo-spatial concepts are given by equation (6).

Semantic_dist=|Dimensional_semantic_distance-Relational_semantic_distance|    (6)

The next section discusses the sample calculation for the proposed MBSM algorithm.

## 4.2    Semantic Similarity Computation Using Manhattan Distance of MBSM Algorithm

Consider the hydrological query concept to be 'river' the related concepts retrieved from geo-spatial ontology are dam, floodplain, sea, pool, pond, etc., is given in the form of tree as shown in the Fig.2.

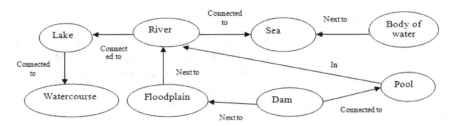

**Fig. 2.** Sample Tree containing the related concepts of the query concept 'river'

MBSM algorithm (Q, O, S, D) // O is the ontology, S is the Shared Vocabulary, D is the data-source.
Input: Query concept Q
Output: Retrieval of semantically similar concepts
1. Pre-processing of the Query concept Q
2. The related concepts from datasource D are retrieved.
3. The quantitative dimensions and relations of the Query concept and the related geo-spatial concepts are obtained from the shared vocabulary S.
4. repeat
5. repeat
     If the quantitative_query_dimensions and datasource_concepts_dimensions are matching
     then
6. Compute Manhattan_distance = $|qd_1-dd_1|+|qd_2-dd_2|.........|qd_n-dd_n|$  //qd is quantitative query dimensions and dd is quantitative datasource dimensions.
7. else
8. Compute standardized_distance //the concept which has dimension is standard- ized distance.
9.    end if
10. Dimensional_semantic_distance=α*standardised_distance+β*manhattan_distance.
11. Until all quantitative_dimensions are matched.
12. Repeat

**Fig. 3.** Proposed MBSM Algorithm

13. if the quantitative_query_relations and datasource_concepts_relations matching
14. then
   Compute Manhattan_distance = |qr1-dr1|+|qr2-dr2|.........|qrn-drn| //qr is Quantitative query dimensions and dr is quantitative related datasource concept dimensions.
15. Else
16. Consider standardised_distance//the concept which has dimension is
17. Standardized distance.
18.   end if
19.   Relational_semantic_distance = α* standardised_distance + β* manhattan_distance.
20.   Until all quantitative_relations are matched
21.   Until all extracted concepts from datasource D are considered.
22.   Semantic_dist=|Dimensional_semantic_distance - Relational_semantic_distance|
23.   Compute precision and recall where,
   precision = |relc ∩ retc|/ retc, recall = |relc ∩ retc|/ relc. // relc is relevant concepts and retc is retrieved concepts.

**Fig. 3.** (*continued*)

The experiments done in this work takes 21 dimensions. For the sample calculation three dimensions are considered and their corresponding dimensional value for the geo-spatial concept is tabulated shown in the Table 1.

**Table 1.** Dimensional Values of the Geo-Spatial Concepts

| Concepts | Dimensions | | | |
|---|---|---|---|---|
| | Elevation(meters) | Gradient (%) | Altitude ence(meters) | Differ- |
| River | 6 | 79 | 8 | |
| Floodplain | 9 | 45 | 5 | |
| Sea | 8 | 77 | 9 | |
| Dam | 8 | 78 | 6 | |
| Lake | 3 | 78 | 6 | |
| Body of water | 1 | 56 | 6 | |
| Watercourse | 2 | 78 | 8 | |
| Pool | 5 | 89 | 6 | |

### 4.2.1 Semantic Similarity Computation Using Manhattan Distance Method

In this sample, all the dimensions between the query concept and the related concept are matching. There are no non-matching dimensions and hence the standardized distance will be zero multiplied to α. Assume α and β values to be 0.8 and 0.2 which yields better precision and recall. The semantic distance between the query concept river and the related concept floodplain is computed here using equations (3), (4), (5). The dimensions of river and floodplain are considered. Dimensional_semantic_distance = α*0+β*[|6|0-950|+|79-45|+|80-54|] = 80. The dimensions of floodplain and dam are considered as the related concept of floodplain is d a m. Relational_semantic_distance =α*0+0.2[|950-890|+|45-78|+|54-67|] =21.2. The semantic distance between the geo-spatial concept river and the related concept is computed by considering the dimensions and the relations. Semantic_dist (river, floodplain) =|80-21.2| = 58.8/10 =5.88. The semantic distance between the query concept river and the related geo-spatial concept Sea is computed here. Dimensional_semantic_distance = $\alpha*0+\beta*[|610-800|+|79-77|+|80-90|]$ = 40.4. The dimensions of Sea and body of water are considered as the related concept of sea is body of water. Relational_semantic_distance =$\alpha*0+0.2[|800-1100|+|77-56|+|90-67|]$ =68.8. The semantic distance between the geo-spatial concept river and the related concept is computed by considering the dimensions and the relations. Semantic_dist (river, sea) = |40.4 – 68.8| = 28.4/10 = 2.84. The semantic distance between the query concept river and the related concept lake is computed here. Likewise the semantic distance between the query concept and all its related geo-spatial concepts are computed. The semantic distance between river and floodplain, sea, lake and pool is computed whose values are 5.88, 2.84 3.82 and 5.36 respectively. The geo-spatial concepts with less semantic distance is said to be more similar and the geo-spatial concepts with more semantic distance is said to be less similar. Here the semantic distance between river and sea is less so the most similar geo-spatial concept to the query concept is sea. The semantically similar geo-spatial concepts will be retrieved for the query c o n c e p t   given.

## 5    Experimental Results and Analysis

This section discusses the experimental results of the Hybrid Model with the Euclidean distance method and the Manhattan distance method. For conducting experiments, the OS MasterMap datasource is used. For viewing and using the OS- MasterMap data, OS GML viewer is used. The JDK platform is used with the Net- beans 7.2.1. About 108 hydrological concepts are considered for conducting exper- iments. The performance of the Euclidean and the Manhattan distance measure is measured using the metrics precision and recall. The precision and the recall are cal- culated for various similarity thresholds. Fig.4 depicts the precision for the Hydrological query concept River for various similarity thresholds 2, 3, 4 and 5 when using Eucli- dean distance method are 0.22, 0.4, 0.55, and 0.82 respectively. The precision in- creases with the increase of the similarity threshold. Fig.5 depicts the recall for the Hydrological query concept River for various similarity thresholds 2, 3, 4 and 5 when using Euclidean distance method are 1, 1, 1 and 0.69 respectively. Fig.6 depicts the precision for various similarity thresholds when using Manhattan distance me- thod. For the Hydrological query concept River the precisions are 0.3, 0.5, 0.6, and 0.91 for the similarity thresholds 2, 3, 4 and 5 respectively. Fig.7 depicts the re- call for various similarity thresholds when using Manhattan distance method. For the Hydrological query concept River the recalls are 1, 0.82, 0.72 and 0.46 for the simi- lar- ity thresholds 2, 3, 4 and 5 respectively. From Fig.4 and 5 it is implied that the Euclid- ean distance method can yield the maximum precision of 80%. From the Fig.6 and 7 it is inferred that Manhattan distance method can yield the maximum precision of 90% when the similarity threshold is 5. For most of the tested concepts, the simi- larity threshold of 5 has yielded maximum precision and recall. Hence the number of the relevant concepts retrieved is more when using the Manhattan distance method than the Euclidean distance method.

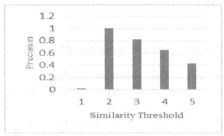

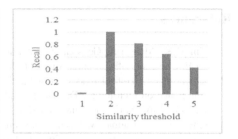

**Fig. 4.** Precision when using Euclidean Distance Method

**Fig. 5.** Recall when using Euclidean Distance Method

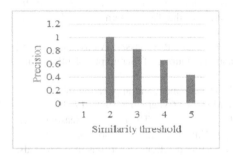

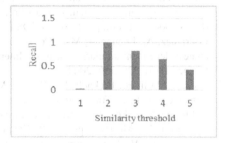

**Fig. 7.** Recall when using Manhattan Distance Method

**Fig. 6.** Precision when using Manhattan Distance Method

## 6 Conclusions and Future Enhancement

In this paper, the existing computational models for estimating semantic similarity between the Geo-spatial concepts are discussed. This paper provides an overview on the drawbacks of the various computational models and depicts how well the Hybrid Model works. In order to improve the information retrieval, the Hybrid model which uses both the properties and relations to describe the Geospatial concept is used. The Euclidean distance is used for measuring the semantic similarity between Geo-spatial concepts which leads to more number of computations and does not yield better precision and recall. So the latest Manhattan distance method has been proposed for easier and efficient computation and also it provides better precision and recall for tested Geo-spatial concepts. Further the MBSM algorithm is proposed and its detailed description is specified. The other semantic similarity distance measures such as Hirst and orge measure, Sussna distance measure and Wu palmer distance measure can be tested for the geo-spatial domain and can depict the best semantic similarity computation measure for retrieving the geo-spatial information.

# References

1. Win, K.K.: Measuring Geospatial Semantic Similarity between Geospatial Entity Classes. IEEE, University of Computer Studies (2006)
2. Schwering, A.: Hybrid model for semantic similarity measurement. In: 4th International Conference on Ontologies, DataBases, and Applications of Semantics (ODBASE 2005), pp. 1449–1465. Springer, Agia Napa (2005)
3. Schwering, A., Raubal, M.: Measuring semantic similarity between geospatial conceptual regions. In: Rodríguez, M.A., Cruz, I., Levashkin, S., Egenhofer, M. (eds.) GeoS 2005. LNCS, vol. 3799, pp. 90–106. Springer, Heidelberg (2005a)
4. Hosseinabady, M., Nunez-Yanez: Run-time stochastic task mapping on a large scale network-on-chip with dynamically reconfigurable tiles. J.L. Computers & Digital Techniques, IET 6(1), 1–11 (2012), doi:10.1049/iet-cdt.2010.0097
5. Gärdenfors, P.: How to make the Semantic Web more semantic Formal Ontology in Information Systems. In: Vieu, L. (ed.) Proceedings of the Third International Conference (FOIS 2004), vol. 114, pp. 153–164. IOS Press (2004)
6. Rodríguez, A., Egenhofer, M.J.: Comparing geospatial entity classes: An asymmetric and context-dependent similarity measure. International Journal of Geographical Information Science 18(3), 229–256 (2004)
7. Rada, R., Mili, H., Bicknell, E., Blettner, M.: Development and application of metric on semantic nets. IEEE Transactions on Systems, Man, and Cybernetics 19(1), 17–30 (1989)
8. Goldstone, R.L., Son, J.: Similarity Cambridge Handbook of Thinking and Reasoning. K. Holyoak and R. Morrison, pp. 13–36. Cambridge University Press, Cambridge (2005)
9. Levenshtein, I.V.: Binary codes capable of correcting deletions, insertions, and reversals. Soviet Physics Doklady 10(8), 707–710 (1966)
10. Vadivel, A., Majumdar, A.K., Sural, S.: Performance comparison of distance metrics in content-based Image retrieval applications. Computer Science and Engineering, Indian Institute of Technology, Kharagpur, vadi@cc.iitkgp.ernet.in
11. Swain, M.J., Ballard, D.H.: Color Indexing. International Journal of Computer Vision 7(1), 11–32 (1991)
12. Jain, A., Vailaya, A.: Image Retrieval using Color and Shape. Pattern Recognition 29(8), 1233–1244 (1996)
13. Sural, S., Qian, G., Pramanik, S.: Segmentation and Histogram Generation using the HSV Color Space for Content Based Image Retrieval. In: IEEE Int. Conf. on Image Processing, Rochester, NY (2002)
14. Sural, S.: Histogram Generation from the HSV Color Space using Saturation Projection. In: Multimedia Systems and Content-based Image Retrieval. Idea Group Publishing, Hershey (2003) (in press)
15. Niblack, W., Barber, R., Equitz, W., Flickner, M., Glasman, E., Pektovic, D., Yanker, P., Faloutsos, C., Taubin, G.: The QBIC Project: Querying Images by Content using Color Texture and Shape. In: Proc. SPIE Int. Soc. Opt. Eng., in Storage and Retrieval for Image and Video Databases, vol. 1908, pp. 173–187 (1993)

# Bridging the Gap – Using External Knowledge Bases for Context-Aware Document Retrieval

Benjamin Köhncke[1], Patrick Siehndel[1], and Wolf-Tilo Balke[2]

[1] L3S Research Center; Hannover, Germany
[2] TU Braunschweig, Germany
{koehncke,siehndel}@L3S.de, balke@ifis.cs.tu-bs.de

**Abstract.** Today, a vast amount of information is made available over the Web in the form of unstructured text indexed by Web search engines. But especially for searches on abstract concepts or context terms, a simple keyword-based Web search may compromise retrieval quality, because query terms may or may not directly occur in the texts (vocabulary problem). The respective state-of-the-art solution is query expansion leading to an increase in recall, although it often also leads to a steep decrease of retrieval precision. This decrease however is a severe problem for digital library providers: in libraries it is vital to ensure high quality retrieval meeting current standards. In this paper we present an approach allowing even for abstract context searches (conceptual queries) with high retrieval quality by using Wikipedia to semantically bridge the gap between query terms and textual content. We do not expand queries, but extract the most important terms from each text document in a focused Web collection and then enrich them with features gathered from Wikipedia. These enriched terms are further used to compute the relevance of a document with respect to a conceptual query. The evaluation shows significant improvements over query expansion approaches: the overall retrieval quality is increased up to 74.5% in mean average precision.

**Keywords:** conceptual query, query expansion, semantic enrichment.

## 1   Introduction

Today's information gathering in many domains is almost entirely focused on Web searches. However, handling the growing amount of available information poses severe challenges even for focused information providers, such as digital libraries and archives. When searching for information, users usually describe their broad information needs with several keywords which are likely to be different from the words used in the actually relevant documents. As a consequence the results returned by the information provider may miss relevant documents with respect to the user's information needs. This leads to a dramatically decreased retrieval quality and thus a bad usage experience. To guarantee high quality retrieval it is therefore important to bridge the gap between the query terms and the documents' vocabulary. The challenge of expressing the user's information need by finding the right query terms is widely known as the vocabulary problem [1]. Users often try to solve this problem by

S.R. Urs, J.-C. Na, and G. Buchanan (Eds.): ICADL 2013, LNCS 8279, pp. 11–20, 2013.
© Springer International Publishing Switzerland 2013

refining their query, i.e. adding or changing query terms in case the retrieval results have not been satisfying [2]. However, considering scenarios where users are searching for information about abstract concepts the problem of word mismatch is even bigger: such abstract concepts or context terms hardly ever occur directly in Web documents. Imagine a user who is interested in *information retrieval*. By entering the conceptual query '*information retrieval*' he only receives documents dealing with this very general concept. Closely related and also relevant documents not containing the exact term, like, for instance, documents about *Web search*, will not be returned. This also holds for more specific conceptual queries, like, e.g., *polyomavirus infections* in the biomedical domain or searches for chemical classes, like, e.g., *alcohol*, in the domain of chemistry.

To solve this problem, in some domains documents are already pre-annotated with suitable context terms. The most prominent example is the MEDLINE corpus which is currently the largest document repository of life science and biomedical documents, containing more than 20 million publications. Each of these documents is manually annotated with several terms from the Medical Subject Heading (MeSH) ontology which offers a controlled vocabulary for indexing and retrieval purposes. However, document collections like MEDLINE are a rare case and most collections lack suitable context annotations. For most domain specific collections no suitable controlled vocabularies or even better, ontologies, are available.

The traditional way of searching for documents relevant for conceptual queries is to use query expansion. It expands the query term issued by a user with suitable related terms, called expansion terms, matching the documents' vocabulary. In general, query expansion leads to higher recall, but strongly decreases the retrieval precision. The reason is that usually the context of the query is not known and thus the expansion terms do not meet the user's search intention. More advanced retrieval models, like Latent Semantic Analysis (LSA), try to solve this by producing sets of concepts related to the documents and their contained terms. However, as we will see in our experiments, the resulting quality is still not sufficient. For digital library providers it is important to enable conceptual queries while also ensuring their high quality requirements. While the context of the query can hardly be determined, the context of each document is defined based on its contained terms. Thus, instead of expanding the query, the idea of this paper is to expand the documents with semantic annotations. To find suitable annotations for semantic enrichment external knowledge bases are necessary.

In previous work we have already shown the usefulness of Wikipedia categories to summarize documents' content [3]. Therefore, in the presented approach we use external knowledge provided by Wikipedia to semantically enrich documents, bridging the gap between conceptual queries and documents' vocabulary. We extract the most important terms from each document and enrich them with several semantic features gathered from Wikipedia. The enriched terms are used to compute the relevance of a document to a conceptual query. Our experiments show that our approach outperforms traditional query expansion methods using statistical query expansion, showing an increase of more than 30% in mean average precision. We also compare against stronger baselines using LSA and Random Indexing showing an improvement of more than 15%. All results have been proven to be statistically significant. Another advantage of our approach is that it can be easily integrated in the metadata enrichment process of a digital library.

The rest of the paper is organized as follows: In section 2 we give an overview of the related work, followed by a detailed description of our approach in section 3. The evaluation is presented in section 4. Finally, we conclude and give an outlook to our future work in section 5.

## 2 Related Work

One major problem of current information retrieval systems is their low retrieval quality caused by the inaccuracy of the query composed of a few keywords compared to the actual user information need. In case the user enters a query containing several topic-specific keywords the system is able to return good results, but in most cases queries are rather short and since language is inherently ambiguous this leads to worse retrieval results [4]. The most critical problem influencing the retrieval quality is the term mismatch problem (also known as the vocabulary problem [1]), meaning that the query terms chosen by the user are often different from the vocabulary used in the documents. In case of conceptual queries one possibility is to let users choose from a fixed set of context terms from a controlled vocabulary, like, e.g., provided by the MeSH ontology. In our scenario a conceptual query is defined as the search for documents relevant for an abstract concept, like, for instance, *Polyomavirus Infections* in the biomedical domain. In current search interfaces this context restriction is offered using facetted browsing, see, e.g., GoPubMed. Other approaches use controlled vocabularies to suggest suitable query terms to the user to avoid the vocabulary problem. In [5] such an approach is presented showing that discipline-specific search term recommendations improve the retrieval quality significantly.

In general, one well known method to overcome the term mismatch problem is automatic query expansion. A good summary of different query expansion approaches is given in [4]. Automatic query expansion approaches can be generally categorized into global and local analysis [6]. Global analysis is usually based on statistics of co-occurrences of pairs of words, resulting in a matrix of word similarities [7]. Although these approaches are relatively robust, the computation of the corpus-wide statistics is computational intensive. In contrast, local analysis uses only a subset of the returned documents for a given query to find suitable expansion terms. This kind of local feedback has the drawback that the documents retrieved in the initial search strongly influence the retrieval quality. These methods have, for instance, been evaluated on TREC datasets, see, e.g., [8] or [9]. Since these methods need to know which documents are relevant for a given query and pseudo relevance needs a multi-phase retrieval process they cannot be applied directly to commercial search engines. Therefore, recently a number of expansion approaches have been developed using query logs. Generally, these approaches also derive expansion terms from (pseudo-) relevant documents, which are extracted from search logs by analyzing user clicks, see, e.g., [10] or [11]. This approach is further extended in [12]. The authors replaced the correlation model with a statistical translation model which is trained on pairs of user queries and the titles of clicked documents. Furthermore, they translated the word-based translation model to a concept-based model. These concepts are used to expand the original query. However, also the idea of representing queries and documents as a set of related concepts rather than a bag of individual words is used in several approaches. The first necessary step is to identify the concepts in queries and documents. Afterwards, the concepts are introduced as hidden variables in the query expansion model to capture term dependencies.

Also methods like Latent Semantic Analysis (LSA) [13] can be used in the proposed scenario. LSA analyzes a set of documents to produce a set of concepts which are related to the documents and terms. The main idea behind this approach is that words which are used in the same context may have a similar meaning. These concepts are generated by applying singular value decomposition to a generated word-document matrix.

Other approaches try to use the knowledge of external information sources to enrich the user query [14], [15]. An interesting approach dealing with effective query formulation is presented in [16]. The authors present a unified framework trying to automatically optimize the use of different information sources for formulating the user query. The experimental results show better results than state-of-the-art baseline approaches performing concept weighting, query expansion or both.

In contrast to these approaches, in our approach we use external knowledge bases to enrich the documents with semantic annotations. In previous work we already analyzed the usefulness of Wikipedia as external source for semantic enrichment [3].

## 3      Semantic Enrichment Using Wikipedia

### 3.1   Architecture Overview

In this section we describe the architecture of our approach. The goal is to semantically enrich documents enabling conceptual queries. Our basic idea is to extract important terms from documents and use community maintained knowledge bases to compute the semantic similarity between these terms. Previous work used Wikipedia to help users finding relevant query terms and interactively guide them on their search [17]. In [3] we used Wikipedia categories to describe the content of chemical documents. Experiments showed that also for specialized domains like chemistry, knowledge gathered from Wikipedia is more useful for domain experts than a domain specific ontology. Since Wikipedia uses the wisdom of the crowds, which has been proven to provide tremendous quality [18], the contained knowledge is growing fast and updated regularly. In our approach we further exploit the provided knowledge by creating semantic features based on the Wikipedia categories and the link structure. Fig. 1 gives an overview of our approach.

The architecture is composed of two basic components. The term extractor is responsible for annotating and extracting important terms from the documents. For annotating the documents we use the Wikipedia Miner toolkit [19]. The main purpose of the Wikipedia Miner is to annotate a given fulltext in the same way a human would annotate a Wikipedia article. The methods are based on a machine learning approach which is used to identify relevant terms and links them to Wikipedia. The approach is two folded in the way that the first task is to disambiguate the terms which occur in a given text, and the second task is to check whether the detected terms are useful links to Wikipedia articles.

**Fig. 1.** Architecture Overview

The extracted terms are further processed by the semantic annotator. For each term its associated Wikipedia categories, and its in- and out-links are extracted. These features are used for computing the semantic similarity between different terms. The measures used for calculating the feature similarities are based upon the Jaccard coefficient and are described in detail in [20].

## 3.2    Retrieval Workflow

The user enters a query and submits it to our system. For retrieving a ranked list of relevant documents the system is composed of two components: the semantic annotator and the ranking engine. Fig. 2 gives an overview of the retrieval workflow.

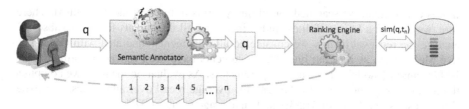

**Fig. 2.** Retrieval Workflow

The query term $q$ is analyzed by the semantic annotator which enriches it with the different similarity features extracted from Wikipedia. The ranking engine receives the enriched query term and creates a ranked list containing all other terms. In case $q$ is already known in our system the semantic similarity ranking is directly received from the relational database. Otherwise, it is necessary to compute the similarity to all terms known to the system. For our repository, containing 34324 different terms, the similarity computation for an unknown term took less than three seconds. Finally, the documents are ranked according to the similarity values of their contained terms. The relevance of a document $d$ to a query $q$ is computed as follows:

$$rel(q,d) = \frac{\left( \Sigma_{t \in q} \Sigma_{t_X \in T_d} \frac{sim(t_X,t) * \tau_{t_X}}{|T_d|} * \frac{\omega_{t_X}}{\Omega_{t_X}} \right)}{|q|} \qquad (1)$$

where $T_d$ is the set of all terms included in $d$ and $\tau$ is a boosting factor to give terms occurring in the document's title a higher weight. Each query $q$ can consist of several terms $t$. Furthermore, $\omega$ denotes the number of times a term occurs in a document. This value is normalized by the number of times the term occurs in the whole collection, denoted by $\Omega$. Finally, the score is normalized by the number of terms in $q$.

# 4     Evaluation

As document repository we use 122640 documents from the PUBMED Central corpus which is part of the MEDLINE repository. Each document in this set is manually annotated with several terms from the MeSH ontology which offers a controlled vocabulary for indexing and retrieval purposes. These terms are abstract concepts describing the general context of the respective document. Therefore, we also use MeSH terms as query terms in our experiments. To find a set of suitable query terms we analyzed the distribution of the MeSH terms in our document collection. As possible query terms we considered all terms occurring in less than 1000 but more than 10 documents. From this set we randomly choose 80 query terms which also occur in Wikipedia. As document set for the experiments we used all documents that have been annotated with at least one of these query terms. The MeSH annotation is done manually by domain experts resulting in high quality. Therefore, for our evaluations we considered all documents annotated with the respective MeSH term as relevant hits. In total our set contains 10791 documents.

## 4.1     Lucene Index, Statistical Query Expansion and Latent Semantic Analysis

In this experiment, we searched for all query terms in the documents' fulltext. Therefore, we created a Lucene fulltext index including all documents from our subset. To analyze the retrieval quality we considered all documents annotated with the respective MeSH term as relevant hits. The documents have been ranked according to the BM25 ranking model using standard parameters. As evaluation measure we computed the mean average precision (MAP) and the average recall over all queries. Our experiment results in a MAP of 31.53% and an average recall of 37%.

To enhance the MAP and the recall we also used a statistical query expansion method. We computed the term-to-term co-occurrence matrix based on the documents of our subset. The position of the term in the document is also taken into account, meaning two terms that are close together will get a higher score. Furthermore, we used popularity thresholds defining a required minimum and maximum popularity. Terms not fulfilling these thresholds are also not used as expansion terms. We used the following retrieval model: Let $q$ be the query term and $C=\{c_1,c_2,...,c_n\}$ the set of all expansion terms. For the expanded query the queries are formulated as $q$ OR $c_1$ OR $c_2$ OR ... OR $c_n$, meaning all documents are returned containing the query term or at least one expansion term. Finally, the query is expanded with the top-k co-occurring terms. Fig. 3a shows the results for the top-k expansion terms.

The best MAP of 40.28% is reached for the top-21 expansion terms. As expected, the more terms are added to the query the higher is the recall. The maximum recall of 81.91% is reached for the top-58 terms.

Beside query expansion we also evaluated how an LSA approach would perform in this scenario. To analyze the performance of an LSA based approach we used the Semantic Vectors[1] toolkit which is build upon Apache Lucene. We used LSA and

---

[1] https://code.google.com/p/semanticvectors

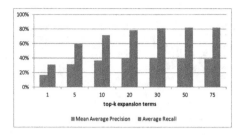 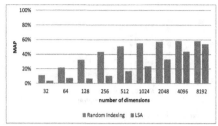

**Fig. 3.** MAP and average recall for the top-k expansion terms (a)MAP for Random Indexing and LSA (b)

Random Indexing for building the vectors for our corpus. Random Indexing is an alternative approach to standard word space models, which is efficient and scalable [21]. For both methods we used the standard parameters and varied the number of dimensions used for the vectors. We started with 32 dimensions and went up to 8192 dimensions. The resulting MAP of booth methods was continuously growing with an increase of the number of dimensions. We did not use a higher number of dimensions because of the runtime complexity and memory requirements for the resulting model. The results are shown in Fig. 3b. We see that the MAP based on Random Indexing is higher in all cases, reaching up to a maximum MAP of 58.2%. Using a very high number of dimensions we archive quite similar results using LSA (54.1%).

### 4.2    Semantic Enrichment Using Wikipedia

In this experiment we evaluate the usefulness of our approach for conceptual queries. For each document and each annotated term a confidence value has been computed describing the reliance of the assignment between Wikipedia article and term. We did two main experiments analyzing the influence of the confidence value. In the first one we computed the MAP using different confidence thresholds. In this experiment, for computing the relevance of a document to a query term only the assigned terms having a higher confidence value than the threshold are used. In the second main experiment we ordered the assigned terms for each document by their confidence values. For the relevance computation only the top-k terms for each document are used. Furthermore, in both experiments we also analyzed the influence of giving terms occurring in the document's title a higher weight. In addition, we also considered the number of times the term appears in the document in the ranking function. To do not prefer frequently used terms that are not descriptive for the respective document, we normalized this value by the number of times the term occurs in the whole collection. Since our method computes the relevance of a query to all documents in our set, the recall is always 100% and therefore not meaningful at all. To evaluate the different rankings and compare them to the baseline approaches we compute MAP.

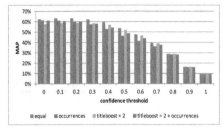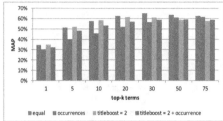

**Fig. 4.** MAP for varying confidence thresholds (a)MAP for top-k terms (b)

Fig. 4a shows the results for the confidence threshold experiment. A confidence threshold of 0 means that all terms have been used for the relevance computation. The results show that giving the terms occurring in the documents' title a higher score leads to a decrease of the MAP. We only show the results for a title boost factor of 2, meaning the title terms are twice as important as other terms. In our experiments we varied the boosting factor from 1 to 15. But, the higher the boosting factor the worse the results. Also the number of occurrences of a term does not lead to better overall results. The combination of title boost an occurrences leads to better results for smaller thresholds than using the features alone, but the overall best results are achieved if all terms are considered as equally important. The best MAP of 63.14% is reached for a confidence threshold of 0.1. The higher the threshold the fewer is the number of assigned terms for each document.

Fig. 4b shows the evaluation results for using the documents' top-k terms. We analyzed the distribution of assigned terms for the documents in our collection. Around 10% of the documents in our collection have more than 75 terms assigned. Therefore, we computed the MAP for up to the top-75 terms. Please note, we always used all documents and only limited the number of assigned terms. As in the confidence threshold experiment the best results are achieved if all terms are considered as equally important. Using a title boost factor or taking the number of occurrences into account does not lead to better retrieval results. The best MAP of 65.14% is reached for using the top-31 terms of each document. The MAP is slightly higher as for the confidence thresholds.

As last experiment we analyzed the different combinations of the features used in our similarity measure. Fig. 5 shows the results for the different combinations. This experiment shows that the categories are performing worst with a best MAP of 59% for the top-31 terms. The overall best MAP of 74.5% is reached for the top-61 terms using only the in-links feature.

Overall we showed that for conceptual queries the proposed method leads to better results than state-of-the-art retrieval models. The best baseline approach was Random Indexing achieving an MAP of 58.2%. Our approach significantly outperforms (p-value of 0.03 using a two-tailed t-test) the best baseline by achieving an MAP of 74.5%.

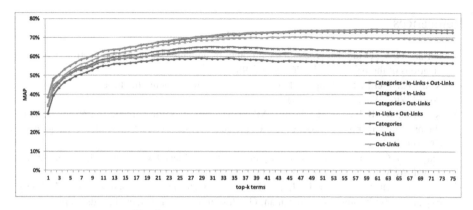

**Fig. 5.** Comparing MAP of different features

## 5    Summary and Outlook

One major problem digital library providers have to solve is the well-known vocabulary problem. Users often search for information using query terms not directly occurring in the documents. Considering conceptual queries this problem is even more
complicated. To allow for suitable document retrieval meeting the high quality standards of a digital library it is important to bridge the gap between the user's query
and the documents' fulltext. State-of-the-art solutions suggest using statistical query
expansion. More advanced approaches are based on LSA or LSI models. However,
especially for conceptual queries their retrieval quality is often still insufficient.

In this paper we presented an approach allowing for conceptual queries using external knowledge as provided by Wikipedia. We took a document collection from the
PubMed Central repository and extracted the most important terms from each document. These terms are semantically enriched with features gathered from Wikipedia.
Finally, the relevance of a document to a conceptual query is computed resulting in a
ranked retrieval list. Our evaluation has shown that our approach outperforms state-
of-the-art query expansion and LSA approaches resulting in an increase of the mean
average precision of 58.2% for LSA to 74.5% for our approach. All results have been
proven to be statistically significant (p-value of 0.03 using a two-tailed t-test). The
proposed method bridges the gap between user queries and documents' fulltext by
using external knowledge sources for semantic enrichment. To summarize, our results
show that even without manual annotating the retrieval quality can be improved meeting the high quality standards of a digital library.

For future work we plan to also consider other knowledge bases instead of Wikipedia to bridge the gap between conceptual queries and documents. Furthermore, we
plan to extend our approach with a personalization component to learn the best similarity measure dependant on the individual user.

# References

1. Furnas, G.W., et al.: The vocabulary problem in human-system communication. Communications of the ACM 30(11), 964–971 (1987)
2. Kraft, R., Zien, J.: Mining anchor text for query refinement. In: Proc. of Int. Conf. on World Wide Web, WWW (2004)
3. Köhncke, B., Balke, W.-T.: Using Wikipedia categories for compact representations of chemical documents. In: Proc. of Int. Conf. on Information and Knowledge Management, CIKM (2010)
4. Carpineto, C., Romano, G.: A Survey of Automatic Query Expansion in Information Retrieval. ACM Computing Surveys 44(1), 1–50 (2012)
5. Lüke, T., Schaer, P., Mayr, P.: Improving Retrieval Results with discipline-specific Query Expansion. In: Zaphiris, P., Buchanan, G., Rasmussen, E., Loizides, F. (eds.) TPDL 2012. LNCS, vol. 7489, pp. 408–413. Springer, Heidelberg (2012)
6. Xu, J., Croft, W.: Query expansion using local and global document analysis. In: Proc. of Int. Conf. on Research and Development in Information Retrieval, SIGIR (1996)
7. Jing, Y., Croft, W.: An association thesaurus for information retrieval. In: Proceedings of RIAO, pp. 1–15 (1994)
8. Cao, G., et al.: Selecting good expansion terms for pseudo-relevance feedback. In: Proc. of Int. Conf. on Research and Development in Information Retrieval, SIGIR (2008)
9. Metzler, D., Croft, W.B.: Latent concept expansion using markov random fields. In: Proc. of Int. Conf. on Research and Development in Information Retrieval, SIGIR (2007)
10. Cui, H., Wen, J., Nie, J., Ma, W.: Query expansion by mining user logs. IEEE Transactions on Knowledge and Data Engineering 15(4), 829–839 (2003)
11. Wang, X., Zhai, C.X.: Mining term association patterns from search logs for effective query reformulation. In: Proc. of Int. Conf. on Information and Knowledge Management, CIKM (2008)
12. Gao, J., Nie, J.: Towards Concept-Based Translation Models Using Search Logs for Query Expansion. In: Proc. of Int. Conf. on Inf. and Knowledge Management, CIKM (2012)
13. Deerwester, S., et al.: Indexing by Latent Semantic Analysis. Journal of the American Society for Information Science 41(6), 391–407 (1998)
14. Hu, J., Wang, G., Lochovsky, F., Sun, J., Chen, Z.: Understanding user's query intent with wikipedia. In: Proc. of Int. Conf. on World Wide Web, WWW (2009)
15. Xu, Y., et al.: Query dependent pseudo-relevance feedback based on wikipedia. In: Proc. of Int. Conf. on Research and Development in Information Retrieval, SIGIR (2009)
16. Bendersky, M., et al.: Effective query formulation with multiple information sources. In: Proc. of Int. Conf. on Web Search and Data Mining, WSDM (2012)
17. Milne, D., et al.: A knowledge-based search engine powered by wikipedia. In: Proc. of Int. Conf. on Information and Knowledge Management, CIKM (2007)
18. Surowiecki, J.: The Wisdom of Crowds: Why the Many Are Smarter Than the Few and How Collective Wisdom Shapes Business. Economies, Societies and Nations (2004)
19. Milne, D., Witten, I.H.: An open-source toolkit for mining Wikipedia. Artificial Intelligence 194, 222–239 (2012)
20. Köhncke, B., Balke, W.-T.: Context-Sensitive Ranking Using Cross-Domain Knowledge for Chemical Digital Libraries. In: Aalberg, T., Papatheodorou, C., Dobreva, M., Tsakonas, G., Farrugia, C.J. (eds.) TPDL 2013. LNCS, vol. 8092, pp. 285–296. Springer, Heidelberg (2013)
21. Sahlgren, M.: An Introduction to Random Indexing. In: Proc. of the Methods and Applications of Semantic Indexing Workshop (2005)

# TrieIR: Indexing and Retrieval Engine for Kannada Unicode Text*

Sumant Kulkarni** and Srinath Srinivasa

International Institute of Information Technology,
Bangalore, 26/C, Electronic City, Bangalore, India
{sumant,sri}@iiitb.ac.in

**Abstract.** Kannada is a phonetic language. In Kannada language, the morphological forms of terms (especially of nouns and verbs) are formed by adding different morphological suffixes to their pure forms. Hence, when queried for morphological forms, search engines based on exact matching fail to identify other semantically similar and morphologically different terms, and thus reduce the quality of the search results. We observe that even though the morphological forms of a term look different, they can be grouped together based on their common prefixes. In this work we propose fuzzy matching based indexing and retrieval algorithms. We propose an indexing mechanism inspired from prefix trees. We also derive our inspirations from the fact that the Unicode encodes the Kannada terms very similar to the way terms are generated using Kannada grammar. We also discuss a *query term truncation* and *decayed score* based retrieval algorithm for better retrieval of the documents for the given query. The indexing and retrieval systems still are based on the *tf-idf* based indexing and retrieval. However, the novelty of the work lies in the way the algorithms bring together the similar terms. This solution can be scaled to work for other South Indian languages with no or little modification as their Unicode encoding and morphological behaviors are similar to Kannada.

## 1 Introduction

Kannada is the Dravidian style language spoken in the South Indian state of Karnataka. According to 2001 census data, Kannada language is spoken by more than 38 million [1]people. There have been many portals [2] which host large amounts of the Kannada content. However, we argue that this data is being underutilized due to the unavailability of efficient indexing and search methodologies.

---

* This work is a part of Kanaja project, conceptualised by *Karnataka Jnana Ayoga*.
** The authors would like to thank Prof. S. Rajagopalan and Aditya Ramana Rachakonda for their valuable inputs.
[1] http://www.censusindia.gov.in/Census_Data_2001/
Census_Data_Online/Language/Statement1.aspx
[2] http://kanaja.in/, http://sampada.net/, http://kn.wikipedia.org

S.R. Urs, J.-C. Na, and G. Buchanan (Eds.): ICADL 2013, LNCS 8279, pp. 21–24, 2013.
© Springer International Publishing Switzerland 2013

Kannada is a phonetic agglutinative language [5]. In Kannada, both verbs and nouns have morphological form(MF)s which look different than the original term as well as the other MFs of the same term. Hence, when we use the strict term search for Kannada language, which matches only the given term, we can not match the other MFs. Even if the MFs are present, they will not be captured in quantities like term frequency(*tf*) [6]. This reduces the quality of the search results. Hence, a strict indexing and retrieval methodology, where only the given term is indexed independent of its morphologically related terms, can not work for Kannada text. In this paper, we propose a new indexing and retrieval mechanism for Kannada Unicode text. The indexing is inspired from *trie*(prefix tree), while the retrieval is done using query term truncate and decay score model.

There have been earlier attempts to understand non-English language IR [2,3,4,5]. A detailed related literature and our approach is available in the technical report [1]. In the further section( 2) we discuss our approach and evaluation. We conclude in section 3.

## 2   Indexing the Document Corpus

In indexing, our main aim is to bring together the different MFs of root term. As discussed, MFs of a term have a single common shorter prefix. However, there can be subsets of MFs having longer common prefixes. This characteristic feature of MFs inspired us to develop a *trie* based indexing mechanism.

A text corpus contains many documents. Each text document is made up of sequence of words. We parse each document in the corpus individually in to a *bag of words*. Then, each word is segmented as a set of core-letter and its dependent vowel. For example, the term *beTTagaLu* is segmented as *ba+e+TTa+ga+La+u*. The Unicode encoding supports this segmentation. The number of these *segments* is the length of the term. Hence, the length of the term *beTTagaLu* is 6. Now on, whenever we mention length in the paper, we refer to this *segment length*.

Next, for each term we truncate these segments iteratively one by one from the back. Truncation terminates when the term reduces by a *truncation factor* ($\alpha$) or the term length reduces below the *termination threshold* (*tt*). Here, $0 \leq \alpha \leq 1$ and and $tt \in \mathbb{N}^0$. The algorithm 1 explains this prefix generation step for a given term. For each document $d_i$ in the corpus, all the prefixes generated are added to *bag of prefixes* ($B_{d_i}$). Hence, $B_{d_i}$ is a super-set of the *bag of words*.

In the next step, called *metric generation*, we generate *prefix frequency(pf)* and *inverse document frequency(idf)*. The *prefix frequency* of prefix $p$ in document $d_i$ is defined as $pf_{p,d_i} = \log(f_{p,d_i} + 1)$, where, $f_{p,d_i}$ is the count of $p$ in $B_{d_i}$. The inverse document frequency for the prefix $p$ is calculated as $idf_p = \log \frac{N}{|D_p|}$, where, $N$ is the number of documents in the corpus and $|D_p|$ is the number of *bag of prefixes* containing $p$ in the corpus. A postings list is maintained to map documents with their *pf* and *idf*s. This part of indexing is inspired by classical tf-idf indexing. However, the novelty of the approach is in the prefixes based indexing which enables the retrieval of documents with other morphologies.

---

**Algorithm 1.** Generate Term Prefixes
**Input:** Term $t_k$, Truncation Threshold $\alpha$, Termination Threshold $tt$
**Description:** Generate all the prefixes for the term $t_k$ bounded by $\alpha$ and $tt$

---

**Require:** $t_k \neq null$, $0 \leq \alpha \leq 1$, $tt \geq 0$
**Output:** Set of *prefixes* in $Q_p$
1: $Q_p \Leftarrow new\ array()$
2: $minimal\_length \Leftarrow (1 - \alpha) * segment\_length(t_k)$
3: $current\_length \Leftarrow length(t_k)$
4: $Q_p.put(t_k)$
5: **while** $current\_length > minimal\_length$ && $current\_length >= tt$ **do**
6: $\quad term \Leftarrow truncate\_last\_segment(term)$
7: $\quad Q_p.put(term)$
8: $\quad current\_length \Leftarrow segment\_length(term)$
9: **end while**

---

### 2.1 Retrieval and Ranking of the Documents

Let the user query be represented as $Q = \{t_1, t_2, ...., t_n\}$, where, $t_1$ to $t_n$ are the terms in it. Initially, we calculate *Individual score* for each query term in the query for each relevant document. For every query term, we generate a set of prefixes using algorithm 1. For each of these prefixes we retrieve exactly matching documents from the postings list. The *pf-idf score* for each document is calculated as $pfidf_{p,d_i} = (1 + pf_{p,d_i}) * (1 + idf_p)$. The *pfidf* calculation does not consider that the documents were retrieved by using the prefixes which are truncated versions of the query term $t_k$. Hence, we reduce the *pfidf* score by of *query truncation error* and calculate the individual score of the document as $score_{p,d_i} = pfidf_{p,d_i} * (1 - \left( \frac{length(t_k)-length(p)}{length(t_k)} \right))$. The $score_{p,d_i}$ decays with the increase in query truncation error. Hence, it is called *decay score* model.

For a term, a document can be scored for more than once due to its prefixes. We calculate the independent score $iscore(t_k, d_i)$ of a document $d_i$ for the query term $t_k$ as the maximum of all *scores* for $d_i$. Finally, *fscore* of a document is calculated by adding its *iscores* for all the query terms. The documents are ranked in the decreasing order of their *fscores*. The detailed explanation on prefix generation, indexing and retrieval is available in technical report [1].

### 2.2 Experiments and Performance Analysis

As there is no established IR model for Kannada, we evaluated TrieIR against the classical TF-IDF based model. The results were evaluated by 24 users on a corpus of 115 documents. We calculated the Mean Average Precision (MAP)s [7] for the results iteratively. The MAP of TrieIR was consistently better than that of TF-IDF based model. We also compared TrieIR with the current Wordpress[3] default search with the help of 7 users. Wordpress search was chosen as there are

---

[3] http://wordpress.org/download/

many Kannada websites[4] hosted using Wordpress. We observed MAP of TrieIR outperformed MAP of Wordpress search by a considerable margin. Finally, we measured the average recall per query term. For comparison between TrieIR and tf-idf, it was 7.3 documents for TrieIR versus 2.5 for tf-idf. Similarly, for comparison between Wordpress and TrieIR, the recall of TrieIR was 5.8 documents and for Wordpress it was 2.8 documents. The recall of TrieIR was considerably higher than that of tf-idf and Wordpress. The evaluations showed that, TrieIR performed considerably better than the TF-IDF and Wordpress searches. The details of the complete evaluation are available in the technical report [1].

## 3  Conclusion and Future Work

This work gives new set of indexing and retrieval methods for Kannada Unicode text. Understanding of the Kannada morphologies and the Unicode encoding of Kannada text inspired the trie based indexing. The indexing enables us to search for lexically similar terms and hence groups similar morphologies. The strategy of indexing and retrieval can be improved by stopword identification and removal, and suffix based stemming. We can also improve the quality of results by quantifying the amount of error getting introduced at the time of truncation based indexing. There are many other Indian languages like Marathi, Tamil, Telugu and Malayalam which are agglutinative and have suffix based MFs. As these languages are structurally similar to Kannada, we can also apply the same methods to these languages. We assert that, the quality of the retrieval will improve there as well. Hence, these indexing and retrieval methods open up a new way of looking at the retrieval for agglutinative languages.

## References

1. Kulkarni, S., Srinivasa, S.: A Novel IR Approach for Kannada Unicode Text. Technical Report, Open Systems Lab (2013),
   http://osl.iiitb.ac.in/reports/trieir_report.pdf
2. Bar-Ilan, J., Gutman, T.: How do search engines handle non-English queries?-A case study. WWW (Alternate Paper Tracks) (2003)
3. Singh, A.K., Surana, H., Gali, K.: More accurate fuzzy text search for languages using abugida scripts. In: Proceedings of ACM SIGIR Workshop on Improving Web Retrieval for Non-English Queries (2007)
4. Vikram, T.N., Urs, S.R.: Development of Prototype Morphological Analyzer for he South Indian Language of Kannada. In: Goh, D.H.-L., Cao, T.H., Sølvberg, I.T., Rasmussen, E. (eds.) ICADL 2007. LNCS, vol. 4822, pp. 109–116. Springer, Heidelberg (2007)
5. Singh, A.K.: A computational phonetic model for Indian language scripts. In: Constraints on Spelling Changes: Fifth International Workshop on Writing Systems (2006)
6. Salton, G., McGill, M.J.: Introduction to modern information retrieval (1986)
7. Manning, C.D., Raghavan, P., Schütze, H.: Introduction to information retrieval, vol. 1. Cambridge University Press, Cambridge (2008)

---

[4] kanaja.in, justkannada.in, oppanna.com, vknews.in, vartamaana.com

# Social Sustainability of Digital Libraries: A Research Framework

Gobinda G. Chowdhury

Department of Mathematics & Information Sciences,
Northumbria University, Newcastle NE1 8ST, UK
gobinda.chowdhury@northumbria.ac.uk

**Abstract.** Major factors related to the social sustainability of digital libraries have been discussed. Some indicators for the social sustainability of digital libraries have been proposed. A conceptual model and a theoretical research framework for study of the social sustainability of digital libraries is proposed. It is argued that the social sustainability of digital libraries can and should be studied at different levels – from the very broad issues of sustainable development of societies and communities to more specific issues of information seeking and retrieval, ICT infrastructure and tools for access to, and use of, digital libraries.

**Keywords:** digital libraries, social sustainability, sustainable digital libraries, information access.

## 1    Introduction

Various social issues of digital libraries have been studied since the beginning of digital library research, e.g. in the digital library workshop[1] organised in 1996, in the DELOS Manifesto of digital libraries[2] published in 2007, and in a number of research literature as reviewed by Liew [1]. However, sustainability issues of digital libraries have not been systematically researched as yet [2]. Study of the sustainability of digital libraries requires us to identify the challenges that are associated with the design, delivery, access and use of digital information [2].

This paper focuses on the social sustainability of digital libraries the target of which is to ensure equitable access to digital information in order to build a better (well informed) and healthy society; and the success can be measured by increase in the accessibility and usability of digital libraries in every sphere of life and society. This paper proposes some indicators for measuring the social sustainability of digital libraries. A framework for study of the social sustainability of digital libraries is then proposed. Different layers of the framework and their implications for studies of the social sustainability of digital libraries have been discussed. Specific examples from

---

[1] http://is.gseis.ucla.edu/research/dig_libraries/
[2] http://www.dlib.org/dlib/march07/castelli/03castelli.html

S.R. Urs, J.-C. Na, and G. Buchanan (Eds.): ICADL 2013, LNCS 8279, pp. 25–34, 2013.
© Springer International Publishing Switzerland 2013

open access digital libraries are drawn to support the discussions. It is argued that the proposed theoretical framework can be used to undertake systematic research and studies in different aspects of the social sustainability of digital libraries.

## 2      Social Sustainability of Digital Libraries

The term sustainability is used to denote continuing development or progress of an organization or business, a product, a service, a process or an activity while at the same time maintaining an ecological balance. According to the US Environment Protection Agency, sustainability "creates and maintains the conditions under which humans and nature can exist in productive harmony, that permit fulfilling the social, economic and other requirements of present and future generations."[3] In order to achieve sustainable development, one needs to consider all the three inter-related dimensions, often called the three pillars, of sustainability, viz. economic sustainability, social sustainability and environmental sustainability [2]. Sustainable information refers to resources that facilitate the integration of all the three parts of sustainable development, and it contributes to the strengthening of the processes in which society is transformed according to the ideals of sustainable development [2]. Broadly speaking social sustainability may be defined as the maintenance and improvement of well-being of the current and future generations [3]. However, the concept of well-being can be defined differently in different contexts ranging from the equity of access to essential services for healthy lifestyle and well-being, for building democratic and informed citizenship, for promotion and sharing of positive relations and culture, and so on. Many indicators of sustainable development have been proposed in literature (see for example [4,5]). For digital libraries the main goal of the social sustainability is to ensure equitable access and use of digital information in every sphere of life and society. Access is a rather broad term here that includes all the activities related to the discovery, access and use/re-use of information for day-to-day business, pleasure, well-being, knowledge and understanding, and so on; and a number of parameters have direct or indirect influence on equitable access.

## 3      Indicators for the Social Sustainability of Digital Libraries

A variety of indicators may be identified for measuring the social sustainability of digital libraries depending on the nature of content and data, the information service providers, the underlying information systems and ICT frameworks, the users and their context, etc. The following ten may be considered as the most important measures for the social sustainability of digital libraries:

- rights to information;
- equity of access to key information relevant for every sphere of life;

---

[3] http://www.epa.gov/sustainability/basicinfo.htm

- equity of access to information among different user generations – present and future;
- community recognition and responsibility for information sharing;
- advocacy in support of all activities for the creation, access and use of information;
- mechanisms for protection of community needs through the use of information;
- involving users in the design and usability of information systems and services;
- transmitting awareness through generations, for example through education and training in information skills, green user behaviour, etc.;
- creation of an information society and a knowledge economy through appropriate legal and policy frameworks; and
- protection of the privacy and security of people in relation to information.

Some of these indicators are related directly to the information systems and services while others are related to the wider society such as awareness, advocacy, participation and regulations. In some cases people may have restricted or no access to some specific information, for example, in military, business and key scientific intelligence. However, in principle, information should be available for all kinds of activities and development, e.g. for research and scholarly information to support education and research, health information to support well-being and healthy lifestyle, political and government information to support informed citizenship, cultural and heritage information for ensuring protection of values and support and promotion of cultural integration as and when desired by individuals and groups, information for sustainable development and for protection of communities, and so on. However, there are a number of barriers, e.g. the equity of access to information is often affected by a number technological, economic and social barriers.

Equity of access to information should be considered for everyone in the present and future generations through appropriate mechanisms of preservation of information. Rights to information should go hand in hand with the sharing of information, as far as practicable. Appropriate mechanisms need to be developed for advocacy at all levels to support all the activities related to the creation and dissemination of information among the various stakeholders and to the general public, as appropriate. Similarly appropriate mechanisms need to be built so that communities can be protected through the right use of information, for example from acts of crime and terrorism, natural disasters, etc. Ease of access and use can be ensured only when information users are involved at every step of the design and evaluation of information systems and services. Since information systems and services change fast with the advancement of technology vis-à-vis changing society and community needs, user involvement and user training should be a continuous process for any successful information service. Finally all these activities, and steps for building a knowledge society, should be governed by the appropriate legal and policy frameworks that can support all the activities related to the development of information systems and services, but at the same time can protect people's rights to privacy and security. Technology and regulations should go hand in hand to promote free flow and easy access to information but at the same time protecting people against misuse of information.

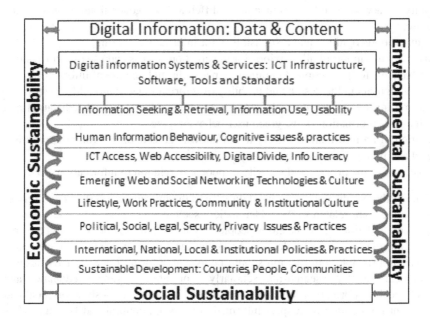

**Fig. 1.** A Framework for Study of the Social Sustainability of Digital Libraries

# 4      A Social Sustainability Model for Digital Libraries

Figure 1 provides a framework for study of the social sustainability of digital libraries. It shows the different issues and challenges that should be considered to study the various factors, and the associated challenges, of social sustainability of libraries. Each of the layers, shown in Figure 1, not only influences the overall social sustainability of digital libraries, but they also influence each other, and they all are also related to, or dependent on, the nature and characteristics of the digital data and information managed by a specific digital library system. These are discussed in more details along with some specific research issues in the following sections.

## 4.1      Digital Libraries for Sustainable Development

As shown in Figure 1, digital library systems and services are created in order to support various activities related to sustainable development. The importance of information and knowledge sharing for sustainable development have been identified and discussed in many international and national policy documents. The recently held *Expert Consultation on Knowledge and Capacity Needs for Sustainable Development in Post Rio+20 Era,* organized by the UN Office for Sustainable Development (UNOSD) together with its partners in Incheon, Republic of Korea on March 6-8, 2013, emphasized on information and knowledge sharing in the following terms [6]:

We are of the view that transition towards sustainability requires efforts on several fronts, but knowledge sharing and capacity building should be the fundamental platform for these efforts (P.1).
UNOSD should collaborate with other knowledge providers, and both promote and facilitate the linking and sharing of data and knowledge through open networks, avoiding the duplication of existing initiatives (P.3).

The UN General Assembly Resolution A/RES/66/288, called *The Future We Want* [7], made a series of recommendations for achieving sustainable development in different areas. Thus at the very broad level the success of a digital library can be measured by its contributions to the overall sustainable development of countries, people and communities. In the context of institutional repositories and open access digital libraries, one measure of success of the social sustainability of digital libraries could be their contributions and impact on the sustainable development in education and research. However, such measures of success depend on a number of other factors as shown by different layers in Figure 1.

## 4.2    Policies and Practices

Digital libraries and information services are governed by a variety of international, national, local and institutional policies and practices. Consequently, the social sustainability of digital libraries depend on these policies. Two different layers in Figure 1 are concerned with, or affected by, the different policy and regulatory frameworks. Let's take the examples of the recently introduced open access policies of various international and national bodies and their implications on the social sustainability of digital libraries.

The European Commission recommends that from 2014 every EU-funded project will have to follow [8]:

- Gold open access where research papers will be made immediately accessible online by the publisher and the researchers will be eligible for reimbursement of the APCs from the Commission; or
- Green open access where researchers will make their papers available through an open access repository no later than six months (or 12 months for articles in the fields of social sciences and humanities) after publication.

The OA policy of the Australian Research Council (ARC) stipulates that with effect from 1st January 2013 any publications arising from an ARC supported research project must be deposited into an OA repository within 12 months from the date of publication [9]. The OA access policy of the US National Institute of Health (NIH) stipulates that all investigators funded by the NIH must submit an electronic copy of their final peer-reviewed manuscript to the National Library of Medicine's PubMed Central no later than 12 months after the official date of publication [10]. The Wellcome Trust have also introduced a similar OA policy that requires electronic copies of all papers, arising from research that has been fully or partly supported by the Wellcome Trust funding, to be made available through PubMed Central (PMC) and Europe PubMed Central within six months of the official date of publication [11]. The Wellcome Trust also promises additional funding, through their institutions, to cover OA charges, where appropriate. The OA policies of the Research Councils in UK (RCUK), introduced from April 2013, show a preference for the Gold OA model [12]:

> The Research Councils UK (RCUK) policy supports both 'Gold' and 'Green' routes to Open Access, though RCUK has a preference for immediate Open Access with the maximum opportunity for re-use (P.1).
>
> Funding for Open Access arising from Research Council-supported research will be available through a block grant awarded directly to research organisations (P.1).

In a policy memorandum released on February 22, 2013, the Office of Science and Technology Policy (OSTP) of the US government directed all US Federal agencies with more than $100M in R&D expenditures to develop plans to make the published results of federally funded research freely available to the public within one year of publication and requiring researchers to better account for and manage the digital data resulting from federally funded scientific research [13].

The OA policies and the corresponding institutional policies and practices will have a significant influence on the social sustainability of digital libraries. While in principle all the OA policies will significantly boost the social sustainability of digital libraries by increasing the ease and equity of access to research information and data, there may be some negative implications as well. For example, different OA policies have proposed different embargo periods for OA publications arising out of the Green OA model. Furthermore, where Gold OA is preferred, as in the case of RCUK policies, management of the funds for payment of APCs will be governed by the re-spective research funding bodies as well as specific universities. These policies may restrict the researchers' choice, and some may be forced to select journals simply because of their lower APCs, which in turn may have an impact on the overall schol-arly communication processes. Furthermore, some researchers, e.g. students, retired or voluntary researchers may not have access to funds for APCs and they may be forced to find alternative routes to publishing, or worst some of their works may not be published ever. Some OA policies, for example, those of RCUK and the Wellcome Trust, require that research papers should be made available with the CC-BY license that permits free use and re-use of content and data, even for commercial purposes. This may disadvantage some authors and researchers because some of their works may be used/re-used by others for commercial benefits without generating any bene-fits or gains for the creators of the original idea or knowledge. From social sustain-ability point of view, there are concerns related to research ethics and data protection. Currently the research ethics and data protection guidelines require that a researcher or a team secures permissions for creation and use of research data sets under specific circumstances for a stated research purpose. Perhaps changes in the research ethics and policies are needed in order to find ways for re-use of research data sets.

## 4.3    Lifestyle, Practices, Community and Work Culture

Research shows that access to, and use of, information resources and services are very much influenced by the lifestyle, practices, community and work culture of people. While these largely form part of the fields of HIB research (discussed below), some regulations, policies and guidelines also influence the lifestyle and culture of people in relation to information access and use. Continuing with the same example of the recently introduced OA policies of various research funding bodies and government organizations, it may be noted that the OA policies will bring a paradigm shift in information access and management in the context of scholarly communications. With the implementation of the OA policies more and more scholarly content and research data will be available in the public domain. So, after a few years, commercial journals and databases will have only a small fraction of their published content that they can charge for. Such content will comprise research papers that are published under the Green OA model and are still within the embargo period, usually 6-12 months. This will cause a major shift from the subscription-based services to open information services. Consequently, this will bring a paradigm shift in the way academics and scholars create and use digital information. More and easier access to scholarly information and data will bring a significant change in the way information is used for research and scholarly activities, and these will in turn promote the creation of more new knowledge. The social sustainability of digital libraries, in promoting the sustainable development of academic and scholarly activities, will be influenced by how quickly academics and scholars can adapt to the new digital environment and change their work culture, for example in terms of classroom teaching, or drawing on large volume and variety of linked data (discussed below in more details).

### 4.4 Accessibility and Literacy Issues

Access to, and effective use of, digital libraries can be significantly affected by digital divide that is often manifested by the [14]:

- social divide characterized by difference in access between diverse social groups
- the global divide which is characterized by the difference in terms of access to the Internet technologies, and
- the democratic divide which is characterized by the different applications and uses of digital information in order to engage and participate in social life.

There are different indicators for assessing these different manifestations of digital divide, and these are not only prevalent in the developing world, but also among various communities within the developed nations. For example, more than a third of the US households do not have a broadband connection yet, and only about two-thirds of the 27 EU countries have a broadband connection at home [14]. So, the vision of the Europeana digital library, to provide digital information and culture to everyone in Europe, still cannot be fully utilized because two-thirds of the EU homes do not yet have a broadband connection. The situation in the third world countries is even worse.

There are other related areas of research like digital literacy, digital divide, social inclusion, etc. Access to, and effective use of, digital libraries can be significantly affected by the poor information and digital literacy skills of people. A November 2012 BBC news[4] reports that 16 million people in Britain, i.e. about one in four, or one in three in the adult British population, do not have the basic Internet skills.

---

[4]  http://www.bbc.co.uk/news/technology-20236708

It may be safely assumed that this is not an isolated case and many countries in the world have comparable, or even worse, information and digital literacy skills causing social exclusion. In the context of digital libraries, social exclusion may be caused by a number of factors ranging from the lack of adequate access to ICT infrastructure and services, to lack of digital and information skills that are the pre-requisites for successful access to, and use of, digital library services.

## 4.5    HIB and IS&R Issues

HIB (human information behavior) and IS&R (information seeking & retrieval) have remained the two most widely researched areas of information science for the past few decades giving rise to several models in information science in general (for details see, [15-17]) and in the context of digital libraries in particular [18,19]. These models discus various personal, contextual, social, cultural and technological issues that influence access to, and use of, digital libraries.

IS&R in the context of digital libraries is also influenced significantly by the emerging web, mobile and social networking technologies. Many digital libraries now offer special services that can be accessed through various handheld and mobile devices [20]. Similarly many digital libraries use social networking and social technologies for providing better retrieval [21]. Various other novel techniques and tools, such as recommendation systems and collaborative filtering [22], and social semantic tagging [23] are now being developed and experimented by researchers. These emerging technologies and their implications on the users and communities have significant implications for the social sustainability of digital information services.

## 4.6    Digital Library Systems

A number of different design models – such as the 5S model (Streams, Structures, Spaces, Scenarios and Societies [24]), the Kahn and Wilensky Framework [25], the DELOS Reference model and a number of software platforms such as DSpace, EPrints, Fedora Commons, Greenstone, etc. have been developed and used for digital library design and development over the past two decades. Similarly a variety of tools, metadata standards and protocols for metadata harvesting, such as the OAI-PMH [26], have also been developed over the past few years. These DL architectures, software, tools and standards aim to facilitate better and easier access to information, and thus improve the social sustainability of digital libraries. However, social sustainability also requires better organization, indexing, linking and retrieval of digital library objects. Furthermore, the usability of digital libraries is often affected by the user needs and expectations that are set, often wrongly, by the search engines. In a usability study of the Europeana digital library it was noted that young users' information needs and search strategies and expectations were quite different from those of more matured users [27]. Changing user behaviour is often caused by the recent proliferation of the easy-to-use search engine services that have created a different set of expectations, especially amongst the younger users.

# 5     Conclusion

In order to build socially sustainable digital libraries, attention should be paid to a number of areas some of which are soft – related to the society, users, culture, regulations and practice issues – others are more technical such as ICT infrastructure, software, metadata, indexing and retrieval, etc. The generic model proposed in this paper shows that research and development activities in the social sustainability of digital libraries should be undertaken at different related layers or phases each of which has a number of key issues and challenges, and together they can contribute to the goals of the social sustainability of digital information systems and services. Furthermore, as shown in Figure 1, social sustainability of digital libraries cannot be achieved in isolation of the economic and environmental sustainability. Overall, the model can serve as a starting point for future research and development with a holistic view of digital libraries, and the various factors that have implications on all the three forms of sustainability in general and the social sustainability in particular.

# References

1. Liew, C.L.: The social element of digital libraries. In: Chowdhury, G.G., Foo, S. (eds.) Digital Libraries and Information Access: Research Perspectives, pp. 97–112. Facet Publishing, London (2012)
2. Chowdhury, G.G.: Sustainability of digital libraries: A conceptual model. In: Aalberg, T., Papatheodorou, C., Dobreva, M., Tsakonas, G., Farrugia, C.J. (eds.) TPDL 2013. LNCS, vol. 8092, pp. 1–12. Springer, Heidelberg (2013)
3. Mak, M.Y., Peacock, C.J.: Social Sustainability: acomparison of case studies in UK, USA and Australia. In: 17th Pacific Rim Real Estate Society Conference, Gold Coast (January 16-19, 2011), http://www.prres.net/papers/ Mak_Peacock_Social_Sustainability.pdf (accessed May 15, 2013)
4. Hutchins, M.J., Gierke, J.S., Sutherland, J.W.: Decision making for social sustainability: a lifecycle assessment approach. In: IEEE International Symposium on Technology and Society, ISTAS 2009, May 18-20, pp. 1–5 (2009)
5. Hutchins, M., Sutherland, J.W.: An exploration of measures of social sustainability and their application to supply chain decisions. Journal of Cleaner Production 16(15), 1688–1698 (2008)
6. United Nations. Sustainable Development Knowledge Platform. United Nations conference on sustainable development, Rio+20, http://sustainabledevelopment.un.org/rio20.html (accessed May 15, 2013)
7. United Nations. General Assembly. Resolution adopted by the General Assembly. A/RES/66/288. The future we want (September 11, 2012), http://daccess-dds-ny.un.org/doc/UNDOC/GEN/N11/476/10/PDF/ N1147610.pdf?OpenElement (accessed May 15, 2013)
8. Europa. Scientific data: open access to research results will boost Europe's innovation capacity, http://europa.eu/rapid/press-release_IP-12-790_en.htm (accessed May 15, 2013)
9. Australian Research Council. ARC open access policy, http://www.arc.gov.au/applicants/open_access.htm (accessed May 15, 2013)

10. National Institutes of Health. National Institutes of Health public access. NIH public access policy details, `http://publicaccess.nih.gov/policy.htm` (accessed May 15, 2013)
11. Wellcome Trust. Open access policy: position statement in support of open and unrestricted access to published research, `http://www.wellcome.ac.uk/About-us/Policy/Policy-and-position-statements/WTD002766.htm` (accessed May 15, 2013)
12. Research Councils UK. RCUK policy with open access and guidance, `http://www.rcuk.ac.uk/documents/documents/RCUKOpenAccessPolicy.pdf` (accessed May 15, 2013)
13. Executive Office of the President. Office of Science and Technology. Memorandum for the heads of executive departments and agencies (February 22, 2013), `http://www.whitehouse.gov/sites/default/files/microsites/ostp/ostp_public_access_memo_2013.pdf` (accessed May 15, 2013)
14. Chowdhury, G.G., Chowdhury, S.: Information users and usability in the digital age. Facet Publishing, London (2011)
15. Wilson, T.: On user studies and information needs. Journal of Documentation, Special publication, 174–186 (2009)
16. Ruthven, I., Kelly, D. (eds.): Interactive information seeking, behaviour and retrieval. Facet Publishing, London (2011)
17. Ingwersen, P., Järvelin, K.: The turn: integration of information seeking and retrieval in context. Springer, Dordrecht (2005)
18. Wilson, T.D., Maceviciute, E.: Users' interactions with digital libraries. In: Chowdhury, G.G., Foo, S. (eds.) Digital Libraries and Information Access: Research Perspectives, pp. 113–128. Facet Publishing, London (2012)
19. Dobreva, M., O'Dwyer, A. (eds.): User studies for digital library development. Facet Publishing, London (2012)
20. Mitchell, C., Suchy, D.: Developing mobile access to digital collections. D-Lib Magazine 18(1/2) (2012), `http://www.dlib.org/dlib/january12/mitchell/01mitchell.html`
21. Lee, K.-P., Kim, H.-G., Kim, H.-J.: A social inverted index for social tagging-based information retrieval. Journal of Information Science 38(4), 313–332 (2012)
22. Rafeh, R., Bahrehmand, A.: An adaptive approach to dealing with unstable behaviour of users in collaborative filtering systems. Journal of Information Science 38(3), 205–221 (2012)
23. Huang, S.-L., Lin, S.-C., Chan, Y.-C.: Investigating effectiveness and user acceptance of semantic social tagging of knowledge sharing. Information Processing and Management 48(4), 599–617 (2012)
24. Gonçalves, M.A., Fox, E.A., Watson, L.T., Kipp, N.A.: Streams, Structures, Spaces, Scenarios, Societies(5S): A Formal Model for Digital Libraries. ACM Transactions on Information Systems 22(2), 270–312 (2004)
25. Kahn, R., Wilensky, R.: A framework for distributed digital object services. International Journal on Digital Libraries 6(2), 115–123 (2006)
26. Lagoze, C., Van de Sompel, H.: The Open Archives Initiative: Building a low-barrier interoperability framework. In: Proceedings of the ACM/IEEE Joint Conference on Digtial Libraries, Roanoke VA, June 24-28, pp. 54–62 (2001)
27. Dobreva, M., Chowdhury, S.: A User-Centric evaluation of the Europeana digital library. In: Chowdhury, G., Koo, C., Hunter, J. (eds.) ICADL 2010. LNCS, vol. 6102, pp. 148–157. Springer, Heidelberg (2010)

# Technological Devices in the Archives: A Policy Analysis

Ciaran B. Trace and Unmil P. Karadkar

School of Information, The University of Texas at Austin
1616 Guadalupe St. Austin, TX 78701-1213, USA
star@ischool.utexas.edu

**Abstract.** Doing research in the archive is the cornerstone of humanities scholarship. Various archives institute policies regarding the use of technological devices, such as mobile phones, laptops, and cameras in their reading rooms. Such policies directly affect the scholars as the devices mediate the nature of their interaction with the source materials in terms of capturing, organizing, note taking, and record keeping for future use of found materials. In this paper, we present our analysis of the policies of thirty archives regarding the use of technology in their reading rooms. This policy analysis, along with data from interviews of scholars and archivists, is intended to serve as a basis for developing mobile applications for assisting scholars in their research activities. In this paper we introduce an early prototype of such a mobile application—AMTracker.

**Keywords:** archive reading room, policies, mobile devices, AMTracker.

## 1    Introduction

The conduct of research in the humanities requires an ongoing process of information work. A crucial aspect of this work that is often overlooked are the information management strategies and techniques used by scholars in order to capture, manage, and cite the primary source documents that form a cornerstone of their research. Such strategies and techniques are highly influenced by the conditions that exist in respect to working with archival materials. Archive policies vary widely: while some allow authors to reproduce the source materials through photocopying, scanning, or taking digital images, others prohibit physical or digital reproduction. Such rules have been found to directly affect and disrupt existing research processes and procedures [20].

Given the impact of archive rules and policies on the information gathering practices on scholars, we studied and analyzed the policies related to researchers' use of technological devices in archive reading rooms. Our current policy analysis is limited to the thirty-six archives that participate in TARO (Texas Archival Resources Online), a site that hosts a compilation of collection descriptions (finding aids) for participating archives in the state of Texas. The policy analysis is accompanied by interview data from archivists and scholars to see what impact these rules and policies have on the ground. This analysis serves as a foundation for designing software that will enhance the information management infrastructure available to scholars while

S.R. Urs, J.-C. Na, and G. Buchanan (Eds.): ICADL 2013, LNCS 8279, pp. 35–44, 2013.
© Springer International Publishing Switzerland 2013

conducting research activities in reading rooms. The initial version of the mobile app described here helps researchers navigate the culture of the archive by summarizing the policies that scholars can expect to encounter when visiting an archive.

The rest of the paper is organized as follows: we survey related work on the information behavior of humanities scholars, following which we present our analysis of the archives' policies with regard to technology use in the archive. This section is accompanied by additional data from archivists and from scholars gathered as part of in-depth interviews about the information management strategies and techniques of scholars, and the role of the archive in supporting this process. The next section presents AMTracker, a mobile application for easy access to TARO archive policies. We then discuss the of implications of the current policies for designing software to aid scholars in capturing and managing primary source documents while in the archives and conclude with directions for continuing this work.

## 2    Related Work

The study of how humanities scholars conduct research is part of a larger research area that studies the information behavior of various social, economic, and occupational groups. Literature reviews of humanities scholars' information behavior post 1970 [16, 18] found that the work is usually solitary, that scholars use various primary and secondary sources in the research process, adopt different approaches to identify material, use search terms focusing on names of persons and places, browse collections, and that information institutions and professionals are an integral part of the research process.

In the last thirty years, research into the information behavior of humanists has deepened and broadened. One strand of research has studied the research environment – including scholars' use of libraries and archives [2, 4, 7, 15], the difference between physical and digital information environments [14], the role of information professionals in the research process, and scholars attitude towards information professionals [7, 8, 11, 15, 18]. Research has also looked at so-called 'derivative elements' of scholarly work, such as investigating the nature of queries, search terms, and information sources favored by scholars [2, 3, 15]. This work has also further delineated the types of sources that scholars use for data and evidence—noting a strong distinction between primary sources and secondary sources [2, 4, 6, 7, 15, 17]. Research in this vein has also explored topic selection [4] and how researchers search for and locate sources in physical and digital environments [1, 2, 3, 6, 7, 8, 9, 14, 15, 17].

Further research into work process has highlighted the importance of reading and note taking practices to humanities research [2], and shed light on scholars' writing processes and habits [2, 4]. Studies have also highlighted additional steps in the research process, including the strategies and tools that scholars adopt in organizing, naming/labeling, and finding analog and digital information [2, 4, 15]. In recent years, research has shown that the introduction of digital cameras complicates information management practices as researchers struggle to capture, organize, describe, contextualize, and access images subsequent to a research trip [15].

Particularly germane to our study, is research that has examined the forms of knowledge that separate novice from expert users of archives. Two of these forms of knowledge—domain (subject) knowledge and artifactual literacy (the ability to interpret and assess records as evidence)—are generally taught within a disciplinary context. The final type of knowledge—archival intelligence (knowledge of archival principles and practices, including "the reasons underlying archival rules and procedures") – relies on the archivist to make this knowledge transparent to patrons [20].

Another area of study directly relevant to our research is that of technology use in the humanities. If, in writing in the early 1980s, Stone [16] felt that it "may be part of the humanistic tradition to be anti-machine" (p. 300), subsequent studies have only served to muddy the waters. Wulf [19], writing in 1995, dismissed the idea of the humanist as technophobe while Massey-Burzio [12] found humanists somewhat ambivalent toward (library) technology in general. Within the past decade research has suggested that humanities scholars have actually "adapted well to rapid technical change," having the ability to "harness information technologies to tried, tested, and somewhat traditional research functions" [2].

Research in this area has also shed light on scholars' preference vis- à-vis material format, the impact of digitization of primary sources and the presence of online finding aids on the research process [1, 15], and the importance of copying or capturing archival sources for continued analysis and interpretation [9, 14, 15]. Research suggests that the impact of technology has also been felt within the immediate physical research environment. In 1991, the photocopier was identified as the device that had most affected historical research [4]. Today, that role has been usurped by digital cameras [10] and other scanning equipment [15], and these tools help facilitate the accurate, efficient, and sophisticated copying, sharing, and analysis of primary source material [5]. The use of this equipment is also changing the nature of the work done in the archive—turning archival visits into what has been dubbed "more of a collection mission" [15], with some scholars thinking about offering these images back to the archive to improve access for others [15].

## 3    Methodology

We selected archives in the state of Texas for this policy analysis. The TARO Web site (http://www.lib.utexas.edu/taro/) aggregates the finding aids created by thirty-six participating archives in the state and facilitates location of relevant collections by making these available through a unified interface. The Web site enables scholars to browse the finding aids for individual archives or locate information within these finding aids via full-text searches. The TARO interface does not include links to the Web pages that describe the policies of individual archives (although limited policy information can be found in the "Administrative Information" and/or "Restrictions" sections of some of the finding aids). Potential patrons must locate the relevant policies on their own initiative, directly from the archive Web sites.

We visited the individual archive Web sites and located the pages that discuss archive and reading room policies. We reviewed, categorized, and analyzed the policy documents hosted on these archive web sites, focusing on parts that relate to technology use in the archive reading rooms. Each policy page was reviewed by two researchers: one recorded and encoded the content from the Web page and a second researcher validated this data. We contextualized our analysis by conducting interviews with a purposeful sample of archive managers who worked for an archive represented in TARO and researchers who have used at least one of these archives. In all, we interviewed three archive managers and four scholars.

To support our objective of eliciting a general overview of the scholars' needs rather than an extensive, deep investigation into the culture of archives themselves, we opted to interview archive administrators representing a small, young academic archive, a large, well-known academic archive, and a public archive. The administrators were all female and each had more than ten years of archival work experience. The administrators are comfortable with using technological devices such as digital cameras, smart phones, tablets, notebook and desktop computers, as well as audio recorders.

We interviewed three female and one male scholar, two of whom are historians, one a media studies researcher, and one a scholar of rhetoric and writing. The scholars were all under the age of 30 and include a post-doctoral scholar, two advanced doctoral students, and a master's student. The scholars possess archival work experience of between one and ten years, each having used at least two archives. Like the administrators, the scholars we interviewed are also comfortable using the technological devices listed above.

# 4    Findings

The archives that participate in TARO are managed by institutions with five distinct profiles—25 are academic (public and private), 8 are governmental (state and local), and 3 are private institutions. Of the 36 archives, we located the policies for 30 on their Web sites—23 from academic, 5 from governmental, and 2 from private institutions.

## 4.1    Policy Documentation on Archive Web Sites

We studied the found policies, focusing on sections related to the use of recent technological advances (such as laptops, tablets, cameras, phones, and scanners). We found that the archive policies, as well as their placement on the Web pages, varies widely. While some archives display prominent links entitled "Research" or "Policies" that enable potential patrons to locate these, other Web sites bury their policies under sections such as "Collections" or "About". While some archives describe policies concisely on one page, others split the discussion of various policies in multiple sections of the Web site. In some cases, the policies are split in up to six different pages and in various formats, such as HTML, MS-Word, and PDF.

Table 1 illustrates the acceptance of devices at various archives based on the archives' publicly stated policies. We classified the range of acceptance into four categories: policies that clearly mentioned that a device could be used in the reading room (allowed), those that mentioned use with significant caveats (conditional), those that expressly excluded their use in the reading room (disallowed) and those that did not mention the device at all (unknown). The policy documents stated three motivations explicitly, although not formally for these policies: the safeguarding of archival materials, ensuring that patron's work does not hinder others' in the reading room, and that the archive gets academic credit or financial remuneration for the use of its materials.

**Table 1.** TARO Technology Related Policies

| | Laptop | Tablet | Still Camera | Video Camera | Mobile Phone | Scanner |
|---|---|---|---|---|---|---|
| Allowed | 20 | 0 | 13 | 1 | 6 | 1 |
| Conditional | 1 | 0 | 3 | 2 | 0 | 0 |
| Disallowed | 1 | 0 | 3 | 2 | 8 | 13 |
| Unknown | 8 | 30 | 11 | 25 | 16 | 16 |

Our analysis showed that laptops are the most commonly addressed devices; only eight archive policies do not mention them. Next to paper and pencil, laptops are the most accepted form of note taking support for scholars. Most archives that allow laptops expressly require patrons to leave laptop bags in lockers. One archive allows laptops but not "video applications running on laptops". While one policy explicitly disallows devices of any kind, including personal computers, one allows patrons to use them, at the discretion of the archive staff, a situation that we have classified as conditional. While administrators as well as scholars are comfortable using tablets, none of the policies we encountered address this class of devices.

Still cameras rank next to laptops in terms of acceptance with 13 permissive policies. Without exception, these policies prohibit the use of flash. Some policies mention digital cameras, while others restrict the use of professional grade cameras or the use of tripods. Three archives that participate in TARO prohibit the use of cameras altogether and eleven do not mention these devices at all. The three conditional cases include those that permit the use of cameras "at the discretion of the department" or "with consent from a librarian or archivist".

Among the devices we studied, scholars have used laptops and digital cameras for the longest duration. Therefore, it is somewhat surprising that about a third of the policies do not mention these devices. Mobile phones, video cameras, and personal scanners go unmentioned in at least half of the policies. At the other end of the spectrum, the use of mobile phones and scanners are expressly prohibited in the reading rooms of at least a quarter of the TARO archives.

Notably, scanners or phones are not permitted for use subject to certain conditions. Six policies state that mobile (or cell) phones may be taken into the reading room if they are switched off or silent. Others require that the phones be stowed in lockers provided at the archive. In some archives, it is unclear from the language in the policy whether or not scanners are permitted. Video cameras are the least mentioned devices in the policies, noted by their absence in 25 out of 30 policy documents.

While our analysis of the public documents provides an insight into the spectrum of technology acceptance in the reading rooms it is but one perspective. We complemented this analysis by seeking the views of the archive administrators who define and implement such policies as well as those of scholars whose research environment is shaped by these policies.

## 4.2   Archive Administrators' Perspectives

Prior to the interview, archive administrators completed a questionnaire regarding the devices permitted in the reading room as well as their experiences with devices used by scholars. The responses to these questions clarify the archives' technology related policies. While one archive mentions only that "personal computers" are permitted and another does not mention technology-related issues at all, the administrators' responses indicate that both archives permit the use of all the technological devices listed in table 1 as long as they do not damage the materials or hinder other scholars. The third archive allows mobile/smart phones in the reading room, contradicting the policy documentation on the Web page. The administrators informed us that video cameras, which are not addressed in any of the archives' policies, are disallowed. The administrators also report that scholars increasingly use tablet computers, which the policies notably do not mention, and that reading room staff do not micro-manage the applications that patrons use on permitted devices.

The administrators reported that most of their patrons are experienced researchers and are familiar with the work culture of the archives. It is the administrators' perception that these scholars arrive at the archive prepared with the necessary information to accomplish their objectives. The administrators felt that reading room staff rarely need to answer clarifying questions about policies. Administrators noted that policies are usually changed only when necessitated by patron or staff requests or in response to changes in technology. The current policies at each of the three archives have been in effect for at least three years and the administrators do not expect major policy changes in the near future.

The administrators are supportive of mobile apps as they expect that some features will reduce the burden on archive staff, in addition to aiding patrons. For example, one administrator requested that the app capture metadata about an artifact when the patron takes a picture. Another would like the app to keep track of the relevant materials that scholars have located in the archive.

## 4.3   Scholars' Perspectives

In our interviews, scholars indicated that they need help in locating policies as the policies are not always easy to find on archives web sites, and when located scholars sometimes find that the rules are not transparent. The issue is exacerbated by the fact that, as one researcher pointed out, no two archives are the same. Policies differ from institution to institution. Even if the policies are located and understood in one context, the rules do not necessarily transfer or translate to another archive.

The interviews also suggest that scholars are sometimes uncomfortable or unwilling to ask reading room staff about policies. This is partly due to the environment of the reading room where researchers feel that any interaction with the reference staff may be disruptive to others working in the space. Researchers try to "fit in" and not make trouble for themselves or the staff.

In addition, we found that researchers characterize what they see as the general culture of the archive, even if they only know the archives by reputation. Part of this characterization comes about through knowing the policies of the archive. Some archives are deemed 'liberal,' 'generous,' or 'open.' While others are deemed 'bureaucratic,' 'picky,' or 'strict.'

Finally, the presence of rules and policies was found to affect researchers directly. This is particularly true in the case of policies that limit the use of personal digital cameras in the reading room. Such a policy may increase the amount of time a researcher spends in an archive, disrupt the preferred method of work process already in place, and result in additional expenses being incurred. As one researcher put it, "…as a grad student your number one priority is not to have any archivist touch anything or do anything for you if you can help it just because it is expensive."

# 5    Implications for Supporting Scholars

The ever-changing nature of technological devices is not yet reflected in archival policies. For example, policies related to cell phones often treat them as devices for making phone calls or text messaging. Over the last six years, cell phones have evolved from being communication devices alone to being computing and information devices that can run multiple applications, access Web-based content, take high-quality photographs, or record videos. Smartphones now span the spectrum of every device listed in table 1. How would an archive that allows laptops and still cameras in the reading room but not personal recorders or video cameras determine the status of a smartphone? Tablet computers pose a similar problem. While iPads and Android tablets are commonplace and archivists permit their use in reading rooms, there is not a consensus on whether these should be treated as small personal computers or large mobile phones. As technologies embed themselves in our work lives it becomes increasingly difficult to pry these out of our hands when entering an institution to, well, work some more.

The lack of clear policies related to commonplace devices is challenging from a design perspective as well. Designing applications for use on the most widely used computing platforms is the best strategy for providing meaningful support to a large community of scholars. As archives follow a contingency-based policy-making model, we anticipate that the increasing number of scholars who bring their devices to the archives will eventually lead to crafting of policy statements that cover only these contingencies. However, the danger with this wait-and-watch approach is that the policies crafted may be shaped by the experience of individual archives and an early negative experience may cast a long shadow on permitting the use of an otherwise relevant device or software. Engaging the archive administrators in a discussion early and addressing their concerns head-on as well as designing prototype applications that assist archivists in dispensing their patron-related duties may be a better approach for harnessing the use of technology in scholarly service.

## 5.1    AMTracker: Mobile Policy Interface

As a first foray into supporting scholars, we have designed a mobile interface that provides a visual snapshot of TARO archive policies in order to help scholars prepare for an archive visit. Currently, scholars who intend to visit an archive must scour the individual web sites to locate their policies. To complicate matters, policies related to different devices may be stated on different Web pages. Our application, entitled AMTracker, presents a unified view of the device-related policies at each archive. The interface favors simplicity of presentation as well as interaction. The application opens to present an initial view that lists the TARO archives as shown in fig. 1(a). The viewer may scroll through the list and tap on the archive of interest to recall its policies. The policy view is illustrated in fig. 1(b). The interface presents abstract yet familiar graphical icons that represent technological devices such as a laptop, a still camera, and a cell phone. The color of the icon indicates the nature of policies related to the device. We use a color mapping that combines traffic lights and Web conventions: red indicates that the device is disallowed, green indicates that it is permitted, and yellow indicates that the device is permitted with certain caveats (the Conditional category used in table 1). In the case of digital cameras, for example, caveats may include limits on supporting equipment, where and how the technology is used, materials handling rules, quantity limits, copyright restrictions, and fees [13]. Gray icons indicate that the application does not contain a record for policies related to this device. In addition to the device-related icons, the interface also contains an icon for the archive's citation policies (the pencil and notepad icon) as well as links to the archive's home page and to its finding aids (Collection Page).

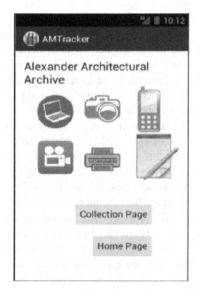

**Fig. 1.** AMTracker (a) Listing of TARO archives. (b) Policy display

The application employs a client-server architecture and the mobile client retrieves the policy information from a server-side database. While the administrators inform us that the policies do not change frequently, the server-side database will enable us to propagate new policies to all clients when these do change, as well as to include policies for other archives and make these available to all patrons with minimal overhead.

# 6      Conclusion and Future Work

Our research broadens the examination of scholarly work related to the humanities in the context of supporting work practices in archive reading rooms. Our policy analysis, coupled with administrator interviews, indicates that archive policies continue to evolve and are increasingly welcoming to technological devices, although the public statements sometimes trail the current policies. On the other hand, scholars are eager to adopt technology in order to use their swiftly dwindling resources more efficiently but are hindered by the lack of clarity regarding archive policies as well as the lack of support when using extant technology for scholarly activities.

The cohesiveness of responses among a small sample of archivists and scholars has encouraged us to design technology to support scholarly work practices as well as increase awareness regarding archive policies. Our mobile app, AMTracker, provides scholars with a snapshot of technology acceptance in archive reading rooms. In the next steps of this project, we will deploy the app among the scholars and study its use. In the near term, we expect to study the reading room policies of other significant archives around the world in order to compare the acceptance of technological devices in various countries and cultures. Simultaneously, we are developing features that will enable scholars to contribute details regarding the policies of other archives. This social feature will broaden the utility of AMTracker to scholars who visit archives other than those included in the TARO database. While AMTracker is currently an Android app, we recognize that humanities scholars also use iOS devices. In order to support scholarly practices on different mobile platforms, we are targeting future development toward using a platform-neutral environment, such as Titanium (http://www.appcelerator.com/platform/titanium-platform/).

We continue to explore the needs of scholars and archivists with a view toward introducing technology for improving the scholarly experience as well as for supporting archivists in their tasks. In addition to surveying archivists and scholars, we are designing features that will enable scholars to capture the metadata related to primary source materials and reduce the cognitive overhead in maintaining the primary source materials that are critical for their research.

**Acknowledgments.** This work was supported in part by the School of Information at The University of Texas at Austin through the John P. Commons fellowship. We also thank Xiaowan Wang for her assistance with this project.

# References

1. Anderson, I.G.: Are you being served? Historians and the search for primary sources. Archivaria 58, 81–130 (2004)
2. Brockman, W.S., Neumann, L., Palmer, C., Tidline, T.J.: Scholarly Work in the Humanities and the Evolving Information Environment. Digital Library Federation, Council on Library and Information Resources, Washington, D.C. (2001)
3. Buchanan, G., Cunningham, S.J., Blandford, A., Rimmer, J., Warwick, C.: Information seeking by humanities scholars. In: Rauber, A., Christodoulakis, S., Tjoa, A.M. (eds.) ECDL 2005. LNCS, vol. 3652, pp. 218–229. Springer, Heidelberg (2005)
4. Case, D.O.: The collection and use of information by some American historians: A study of motives and methods. The Library Quarterly 61(1), 61–82 (1991)
5. Cox, R.J.: Machines in the archives: Technology and the coming transformation of archival reference. First Monday 12(11) (2007)
6. Dalton, M.S., Charnigo, L.: Historians and their information sources. College & Research Libraries 65(5), 400–425 (2004)
7. Delgadillo, R., Lynch, B.R.: Future historians: Their quest for information. College & Research Libraries 60(3), 245–259 (1999)
8. Duff, W.M., Johnson, C.A.: Accidentally found on purpose: Information-seeking behavior of historians in archives. The Library Quarterly 72(4), 472–496 (2002)
9. Duff, W., Craig, B., Cherry, J.: Historians' use of archival sources: Promises and pitfalls of the digital age. The Public Historian 26(2), 7–22 (2004)
10. Dooley, J.M., Luce, K.: Taking our pulse: The OCLC Research survey of special collections and archives. OCLC Research, Dublin (2010)
11. Johnson, C.A., Duff, W.M.: Chatting up the archivist: Social capital and the archival researcher. The American Archivist 68(1), 113–129 (2005)
12. Massey-Burzio, V.: The rush to technology: A view from the humanists. Library Trends 47, 620–639 (1999)
13. Miller, L., Galbraith, S.K.: Capture and Release: Digital Cameras in the Reading Room. OCLC Research, Dublin (2010)
14. Rimmer, J., Warwick, C., Blandford, A., Gow, J., Buchanan, G.: An examination of the physical and the digital qualities of humanities research. Information Processing and Management 44(3), 1374–1392 (2008)
15. Rutner, J., Schonfeld, R.C.: Supporting the Changing Research Practices of Historians. Final Report from ITHAKA S+R (2012)
16. Stone, S.: Humanities scholars: Information needs and uses. Journal of Documentation 38(4), 292–313 (1982)
17. Tibbo, H.R.: Primarily history in America: How U.S. historians search for primary materials at the dawn of the digital age. The American Archivist 66(1), 9–50 (2003)
18. Wiberley Jr., S.E., Jones, W.G.: Patterns of information seeking in the Humanities. College & Research Libraries 50(6), 638–645 (1989)
19. Wulf, W.A.: Warning: Information technology will transform the university. Issues in Science & Technology 11, 46–52 (1995)
20. Yakel, E., Torres, D.A.: AI: Archival intelligence and user expertise. The American Archivist 66, 51–78 (2003)

# A New Plug-in System Supporting
# Very Large Digital Library

Jin Wang, Yong Zhang, Yang Gao, and Chunxiao Xing

Research Institute of Information Technology
Tsinghua National Laboratory for Information Science and Technology
Department of Computer Science and Technology, Tsinghua University, Beijing 100084, China
{wangjin12,yang-gao10}@mails.tsinghua.edu.cn,
{zhangyong05,xingcx}@tsinghua.edu.cn

**Abstract.** In the era of Big Data, actual demands of collecting large volumes of complex digital information have brought new challenges to digital library software. This scenario calls for the construction of Very Large Digital Library (VLDL). New approaches and technologies are needed to deal with the various issues in designing and developing VLDL. In this paper, we design a plug-in system—PuntStore as a general solution to very large digital library. PuntStore supports different kinds of storage engines and index engines to deal with the problem of storing and retrieving data efficiently. We also design a new index engine pLSM in PuntStore to meet the specific needs in digital libraries. The successful adoption of PuntStore in the project of the Digital Library on History of Science and Technology in China (DLHSTC) shows that PuntStore can function effectively in supporting VLDL systems.

**Keywords:** VLDL, plug-in system, PuntStore, storage engine, index.

## 1 Introduction

In the era of Big Data, the actual demands of data collection and repository have brought new challenges to digital library software. The past few years have witnessed the soaring volume as well as complex kinds of digital information to be collected and stored. Thus a variety of measures should be taken to deal with various data forms, large volumes, metadata heterogeneous, strictly demands of the data exchange and sharing, widely distributed content and long-term preservation. This calls for the construction of Very Large Digital Library (VLDL), which has raised many new issues.

Nevertheless, the definition of VLDL still remains to be an open problem. It cannot be considered as very large databases storing digital contents. As described in [2], digital library systems should deal with architecture management, functionality, user management besides content management. Similar to Big Data, the matter of "very largeness" includes the features of volume, velocity and variety. Digital Libraries becomes "very large" when any of these aspects reaches a magnitude that requires specialized methods [4]. Thus a variety of new approaches and technologies are needed in VLDL's data management, including data integration, data storage and access, and data ranking. Some existing DL systems have made some adaption to

S.R. Urs, J.-C. Na, and G. Buchanan (Eds.): ICADL 2013, LNCS 8279, pp. 45–52, 2013.
© Springer International Publishing Switzerland 2013

VLDLs. For example, J. Thompson has made an attempt to improve the performance of Greenstone in National Library of New Zealand's PapersPast digital library by applying parallel processing [7]. The Europeana project has also taken some measures in metadata management in the background of VLDL, such as storing the metadata of contents, using the Semantic Element as its data model [9].

In order to satisfy the specific needs of VLDL, it is crucial to have an efficient way of storing and retrieving contents with different formats or even different structures. We have designed a plug-in system PuntStore, as a general solution. PuntStore can fulfill the task of supporting heterogeneous application by dividing this task into specific steps and providing a variety of plugs for different steps. As a plug-in system, PuntStore provides a universal interface through which storage and index mechanisms of other DBMS could be integrated into the PuntDB, the database system offered by PuntStore. PuntStore also makes optimization in storage, distribution, scalability, heterogeneity and security. To reach the goal of efficiently retrieving heterogeneous data, we design a new index engine pLSM for PuntStore.

The paper is organized as follows: Section 2 describes an overview of PuntStore. Section 3 presents its adoption in the practical project of Digital Library on History of Science and Technology in China (DLHSTC). Section 4 provides the detail of storage engine and index engine in PuntStore and the design of pLSM index engine. Section 5 is concerned with two experiments: one is about multiple storage engines on different datasets, another is pLSM index, showing how it outperforms state-of-art index engines. Finally, we conclude in Section 6.

## 2    System Overview

The main problem that PuntStore is faced with is to deal with massive, complex, heterogeneous and continuous changing digital information. Yet there also exists a large amount of structured data which should be managed by relational DBMS. PuntStore also has to satisfy various kinds of needs for information retrieving. Based on the above consideration, we design the three-layer architecture for PuntStore.

### 2.1    The Architecture of PuntStore

As is shown in Figure 1, PuntStore consists of three layers:

- Storage Layer: Storage Layer is the core of PuntStore. The main function of Storage Layer is to store and manage data, create and maintain indexes. The Storage Layer consists of many PuntDBs, which consists of many PuntTables. There is a record library and an index library in each PuntTable. PuntDB and PuntTable will be described in details in 2.2. To manage metadata in PuntStore, we design a structure named Punt Digital Object (PDO), which will be described in 2.3.
- Management Layer: Management Layer is responsible for parsing requests submitted by Service Layer. Then it would finish the practical manipulations on PuntTable and PuntDB according to the interfaces offered by Storage Layer. In order to transmit messages between different layers, we design Message Object (MO), which will also be described in 2.3.

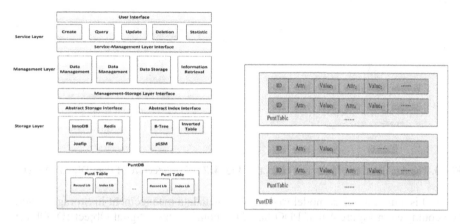

**Fig. 1.** The Overall Architecture of PuntStore      **Fig. 2.** The Data Model of PuntDB

- Service Layer: Service Layer offers different services to users according to data and index management interface provided by Management Layer. These services include creating database, table and index, manipulating insertion, query, updating, deletion and analysis on data.

## 2.2    PuntDB

PuntDB is an optimized NoSQL database to support the storage and analysis of massive data. Just like the SAP HANA database in the SAP HANA Application [3], high-level applications in PuntStore are based on the storage functions provided by PuntDB. The data model of PuntDB is shown in Figure 2.

Every PuntDB can include many PuntTables, which are the actual "repositories" in the PuntStore system. A PuntTable encapsulates multiple storage systems and provides a uniform data management interface for the applications. Applications can choose its storage strategy or make combination strategies without modifying their data operations. Each PuntTable in PuntDB has multiple records. Every record has an ID as the unique identifier, just like the primary key in relational database. The rest part of a line consists of a key and the corresponding value, just like the property and its value in relational database. What is different from relational database is that PuntStore does not have a global schema, the property and number of elements in each line can be different from those of other lines. Moreover, because of trading off ACID properties, PuntDB could be easily scaled up. Thus the scalability of PuntStore could be ensured.

## 2.3    Introduction of MO and PDO

As is shown in Figure 3, MO is the object to transfer information between different layers. It could also be regarded as a service model. MO could be used to provide different services, such as file, log, user, tag and metadata service. We could encapsulate the services inside it and provide a single interface to the outside world. With the features of low coupling and naturally distributing, the design goal of distributed storage could be reached by implementing MO in the Storage Layer.

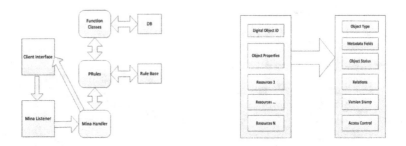

**Fig. 3.** The Architecture of Message Object    **Fig. 4.** The Architecture of Punt Digital Object

PDO is a digital object model to deal with metadata management in Storage Layer. We could see in Figure 4 that PDO has three components: Digital Object ID, Object Properties and a list of resources. One PDO could contain different kinds of data resources. Each resource has an identifier and its own contents. With the design of PDO, we could provide a uniform model for heterogeneous data. In this way, we could offer a concrete solution to metadata management in PuntStore to meet the needs of VLDL system.

## 3    Application

PuntStore has been deployed in the practical project of Digital Library on History of Science and Technology in China (DLHSTC) . Figure 5 shows its overall architecture. Like Bonolo [6], DLHSTC is a project to facilitate ubiquitous access to knowledge. The DLHSTC project aims at building an open digital library to the public and researchers in specific fields. Its main task is to collect, categorize and rescue the relics of science and technology history in China. By the end of 2012, the DLHSTC had included the parts of engineering, mathematics, mechanics, and water conservancy history of China. The DLHSTC system has 10 sub-systems, 85 programs, and 10 sub-databases, and its scale of data has increased to 900GB, including about 250,000 full text data. It is an information-rich, open resource library. A large scale of comprehensive resources are integrated in DLHSTC, including full text of historical documents, microscopic images, synopsis, catalogues, manuscripts, pictures, audios, videos, and animations. Nowadays, DLHSTC has become the largest comprehensive scientific data center in China.

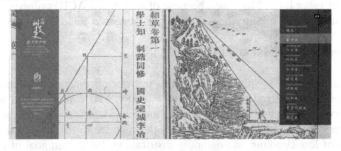

**Fig. 5.** The Project of DLHSTC

# 4    Storage and Index Engines

## 4.1    Storage Engine Overview

The structure of a record library is shown in Figure 6. Since PuntStore is faced with data with different structures, various kinds of storage mechanisms are needed in the record library to satisfy the needs for different applications. So PuntStore has a plug-in storage engine. Storage mechanisms in other DBMS could be easily implemented into PuntStore. Moreover, PuntStore may also support user defined storage mechanisms. The four main kinds of storage mechanisms in PuntStore are InnoDB, Redis, Joafip and File. To improve the efficiency of reading and writing files, optimizations have been made to file storage mechanism in PuntDB.

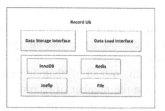
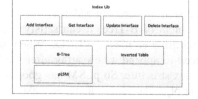

**Fig. 6.** The Record Library of PuntStore          **Fig. 7.** The Index Library of PuntStore

## 4.2    Index Engine Overview

Index is a data structure that improves the speed of data retrieval operations on a database table at the cost of slower writes and the use of more storage space [10]. A highly efficient index could improve the speed of data retrieval operations on a database table. To accelerate information retrieval in PuntDB, PuntStore offers efficient index library and provide a plug-in index engine. Users could create or drop some kinds of indexes according to specific requirements. As is shown in Figure 7, PuntDB provides three kinds of indices: B-Tree, Inverted Table and pLSM—a new index engine we developed. With the collaboration of Inverted Table and B-Tree, PuntDB could also support union query between different fields and keywords.

However, after frequent insertion and updating operations, the logically continuous leaf nodes of B-Tree would not be physically adjacent, thus a large number of random I/O would occur when doing query operations. This problem is known as "aging" problem of B-Tree. To eliminate the aging problem and improve the write throughput, we present pLSM-Tree index as an index engine in PuntStore to replace B-Tree.

## 4.3    Implementation of pLSM Index

The pLSM index structure is based on the traditional LSM-Tree index framework [5]. There are two components in pLSM index. The in-memory component is a light weight data structure—Skip List, while the external-memory component consists of multiple levels of fractional sorted runs.

The insertion happens only in the in-memory component. When this component is full, it will be merged out to disk. When a sorted run on disk reaches its limited size, it will also be merged into the next smaller run. Under the LSM-Tree framework, pLSM can transform random I/Os into sequential ones by perform batch writing. By implementing the logarithm method [1] on the size of sorted runs on disk, the merging operation would be I/O efficient. In order to improve the read performance of pLSM, we add an auxiliary data structure Bloom Filter to the external component. Bloom Filter is a random data structure with high space efficiency. Another advantage of pLSM is that it supports efficient bulk deletion. This feature can help to efficiently create and drop indices. The specific implementation mechanisms are omitted here due to limited length of the paper. More details can be found in our previous work [8].

### 4.4    Summary of pLSM

To sum up, since pLSM performs much better in insertion and eliminates the aging problem of B-Tree, it can satisfy the speed requirements for collecting, processing and using entities in VLDLs. When more records are needed to be indexed, we only need to append a new array after the last sorted runs instead of changing the whole index structure. So pLSM has good scalability when the number of records increases sharply. The above features make pLSM a proper choice as the index structure in VLDL systems.

## 5    Experiment

In order to evaluate the efficiency of our storage engine and pLSM index engine, we perform several experiments. All the following experiments are set up on a server machine with 32GB RAM and a 2.40GHz Intel(R) Xeon E5620 CPU with 2 cores. The environment for our workbench is Windows server 2008. Storage of different structured data

To test the efficiency of our plug-in storage engine, we import three different datasets into PuntStore using different storage mechanisms. Due to the requirement of our system, the insertion cost is usually the bottleneck of our system. So we do the insertion experiment here. The datasets are real workloads from the project of DLHSTC:

A. Dataset Text consists of full text contents. The size is 534MB.
B. Dataset Small Records is part of metadata from the DLHSTC project, which are structured data. The size is 4420MB.
C. Dataset Image consists of image records to be displayed in the digital library. The size is 1530MB.

From Figure 8, we can see that using file as storage has the best time efficiency. This is because file has a much simpler storage mechanism than DBMS. However, file is not able to guarantee usability in some cases since it cannot support data schema and transactions. Redis performs better than MySQL InnoDB for dataset Image but much worse for dataset Small Records, which is structured data. With multiple storage mechanisms implemented, we can make flexible choices according to the characteristics of data, thus enhancing the flexibility of PuntStore.

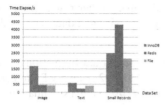

**Fig. 8.** The Result of Insertion Using Different Storage Engines

## 5.1    Performance of pLSM

To verify the efficiency of pLSM, we make two experiments comparing pLSM with B-Tree index. The size of each index entry is 64B. The first experiment is insertion test of the two indexes. The result in Figure 9 shows that pLSM has a much better insertion performance than B-Tree.

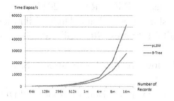
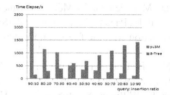

**Fig. 9.** Result of Insertion Experiment        **Fig. 10.** Result of Mixed Workload Experiment

The second experiment is a mixed workload with the variation of ratio between query and insertion. We added 1 million records to each index in bulk to do the initialization. Figure 10 indicates that with the increasing of insertion ratio, the time elapse of pLSM decreases sharply, and the time elapse of B-Tree increases along with the insertion ratio. From the experiment, we find that when index size is larger than 1 GB, B-Tree's aging problem becomes so serious that it will cost more than one day to continue inserting into B-Tree index. So our experiment stops here. Although B-Tree's query performance is better, it is not practical to use B-tree since insertion time dominates in this situation. Instead, pLSM would be more efficient.

## 6    Conclusion

Very Large Digital Library has brought new challenges in almost every issue of Digital Library. In term of the system aspect, we provide PuntStore, a plug-in system as a concrete solution to support VLDLs and adopt it into the project of Digital Library on History of Science and Technology in China. In term of the specific aspect, we design a new index method pLSM. The results show that pLSM could overcome the aging problem of B-Tree and perform well in the occasion of VLDL. As the practical result depicted above, our designs are proper to be implemented in VLDL system. For future work, we would like to perform large scale distribution of PuntTable in more practical projects. There are also many other research topics in VLDL such as architecture model, security, quality of service and data ranking that can be studied.

**Acknowledgement.** Our work is supported by National Basic Research Program of China (973 Program) No.2011CB302302, Key S&T Projects of Press and Publication under Grant No GXTC-CZ-1015004/02, and Tsinghua University Initiative Scientific Research Program.

# References

1. Bentley, J.L.: Decomposable searching problems. Inf. Process. Lett. 8(5) (1979)
2. Candela, L., Athanasopoulos, G., Castelli, D., Raheb, K.E., Innocenti, P., Ioannidis, Y., Katifori, A., Nika, A., Vullo, G., Ross, S.: The Digital Library Reference Model. Deliverable D3.2b, DL.org (April 2011)
3. Farber, F., Cha, S.K., Primsch, J., Bornhovd, C., Sigg, S., Lehner, W.: SAP HANA Database - Data Management for Modern Business Applications. SIGMOD Record (2011)
4. Manghi, P., Pagano, P., Ioannidis, Y.: Second Workshop on Very Large Digital Libraries:in conjunction with the European Conference on Digital Libraries. SIGMOD Rec. 38, 46–48 (2010)
5. O'Neil, P., Cheng, E., Gawlick, D., O'Neil, E.: The log-structured merge-tree (LSM-tree). Acta Informatica 33(4), 351–385 (1996)
6. Phiri, L., Williams, K., Robinson, M., Hammar, S., Suleman, H.: Bonolo: A General Digital Library System for File-Based Collections. In: Chen, H.-H., Chowdhury, G. (eds.) ICADL 2012. LNCS, vol. 7634, pp. 49–58. Springer, Heidelberg (2012)
7. Thompson, J., Bainbridge, D., Suleman, H.: Towards Very Large Scale Digital Library-Building in Greenstone Using Parallel Processing. In: ICADL 2011, pp. 332–341 (2011)
8. Wang, J., Zhang, Y., Gao, Y., Xing, C.: pLSM: A Highly Efficient LSM-Tree Index Supporting Real-Time Big Data Analysis. In: COMPSAC 2013, pp. 240–245 (2013)
9. Union E. Europeana (EB/OL) (2012), http://www.europeana.eu/portal/
10. Wikipedia. Database index (EB/OL) (2013), http://en.wikipedia.org/wiki/Database_index

# SRec: An Automatic Slide Capturing and Sharing System

Zhenkun Zhou, Weiming Lu, and Wenjia An

College of Computer Science and Technology, Zhejiang University,
Hangzhou 310027, China
{zkfzle,luwm,anwengel}@zju.edu.cn

**Abstract.** With the popularity of social media services, academic lecture slides could be shared immediately and discussed among hundreds of friends, which may extend the audience scope. Aiming at slide recording in speaker-occlusion scenes, we present our prototype system SRec, an automatic real-time slide capturing and sharing system. Based on depth information, it filters speaker body occlusion, recovers slide content, generates image/voice digital notes and shares them through social media services. The experiment shows SRec could capture and recover common text and picture slides shown in LCD and projector screens efficiently.

**Keywords:** Depth Information, Lecture slide recording, Digital note, Social media sharing.

## 1 Introduction

In universities and research institutions, attending academic lectures is a common activity, in which new ideas and approaches are shared and discussed. For the audiences, note taking is an important work, which helps to spread ideas, understand knowledge, as well as reserve resources for future use. Among various of resource formats, the slides play an important role in online education and digital libraries [10]. According to an investigation by Wolf et al. [18], 40% of the students are following the course in the lecture halls while the other 60% are watching the e-lectures slides online. With the popularity of mobile devices

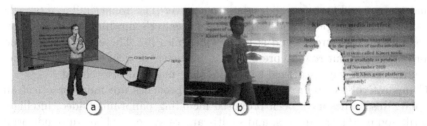

**Fig. 1.** SRec system. (a) Components, including a Microsoft Kinect camera and a laptop. (b) Application scene with LCD screen walls. (c) Based on depth information, speaker body occlusion is detected and filtered.

S.R. Urs, J.-C. Na, and G. Buchanan (Eds.): ICADL 2013, LNCS 8279, pp. 53–62, 2013.
© Springer International Publishing Switzerland 2013

and social media services, more and more people take photos of slide, integrate them in digital notes and post them through social media services. His followers, potentially with the similar research interest, could discuss slide content and feedback their comments immediately. The present listener summarizes the comments and could even discuss with the speaker in the Q&A session. The audience scope is extended and the interactive discussion could be in real-time. In recent years, such discussion has began to appear in many academic conferences. More relevant researchers are involved in the lecture.

The basic requirement of above activity is slide capturing. Various of research effort has been made on lecture recording and slide capturing. Most of these systems are not designed to solve the speaker-occlusion problem, for example, in small space speakers' activities may block the displayed slides, especially where the speaker often tap or draw on touch screen. What's more, the installation difficulty and price limits their further popularized. Users need an automatic system for slide capturing, digital note generating and social media sharing.

We propose our prototype system called SRec (**S**lide **Rec**ord). With depth data, SRec detects and filters speaker occlusion. Based on inter-frame region and switch events, slide content is recovered. The digital notes combining slide image and speaker voice is generated and shared immediately via social media systems.

The main contributions of our study include:

- An automatic slide recording system, which could solve speak-occlusion problem.
- Using off-the-shelf devices, it is low cost and easily deployed, especially suitable for institutions in developing countries.
- With social media services, it could be a new attempt, which pushes immediate information to specific research group with similar interests.

## 2   Related Work

Many online learning website, for example Open Course Ware [13], generally provide course or lecture slides. A variety of approaches have been proposed for capturing slides. Some systems capture slides by requiring the presenter to submit, or installing a plug-in on the presenting computers, which analyses the visual content and transfers slides data to a server [11]. Some similar approaches have used screen-capture software on the presenter's machine [8] or split projector input VGA stream and store as video files [9]. These systems get good recording results but require pre-installed 'intrusive' devices or software. What's more, it is not always practical to require slide material beforehand.

Comparatively, camera based recording approaches are more practical and popular. Researches have been proposed including panoramic video, intelligent pan-tilt-zoom (PTZ) cameras, and multi-camera systems. The Autoauditorium [5] system supports speaker motion tracking with a PTZ camera and proposes a virtual director that automatically selects the view from one of four cameras. Mukhopadhyay et al. [14] developed a system that combines video streams from a static overview camera and a slide tracking camera to create a synchronized presentation media. Rui et al. introduced their works [15][16] with multiple cameras to record lecture and broadcast online. Generally, these systems are designed for large halls with pre-installed cameras, where the slide is displayed on hung-above screens. The slide content is easy to be captured because speaker body and his activities don't block the camera visual field. However, in academic scenarios, most common presentations are often given in relatively narrow space, e.g. a lab meeting room, in which the speaker and audiences share space. The speaker doesn't stand still behind his speech table but walks around and interacts with listeners. His activities may block and occlude the slide content (see Fig.1b).

Organizing slide-centric multi-modal resources could enhance the research more accessible. SlideSeer [12] aligns academic papers and their corresponding report slides to provide a simultaneous view. Xianyu et al. [19] use SIFT features to align slide images with report videos. Bahrani et al. [3] use a three-pronged alignment system for aligning scholarly documents to corresponding presentations. In this paper, we focus on content sharing, including slide images and voice.

The differences of our system and mentioned above systems are:

- It aims to solve speaker-occlusion problem in many ordinary meeting rooms but not only large halls, which most other approaches may face;
- It is low cost and easily deployed, not limited by high price and installation difficulty;
- It focuses on generating and sharing slide-centric digital notes.

## 3   SRec System

### 3.1   Hardware Components

As shown in Fig.1a, SRec consists of one laptop and a Microsoft Kinect. The Kinect is placed against the display screen. Its captured data, RGB and depth streams, is sent to laptop via USB cable.

The Kinect has been calibrated beforehand using the method proposed by Nicolas Burrus [7]. From the configuration parameters, matrix $Hrgb2depth$ and $Hdepth2rgb$ can be calculated, by which the depth information for every RGB pixel could be calculated, and vice versa.

### 3.2   Workflow

The system work flow be generally divided into several functional stages.

- **Data pre-processing**. The horizontal stripes caused by low sample rate are removed.
- **Slide area deformation**. For every frame, slide area is detected via border detection or set manually. A perspective transform matrix helps to map the region into a normal rectangle form.

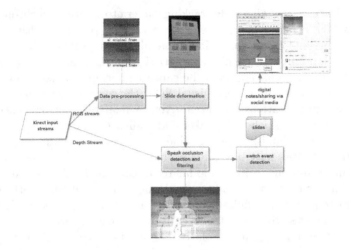

**Fig. 2.** Overview of the recording and sharing workflow of SRec system

- **Speaker occlusion filtering**. Depth difference is used to detect and remove speaker occlusion. The left holes are filled using a dynamically updated reference frame.
- **Switch event detection**. LLAH (*Locally Likely Arrangement Hashing*) [17] based switch detection process generates slide images.

**Data Pre-processing.** In our experiment, the acceptable RGB resolution is 1280x1024, with a low refresh rate of 12HZ, limited by Kinect. The low sample rate generates horizontal stripes in captured RGB frames. We adopt a pre-processing step to remove them (see Fig. 3a). In order to reduce computation complexity and provide reasonable performance, in implementation we adopt a simple smooth function. For every original frame $f_i$, a new frame $f_i'$ is generated by averaging the latest $k$ frames.

$$f_i' = \sum_{i-k+1}^{i} f_i/k \qquad (1)$$

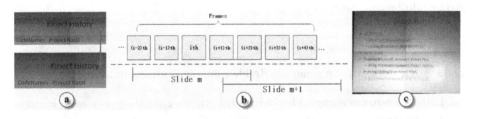

**Fig. 3.** Data pre-processing. (a)Horizontal stripes removal.(b)Smoothing may involve more than one slide with inappropriate $k$ value (slide $m$ and $m + 1$ get overlapped).(c)Overlap with $k$=5. (see clear color image)

Smooth frame parameter $k$ affects the output quality. In a certain range, larger $k$ will produce better smooth performance but it also increases the possibility of slide overlapping. If parameter $k$ value is too large, more than one slide content may be involved in a time slot and the smoothing process may produce overlapping (see Fig. 3b).

We did some experiments to evaluate $k$ value influence. We chose an empirical value $k=4$ (with 12 HZ refresh rate, if $k$ is larger than 6, smoothing time slot is larger than 0.5 second.). As shown in Table 1, the evaluation measurement result includes height of color stripes, human subjective feelings and slide overlapping rate.

**Table 1.** Smooth parameter $k$ experiment

| $k$ value | Height of stripe (in pixels) | Stripe visibility (subjective feeling) | Slide overlap rate |
|---|---|---|---|
| 1 | 50 | Obvious Stripes | No overlapping |
| 2 | 45 | Obvious Stripes | No overlapping |
| 3 | 38 | Slight obvious stripes | No overlapping |
| 4 | **18** | **Not obvious stripes** | **No overlapping** |
| 5 | 13 | Not obvious stripes | Start to overlap |
| 6 | almost 0 | Almost invisible | overlap |

**Slide Area Deformation.** Slide deformation, or formally image registration, is the process of mapping sensed slide image into a normal coordinate form. In deployment, it is impractical to require that the Kinect is always well placed against screen. In order to get a normal form of slide content, a frame deformation is made to map pixels into normal rectangle region (see Fig.4). Roughly the process includes feature detection, feature matching, transform modelling and data warping. Unlike manuscript image registration approach[4][6], we use a perspective matrix to model a rigid-body transform, because there is rarely nonlinear distortion on display screen.

The coordinates of four corners are needed to calculate the perspective matrix. They can be specified manually, or detected automatically. Assuming the slide area with apparent visual boundary, the four corners can be recognized by applying Hough transformation on black-white video frame (see Fig. 4c). A perspective matrix is calculated and used to map each pixel inside borders into a normal normal form image. Even if the corner couldn't be detected automatically, user can manually appoint them.

**Speaker Occlusion Filtering.** With pre-calibrated matrix $Hrgb2depth$, every pixel $p = (x, y)$ in RGB frame can get its corresponding depth value $z$, i.e. the distance from Kinect camera. A mathematical 'slide plane' is built using the 4 corners' $(x, y, z)$ coordinates. With this plane parameters, any pixel in RGB image can be classified whether on the screen or part of body occlusion.

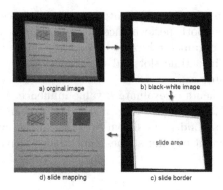

**Fig. 4.** Slide area deformation. Original image is turned into black-white form. Four corners are extracted and the inner pixels are 'mapped' into a normal form.

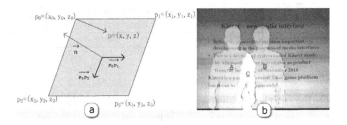

**Fig. 5.** Occlusion detection and filtering. (a)'Slide plane' construction with four point coordinates. (b) Occlusion filtering. For one slide, $A,B$ stands for occlusion areas in different frames which could be 'filled' by reference frame $F_{ref}$, while $C$ could't.

As shown in Fig. 5a, the four corners $p_0....p_3$ of slide are used to calculate a plane normal vector $\vec{n}$. $I(p)$ stands for whether pixel p is on the 'slide plane' (i.e. part of the slide contents) or not. $\varphi_t$ is a threshold.

$$\vec{n} = \frac{\overrightarrow{p_0p_1} \times \overrightarrow{p_0p_2}}{|\overrightarrow{p_0p_1} \times \overrightarrow{p_0p_2}|} \tag{2}$$

$$I(p) = \begin{cases} 1 \text{ if } \left|\arccos \frac{\overrightarrow{pp_0} \cdot \vec{n}}{|\overrightarrow{pp_0}| \times |\vec{n}|} - \frac{\pi}{2}\right| < \varphi_t, \\ 0 \text{ otherwise} \end{cases} \tag{3}$$

If point $p$ is not in slide plane, corresponding pixels in RGB image are set to -1, a value that doesn't exist in RGB color space. This step generates some holes (see Fig. 5b).

For certain slide display interval, while speaker is in different positions, the inter-frame redundancy information provides possibility to fill occlusion holes.

A RGB reference frame $F_{ref}$ is maintained and updated dynamically. In the very beginning, $F_{ref}$ is set to first frame. When new video frame $F_{new}$ comes, the difference of $F_{ref}$ and $F_{new}$ is calculated by counting percentage of different pixels both in non-hole-area $F_{ref}$ and $F_{new}$. If the difference exceed a threshold, reference frame $F_{ref}$ is updated with frame $F_{new}$. In our implementation, difference threshold is set to a empirical value 10%. Otherwise the pixel in occlusion area is set to corresponding value in the reference frame $F_{ref}$ and update the reference frame.

**Switch Event Detection.** In this step, slide switch events extracted different slides from video stream.

Unlike key-frame detection approaches and SIFT based feature extraction approaches, we adopt online document LLAH algorithm to recognize different slides. In a certain report, slides may have same color theme, and their traditional image difference features, for example, color histogram, are not significant. On the other hand, text is the main basis to distinguish different slides. The character space distribution feature is extracted and used to detect slide switches. Every character consists of several pixels. For every pixel, its descriptor is computed using different contributions of nearest neighbour points. Every key point and its descriptors are pushed into a hash table. Slide similarity can be represented as difference of two hash tables. Frame hash tables are compared. If their distance is larger than a threshold, the new frame is recognized as a new slide.

### 3.3 System Implementation

We implemented SRec system with C and C#. The application processes data input from Kinect and generates digital notes consisting slides and speaker voice (optional).

In the upper left corner of Fig.6a, filtered stream is shown. The generated slides are list below. Users can select one or some of slide notes to generate digital notes, and post them on social media services. SRec output could also be integrated with some popular note taking applications, such as Evernote [1]. With their API, the digital note is inserted and organized automatically (see Fig.6b). For social media service, we chose Sina micro-blog [2] as our test platform, which is one of the largest social media service in China with more than 500 million registered users, as shown in Fig.6c. We didn't test Twitter because most participants of our user study could not access its service from China mainland.

## 4 Experiment and User Study

We conducted a user study in order to collect user feedback on recording quality and system usability. Twenty participants (ten female) were invited. The average age was 25, ranging from 19 to 32. Fifteen of them were students from college and the other five were engineers from R&D department of IT company. They all have

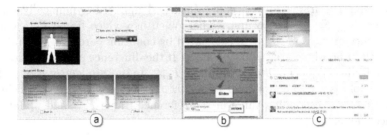

**Fig. 6.** SRec system and its output (please see clear color image). a) The running interface. b) SRec exports digital notes into Evernote. c) Slide sharing using Sina micro-blog and its comments.

at least Bachelor degree and are familiar with academic or technology lectures. All of them have used Sina micro-blog more than one year. Five participants have Twitter and Facebook accounts. For all the participants, we firstly introduced the main functions of SRec and divided them into four 5-person groups. The experiment was held indoor.

### 4.1   Recording Quality

We collected some lecture slides and divided them into four types according to their main content: English text, Chinese text, pictures and videos. For each 5-person group, one randomly selected 25-page slide of each type was shown in LCD display and projector screen respectively. During this process, one *speaker* walked in even speed in front of the screens. SRec captured the slides and each participant were required to give their subjective judge of the recording quality, in *Good, Just OK, Bad* 3 levels. The percent of well recorded slides was calculated and shown.

**Table 2.** Recording quality feedback

| content screen | English text | | Chinese text | | Picture | | Video | |
|---|---|---|---|---|---|---|---|---|
| LCD | 92% | Just OK | 88% | Just OK | 80% | Good | 64% | Bad |
| Projector | 96% | Good | 92% | Good | 84% | Good | 68% | Just OK |

- For text or picture slides, recording performance is acceptable. But for video content, because we use character spatial distribution features to detect switch event, recording accuracy is not good. However, video content is not the main component of academic slides and it is not our main focus.
- In diffuse reflection material (projector screen), recording quality is better than LCD. On LCD screen, there was some high-light area because of external illumination, such as LED light.

## 4.2  User Feedback

Participants were introduced and shown the way SRec shares academic lectures. 85% of the participants thought that SRec is better than traditional note taking and sharing methods. Participants rated highly on the convenience in sharing the generated digital notes.

## 4.3  Limitations

The experiment shows that there exists some limits of SRec.

- For screens with mirror reflection, sometimes the environment lighting may cause high-light area in final output, which requires adjusting the position and orientation of Kinect camera.
- If the speaker stands still in front of the screen, because of the information loss, the system couldn't fill the left occlusion holes. Adopting multiple Kinect sensors could solve this problem.

## 5  Conclusion

In this paper, we propose an automatic slide recording and note sharing system SRec. It combines depth and RGB video input to solve speaker-occlusion problem. Using off-the-shelf devices, its low cost and flex deployment suits widely for small rooms and lab scene. The experiments and user feedback show that SRec system is worthwhile in assisting people in academic reports.

As a preliminary idea and implementation, there are still some potential improvements. For example, using more than one Kinect device will reduce the possibility of 'left holes' in output. Slide keywords and scripts could be automatically generated from slide OCR or voice recognition and used to classify/search corresponding materials. We will improve SRec in the future work.

**Acknowledgments.** This work is supported by National Natural Science Foundation of China (No.61070066 and No.61103099), the CADAL Project and Research Center, Zhejiang University.

## References

1. Evernote, http://www.evernote.com
2. Sina micro-blog, http://t.sina.com
3. Bamdad Bahrani, M.Y.K.: Multimodal alignment of scholarly documents and their presentations. In: Proceedings of the 13th ACM/IEEE-CS Joint Conference on Digital Libraries, pp. 281–284. ACM (2013)
4. Baumann, R., Seales, W.B.: Robust registration of manuscript images. In: Proceedings of the 9th ACM/IEEE-CS Joint Conference on Digital Libraries, pp. 263–266. ACM (2009)

5. Bianchi, M.: Autoauditorium: a fully automatic, multi-camera system to televise auditorium presentations. In: Proc. of Joint DARPA/NIST Smart Spaces Technology Workshop (1998)

6. Brown, M.S., Brent, W.: The digital atheneum: new approaches for preserving, restoring and analyzing damaged manuscripts. In: Proceedings of the 1st ACM/IEEE-CS Joint Conference on Digital Libraries, pp. 437–443. ACM (2001)

7. Burrus, N.: Kinect calibration 3(4), 30 (2011)

8. Chiu, P., Boreczky, J., Girgensohn, A., Kimber, D.: Liteminutes: an internet-based system for multimedia meeting minutes. In: Proceedings of the 10th International Conference on World Wide Web, pp. 140–149. ACM (2001)

9. Chiu, P., Kapuskar, A., Reitmeier, S., Wilcox, L.: Room with a rear view. meeting capture in a multimedia conference room. IEEE Multimedia 7(4), 48–54 (2000)

10. Huber, J., Steimle, J., Olberding, S., Lissermann, R.: Huber, J., Steimle, J., Olberding, S., Lissermann, R., Muhlhauser, M.: Browsing e-lecture libraries on mobile devices: A spatial interaction concept. In: 2010 IEEE 10th International Conference on Advanced Learning Technologies (ICALT), pp. 151–155. IEEE (2010)

11. Kameda, Y., Nishiguchi, S., Minoh, M.: Carmul: Concurrent automatic recording for multimedia lecture. In: Proceedings of the 2003 International Conference on Multimedia and Expo, ICME 2003, vol. 2, pp. II–677. IEEE (2003)

12. Kan, M.Y.: Slideseer: A digital library of aligned document and presentation pairs. In: Proceedings of the 7th ACM/IEEE-CS Joint Conference on Digital Libraries, pp. 81–90. ACM (2007)

13. MIT: Mit opencourseware, http://ocw.mit.edu

14. Mukhopadhyay, S., Smith, B.: Passive capture and structuring of lectures. In: Proceedings of the Seventh ACM International Conference on Multimedia (Part 1), pp. 477–487. ACM (1999)

15. Rui, Y., Gupta, A., Cadiz, J.J.: Viewing meeting captured by an omni-directional camera. In: Proceedings of the SIGCHI Conference on Human Factors in Computing Systems, pp. 450–457. ACM (2001)

16. Rui, Y., Gupta, A., Grudin, J., He, L.: Automating lecture capture and broadcast: technology and videography. Multimedia Systems 10(1), 3–15 (2004)

17. Uchiyama, H., Pilet, J., Saito, H.: On-line document registering and retrieving system for ar annotation overlay. In: Proceedings of the 1st Augmented Human International Conference, p. 23. ACM (2010)

18. Wolf, K., Linckels, S., Meinel, C.: Teleteaching anywhere solution kit (tele-task) goes mobile. In: Proceedings of the 35th Annual ACM SIGUCCS Fall Conference, pp. 366–371. ACM (2007)

19. Xiangyu, W., Ramanathan, S., Kankanhalli, M.: A robust framework for aligning lecture slides with video. In: 2009 16th IEEE International Conference on Image Processing (ICIP), pp. 249–252. IEEE (2009)

# Analyzing Trust-Based Mixing Patterns
# in Signed Networks

Amit Singh Rathore[1], Mandar R. Mutalikdesai[2], and Sanket Patil[2]

[1] International School of Information Management,
University of Mysore, Mysore, India
amit@isim.net.in
[2] DataWeave Software Pvt. Ltd., Bangalore, India
{mandar,sanket}@dataweave.in

**Abstract.** In some online social media such as Slashdot, actors are allowed to explicitly show their *trust* or *distrust* towards each other. Such a network, called a *signed network*, contains *positive* and *negative* edges. Traditional notions of assortativity and disassortativity are not sufficient to study the mixing patterns of connections between actors in a signed network, owing to the presence of negative edges. Towards this end, we propose two additional notions of mixing due to negative edges – *anti-assortativity* and *anti-disassortativity* – which pertain to the show of *distrust* towards "similar" nodes and "dissimilar" nodes respectively. We classify nodes based on a local measure of their trustworthiness, rather than based on in-degrees, in order to study mixing patterns. We also use some simple techniques to quantify a node's bias towards assortativity, disassortativity, anti-assortativity and anti-disassortativity in a signed network. Our experiments with the Slashdot Zoo network suggest that: (i) "low-trust" nodes show varied forms of mixing – reasonable assortativity, high disassortativity, slight anti-assortativity and slight anti-disassortativity, and (ii) "high-trust" nodes mix highly assortatively while showing very little disassortativity, anti-assortativity or anti-disassortativity.

**Keywords:** signed networks, social network analysis, mixing patterns, assortativity, disassortativity, anti-assortativity, anti-disassortativity.

## 1 Introduction and Prior Work

Online social media such as Facebook, Twitter and Slashdot can be modeled as graphs or networks. In these networks, actors (or users) share various kinds of information with each other. While some actors seem to earn the trust of the population, some actors seem to earn the distrust of the population in these networks. In a few such networks, such as Slashdot,[1] actors are allowed to explicitly show their trust or distrust towards each other. These networks are known as *signed networks*.

---

[1] http://www.slashdot.org

S.R. Urs, J.-C. Na, and G. Buchanan (Eds.): ICADL 2013, LNCS 8279, pp. 63–72, 2013.
© Springer International Publishing Switzerland 2013

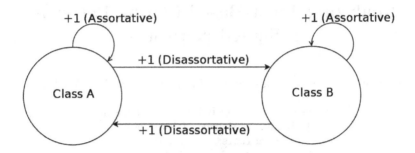

**Fig. 1.** Illustration of assortativity and disassortativity in unsigned networks

A signed network, $\mathcal{G}$, can be defined as a directed graph $\mathcal{G} = (V, E, s)$, where:

1. $V$ is the set of actors (or nodes)[2] in the network.
2. $E \subseteq V \times V$ is the set of edges such that $(u, v) \in E$ indicates a connection between $u \in V$ and $v \in V$.
3. $s : E \rightarrow \{+1, -1\}$ assigns a weight to each edge indicating the connection type, viz. *friend/trust* or *foe/distrust*. In this sense, a signed network is allowed to have "negative" edges.

In this paper, we address the problem of analyzing the "mixing patterns" of actors within the Slashdot signed network. Mixing patterns of nodes in a network pertain to the propensity of the nodes of a given "class" to connect to other nodes that may be either of the same "class" or of another "class". For instance, in an unsigned directed network, mixing patterns could pertain to the tendency of high in-degree nodes to connect to either other nodes of similarly high in-degree or other nodes of low in-degree.

In unsigned networks, the mixing pattern where nodes of a given class tend to connect to other nodes within the same class, is known as *assortative mixing*. On the other hand, the mixing pattern in which nodes of a given class tend to connect to other nodes outside their own class, is known as *disassortative mixing*. These two types of mixing are sufficient to study the mixing patterns in unsigned networks, since all the edges are treated as "positive" edges. An illustration of assortative mixing and disassortative mixing in unsigned networks is shown in Figure 1.

However, a signed network is made up of two kinds of edges: positive (with edge weight $+1$), and negative (with edge weight $-1$). While the traditional notion of assortative mixing and disassortative mixing can be extended to study the incidence patterns of *positive* edges in signed networks, we need to define different notions of mixing to study the incidence patterns of *negative edges* between nodes. In this paper, therefore, we define two additional types of mixing: (i) *Anti-assortative Mixing*, and (ii) *Anti-disassortative Mixing*. In this backdrop, we define the following types of mixing for signed networks.

*Assortativity* is the mixing pattern in which nodes from a given class connect to other nodes within the same class using *positive* edges. *Disassortativity* is the

---

[2] In the rest of this paper, we shall use the terms *actor* and *node* interchangeably.

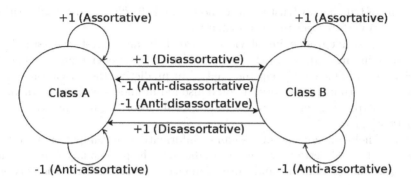

**Fig. 2.** Illustration of assortativity, disassortativity, anti-assortativity and anti-disassortativity in signed networks

mixing pattern in which nodes from a given class connect to other nodes outside their own class using *positive* edges. *Anti-assortativity* is the mixing pattern in which nodes from a given class connect to other nodes within the same class using *negative* edges. *Anti-disassortativity* is the mixing pattern in which nodes from a given class connect to other nodes outside their own class using *negative* edges. Figure 2 illustrates the above types of mixing in signed networks.

## 1.1 Positioning Our Work

The notion of mixing patterns in networks, in general, has been widely studied, e.g. [5,10,11,12]. However, these studies are in the context of unsigned networks. To the best of our knowledge, there exists no other work that considers the mixing patterns between nodes owing to negative edges. Hogg, et al. [5] study assortativity and disassortativity in networks with multiple relationship types. However, they do not seem to take negative edges – explicit shows of distrust or "foeship" – into account. In contrast to these works, we propose novel notions for capturing the mixing patterns due to negative edges. Also, nodes have traditionally been classified based on their degree in order to study mixing patterns. In contrast, we classify nodes based on a local measure of their trustworthiness.

The following applications in social media analytics motivate our attempt to study mixing behaviors among nodes in a signed network based on trustworthiness measures:

1. It allows an analyst in gaining insights into the extent of *homophily* and *heterophily* inside the network [8,14]. Such an insight helps the analyst in identifying the density and expanse of community structures in the network.
2. An analyst can understand the tendencies of nodes with respect to trusting or distrusting other nodes that are deemed to be trustworthy (or untrustworthy) by the population in general. This helps the analyst in addressing problems such as identifying: (i) preferential attachment (c.f. [2]) patterns in

terms of trusting/distrusting other nodes, and (ii) "hubs" and "authorities" (c.f. [6]) with respect to trust/distrust.

3. From a sociological point of view, it can help an analyst understand the underlying mechanisms with which trust relationships emerge in online social media. This could help the analyst in predicting the formation of new linkages within the network. It could also aid in understanding the theoretical underpinnings of the process model itself, according to which the signed network grows.

4. It can help an analyst in designing information dissemination strategies within a social network. Such an insight could help the analyst in planning targeted advertisements and word-of-mouth campaigns within the network.

### 1.2   Contributions of This Paper

The main contributions of this paper can be summarized as follows:

1. We define the notions of anti-assortativity and anti-disassortativity to account for mixing due to negative edges in signed networks (discussed above).
2. We then present a simple model to measure the localized "trust quotient" of an actor in a signed network, based on which we classify the nodes as *high-trust nodes* or *low-trust nodes* (Section 2).
3. Further, we study the above types of mixing behaviors with respect to these two classes of nodes. We present some techniques to measure the extent to which a node contributes to the different types of mixing in a signed network. Using these measures, we study the distributions of such contributions across nodes in the network (Section 3).

We have conducted our experiments on two samples of the Slashdot Zoo network [7].[3] The first dataset, sampled in November 2008, has $77,357$ nodes and $516,575$ edges. The second dataset, sampled in February 2009, has $82,144$ nodes and $549,202$ edges. However, owing to space constraints, we will largely describe our experiences with the 2008 dataset alone. We note that identical empirical results and mixing behavior are observed with the 2009 dataset as well.

## 2   Modeling Trust Quotients

In a signed network, we define the *positive in-degree* of a node as the number of incoming positive edges to that node. Along similar lines, the terms *negative in-degree*, *positive out-degree* and *negative out-degree* refer to the number of incoming negative edges, the number of outgoing positive edges, and the number of outgoing negative edges, respectively.

---

[3] These datasets are available at
`snap.stanford.edu/data/soc-sign-Slashdot081106.html` and
`snap.stanford.edu/data/soc-sign-Slashdot090221.html` respectively.

Given a node $u$, its positive in-degree, negative in-degree, positive out-degree and negative out-degree are denoted by $I^+(u)$, $I^-(u)$, $O^+(u)$ and $O^-(u)$, respectively.

In the immediate neighborhood of a node $u$, we measure the trustworthiness of $u$ in terms of its *trust quotient*, denoted by $T(u)$, as follows:

$$T(u) = \frac{(I^+(u))^2}{I^+(u) + I^-(u)} + 1 \tag{1}$$

Equation 1 is designed such that no node has a trust quotient of 0 (by adding 1 to the ratio). This makes it easy for us to visualize the distribution of the trust quotients on a log-scale. For a brief while, we ignore the addition of 1 to the above equation, in order to explain the essence behind the computation of trust quotients.

The trust quotient is basically the ratio of the positive in-degree to the total in-degree, i.e. a measure of the proportion of trust earned by a node from all its neighbors. Further, this ratio is rewarded by multiplying it with the positive in-degree. Consider a node $u$ having $I^+(u) = 4$ and $I^-(u) = 4$. Consider another node $v$ having $I^+(v) = 1$ and $I^-(v) = 1$. If we were to consider just the ratio of the positive in-degree to the total in-degree, both $u$ and $v$ would have a trust quotient of 0.5. However, $u$ has accrued more units of trust than $v$. We therefore multiply this ratio with the positive in-degree, in order to reward the accrual of trust from a large number of nodes.

The trust quotient of a node is a measure of its "localized" trustworthiness in its immediate neighborhood. It does not correspond to a global measure of the trustworthiness of the node as computed in the case of PageRank for unsigned networks [13]. Currently, we do not compute any fixpoint of trustworthiness measures for the signed network. Recently, there has been an effort to compute the global trustworthiness of a node in a trust network [9]. However, in the context of the current work, we only compute a local measure of the trustworthiness of a node. In the future, we plan to consider global measures of trustworthiness in studying the proposed mixing patterns.

For both our datasets, we computed the trust quotient for each node. If a node $u$ had 0 in-degree (i.e. $I^+(u) + I^-(u) = 0$), it was not considered for computing the trust quotients. There were $11,886$ such nodes in the 2008 network and $11,860$ such nodes in the 2009 network. Figure 3 shows the log-scale Pareto-CDFs[4] (c.f. [1]) of the trust quotient distribution for both of our networks. The trust quotient of each node was rounded off to two decimal places for the computation of these distributions.

The distribution of trust quotients in both the networks seems to follow a power-law with an exponent of 2.26. This indicates that both the networks have a large number of nodes with a low trust quotient and a small number of nodes with a high trust quotient. Based on this distribution, we chose a threshold trust quotient of 5 in order to distinguish between high-trust nodes and low-trust nodes.

---

[4] Pareto Cumulative Distribution Function.

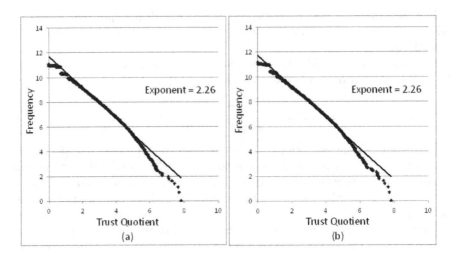

**Fig. 3.** Trust quotient distribution (Pareto-CDF in log-scale) for (a) the 2008 Slashdot Zoo network, and (b) the 2009 Slashdot Zoo network

From our distributions, we observe that only 19.76% of the nodes in the 2008 network, and only 19.8% of the nodes in the 2009 network, have a trust quotient higher than 5. In both the networks, since only a small number of nodes seem to have such high trust quotients, they may be seen as being genuinely *high-trust nodes*. The remaining nodes are classified as *low-trust nodes*.

## 3   Analyzing Patterns of Mixing

Given a node $u$ and its class $C$, we measure its *biases* towards assortativity $(A(u))$, disassortativity $(D(u))$, anti-assortativity $(A'(u))$ and anti-disassortativity $(D'(u))$, in order to evaluate its mixing tendencies.

The assortativity bias of $u$, $A(u)$, is the proportion of $u$'s total out-degree that it contributes to nodes *within* $C$ using *positive* edges.

$$A(u) = \frac{O_C^+(u)}{O_C^+(u) + O_{\overline{C}}^+(u) + O_C^-(u) + O_{\overline{C}}^-(u)} \qquad (2)$$

The disassortativity bias of $u$, $D(u)$, is the proportion of $u$'s total out-degree that it contributes to nodes *within* $C$ using *negative* edges.

$$D(u) = \frac{O_{\overline{C}}^+(u)}{O_C^+(u) + O_{\overline{C}}^+(u) + O_C^-(u) + O_{\overline{C}}^-(u)} \qquad (3)$$

The anti-assortativity bias of $u$, $A'(u)$, is the proportion of $u$'s total out-degree that it contributes to nodes *outside* $C$ using *positive* edges.

$$A'(u) = \frac{O_C^-(u)}{O_C^+(u) + O_{\overline{C}}^+(u) + O_C^-(u) + O_{\overline{C}}^-(u)} \qquad (4)$$

The anti-disassortativity bias of $u$, $D'(u)$, is the proportion of $u$'s total out-degree that it contributes to nodes *outside* $C$ using *negative* edges.

$$D'(u) = \frac{O_{\overline{C}}^{-}(u)}{O_C^{+}(u) + O_{\overline{C}}^{+}(u) + O_C^{-}(u) + O_{\overline{C}}^{-}(u)} \tag{5}$$

In Equations 2, 3, 4 and 5, the denominator is the total out-degree of $u$. In these equations:

1. $O_C^{+}(u)$ is the number of outgoing positive edges from $u$ to other nodes within class $C$.
2. $O_{\overline{C}}^{+}(u)$ is the number of outgoing positive edges from $u$ to other nodes outside class $C$.
3. $O_C^{-}(u)$ is the number of outgoing negative edges from $u$ to other nodes within class $C$.
4. $O_{\overline{C}}^{-}(u)$ is the number of outgoing negative edges from $u$ to other nodes outside class $C$.

The biases defined in the above equations can now be used to measure the mixing tendencies of nodes within a signed network. It might help to study how each kind of bias is distributed across the signed network, in order to understand the nature of mixing patterns in it.

In the previous section, we have described how we classify the nodes in our network into high-trust nodes and low-trust nodes. We computed the above biases for each node of both classes in our 2008 network. For the class of low-trust nodes, the frequency distributions of assortativity biases, disassortativity biases, anti-assortativity biases and anti-disassortativity biases are shown in Figure 4. Figure 5 shows the frequency distributions of the above mixing pattern biases for the high-trust nodes. The respective biases have been rounded off to two decimal places to compute these distributions.

An interesting observation about the 2008 network is that 43.96% of its nodes have an out-degree of 0. We see a similar proportion of nodes with 0 out-degree in the 2009 network as well. We have not considered such nodes for the computation of our mixing pattern biases.

The distribution in figures 4 and 5 do not take into account nodes that have mixing pattern biases of 0. However, we do include such nodes in drawing our interpretations about the mixing patterns in our network.

In the low-trust class for the 2008 network:

1. 76.76% of the nodes have an assortativity bias ($A(u)$) of 0.
2. 68.6% of the nodes have a disassortativity bias ($D(u)$) of 0.
3. 91.75% of the nodes have anti-assortativity bias ($A'(u)$) of 0.
4. 88.27% of the nodes have an anti-disassortativity bias ($D'(u)$) of 0.

This indicates that low-trust nodes mostly tend neither to trust nor distrust other nodes – both within their own class as well as outside of it. The analysis of mixing biases for the remaining nodes is as follows:

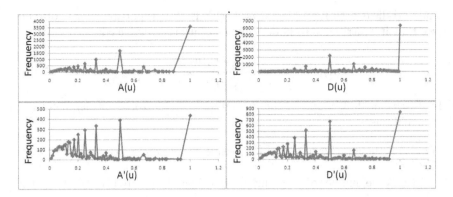

**Fig. 4.** Frequency distributions of $A(u)$, $D(u)$, $A'(u)$ and $D'(u)$ (non-zero values) for the low-trust nodes of the 2008 network

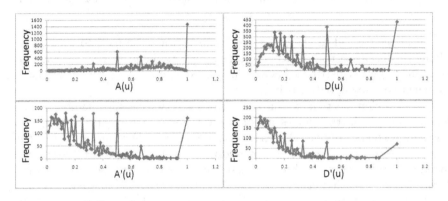

**Fig. 5.** Frequency distributions of $A(u)$, $D(u)$, $A'(u)$ and $D'(u)$ (non-zero values) for the high-trust nodes of the 2008 network

Figure 4 shows that almost half of the low-trust nodes (48.55%) show high assortativity $(A(u) \geq 0.5)$. In fact, 29.03% of the nodes show a complete bias towards assortativity $(A(u) = 1)$. The remaining nodes (about 51.45%) show low assortativity. A large majority (83.64%) of the low-trust nodes show significantly high disassortativity $(D(u) \geq 0.5)$, with 38.4% of the nodes showing a complete bias towards disassortativity $(D(u) = 1)$. This indicates that low-trust nodes generally show trust to other low-trust nodes, but tend to reaffirm the trust of high-trust nodes much more.

Figure 4 also shows that about 22.48% of the low-trust nodes show high anti-assortativity $(A'(u) \geq 0.5)$. Also, about 34.25% of the nodes show high anti-disassortativity $(D'(u) \geq 0.5)$. This indicates that a significant minority of the low-trust nodes tend to show distrust towards other nodes within their own class as well as outside their own class.

In the high-trust class for the 2008 network:

1. 31.91% of the nodes have $A(u) = 0$.
2. 45.45% of the nodes have $D(u) = 0$.
3. 64.74% of the nodes have $A'(u) = 0$.
4. 73.39% of the nodes have $D'(u) = 0$.

This indicates that only a minority of the high-trust nodes tend to show no trust at all in other nodes (of either class). Also, a majority of the high-trust nodes tend to show no distrust at all in other nodes (of either class). However, no show of trust does not imply a show of distrust, and vice-versa. The analysis of the non-zero mixing biases is as follows:

Figure 5 shows that a large majority (82.15%) of the high-trust nodes show high assortativity ($A(u) \geq 0.5$). In fact, 16.62% of the nodes show a complete bias towards assortativity ($A(u) = 1$). Also, only 5.37% of the high-trust nodes show high disassortativity ($D(u) \geq 0.5$). This indicates that high-trust nodes tend to show trust to other high-trust nodes rather than low-trust nodes.

Figure 5 also shows that only 13.42% of the high-trust nodes show high anti-assortativity ($A'(u) \geq 0.5$). Also, only 5.37% of the high-trust nodes show high anti-disassortativity ($D'(u) \geq 0.5$). This indicates that high-trust nodes do not tend to show distrust to other nodes within their own class or outside their own class.

# 4    Concluding Remarks

In this paper, we have discussed various kinds of mixing patterns among nodes in signed networks. The novelty of our work lies in the fact that we study mixing patterns taking into account negative edges as well. We have therefore proposed the notions of anti-assortativity and anti-disassortativity. Also, instead of classifying nodes based on degree, as is traditionally done in the case unsigned networks (c.f. [5,10,11,12]), we have classified the nodes based on trustworthiness.

We have presented a study of the mixing patterns in the Slashdot Zoo network. In this network, low-trust nodes tend to be significantly more disassortative than assortative in terms of showing trust to other nodes. Also, they tend to be slightly anti-assortative as well as slightly anti-disassortative. High-trust nodes tend to be highly assortative in terms of showing trust to other nodes. However, they show very little anti-assortativity or anti-disassortativity.

In the near future, we intend to study the mixing patterns in the Slashdot Zoo network by classifying nodes based on a "global" measure of their trustworthiness (c.f. [9]). As a follow-up to the current work, we are currently studying mixing patterns in signed networks by classifying nodes into multiple classes based on other properties such as their reciprocal behavior (c.f. [3]) and equivalence (c.f. [4]) with other nodes.

We conclude with the assertion that the techniques presented in this paper are general enough to be applied to different types of signed networks.

**Acknowledgments.** The authors would like to thank Ashwini K. and Mathews Babu for their insightful comments and suggestions, which helped in improving this work.

# References

1. Adamic, L.A.: Zipf, power-laws, and pareto – a ranking tutorial. Xerox Palo Alto Research Center, Palo Alto,
   `http://www.hpl.hp.com/research/idl/papers/ranking/ranking.html`
2. Barabási, A.L., Albert, R.: Emergence of scaling in random networks. Science 286(5439) (1999)
3. Garlaschelli, D., Loffredo, M.I.: Patterns of link reciprocity in directed networks. Physical Review Letters 93(26), 268701 (2004)
4. Hanneman, R.A., Riddle, M.: Introduction to social network methods (2005)
5. Hogg, T., Wilkinson, D., Szabo, G., Brzozowski, M.: Multiple relationship types in online communities and social networks. In: Proc. of the AAAI Symposium on Social Information Processing (2008)
6. Kleinberg, J.: Authoritative sources in a hyperlinked environment. Journal of the ACM (JACM) 46(5), 604–632 (1999)
7. Leskovec, J., Huttenlocher, D., Kleinberg, J.: Signed networks in social media. In: Proceedings of the 28th International Conference on Human Factors in Computing Systems. ACM (2010)
8. McPherson, M., Smith-Lovin, L., Cook, J.M.: Birds of a feather: Homophily in social networks. Annual Review of Sociology 27 (2001)
9. Mishra, A., Bhattacharya, A.: Finding the bias and prestige of nodes in networks based on trust scores. In: Proceedings of the 20th International Conference on World Wide Web. ACM (2011)
10. Newman, M.E.J.: Assortative mixing in networks. Physical Review Letters 89(20) (2002)
11. Newman, M.E.J.: Mixing patterns in networks. Physical Review E 67(2) (2003)
12. Newman, M.E.J., Girvan, M.: Mixing patterns and community structure in networks. Statistical Mechanics of Complex Networks (2003)
13. Page, L., Brin, S., Motwani, R., Winograd, T.: The pagerank citation ranking: Bringing order to the web (1999)
14. Rogers, E.M.: Diffusion of innovations. Free Press (1995)

# A Cluster-Based Incremental Recommendation Algorithm on Stream Processing Architecture

Yuqi Wang, Yin Zhang, Yanfei Yin, Deng Yi, and Baogang Wei

College of Computer Science, Zhejiang University, Hangzhou, China
possible2736@gmail.com
{zhangyin98,yinyanfei,yideng,wbg}@zju.edu.cn

**Abstract.** By helping users discover books they may be interested in, recommender systems fully exploit the resources of digital libraries and better facilitate users' reading demands. Traditional memory-based collaborative filtering (CF) methods are effective and easy to interpret. However, when datasets become larger, the traditional way turns to be infeasible in both time and space. In order to address this challenge, we propose an incremental, cluster-based algorithm on Stream Processing Architecture, which is scalable and suitable to real-time environment. Our experimental results on MovieLens datasets and CADAL user-chapter logs show our algorithm is efficient, while still maintains comparable accuracy and interpretability.

**Keywords:** Incremental Recommendations, Cluster-based, Stream Processing Architecture.

## 1 Introduction

Nowadays, users of digital libraries are enjoying an ever increasing amount of books on-line, while are also more vulnerable to get drowned in these tremendous information. With the help of recommender systems, digital libraries are able to make the best use of their resources, and users can also take advantage of this to find their favoured books easier, or even discover their new interests.

China Academic Digital Associative Library (CADAL)[1] has offered 1.5 million digital books and a myriad of multimedia resources to the public. Besides, there are tens of thousands of users visiting CADAL every day, which generate a great deal of logs. Given such a large amount of data, an efficient and scalable recommender system is badly needed, and it will definitely improve user experience.

So far, One of the most successful technologies in recommender systems is collaborative filtering. Collaborative filtering (CF) can be basically categorized into two general classes, memory-based methods [4, 8] and model-based methods [9, 11]. Memory-based methods use the whole datasets to make their recommendations. Generally, they use similarity measures to select users (or items)

---

[1] http://www.cadal.zju.edu.cn

S.R. Urs, J.-C. Na, and G. Buchanan (Eds.): ICADL 2013, LNCS 8279, pp. 73–82, 2013.

that are similar to the active user. Then, the recommendations are made from the ratings of these neighbors(This is why they are also called neighbor-based). Model-based methods first construct a model to represent the behavior of the users, then use the model to make recommendations. The parameters of the model are estimated off-line using the training data.

Traditional memory-based CF methods learn about users' preference by finding users with similar tastes or items that have been similarly rated. Although these methods are effective and easy to interpret, the learning procedure typically involves storing and examining the whole datasets, which is very time and space consuming. With rapidly increasing data size, this approach is becoming more inefficient, thereby strictly constrained by the limited time and resources available. Besides, one of the drawbacks in current CF approaches is that they are set for static settings. But in real world problems, there are always new users and items that should be incorporated into the model in an online manner.

To deal with the above problems, one may resort to Incremental Collaborative Filtering (ICF) [5] methods that can efficiently handle new data arriving in a stream, instead of retraining the whole model from the scratches. Papagelis et al. [7] proposed a method for addressing the scalability problem based on incremental updates of user-to-user similarities for online application, while Yang et al. [10] designed the incremental update strategies in item-based CF to increase the efficiency in recommendations. The incremental ability of a recommendation algorithm can not only reduce its computational cost, but also make it applicable to large-scale datasets and real-time environment.

In this paper, we propose a cluster-based method on Stream Processing Architecture, which incrementally generates recommendations for users and automatically updates itself to keep fitting data. The rest of this paper is organized as follows. In Section 2, we first provide an overview of the stream processing architecture CADAL uses, then introduce our method in details. We describe our experiments and analyze the results in Section 3. In the end, Section 4 presents the conclusions.

## 2    Incremental Recommendation

### 2.1    Stream Processing Architecture

Our stream processing architecture is shown in Figure 1.

When CADAL users read books on the website, users' behavior data are generated, this is where data stream starts. Then we use Kafka[2], an efficient and scalable distributed message system that can collect and deliver high volumes of log data with low latency, to collect users' behavior data. The next step is to deliver these data to Storm[3], a distributed realtime computation system that is scalable and fault-tolerant. After Storm stores users' behavior data to Cassandra[4], a popular NoSQL database that offers scalability and high availability,

---

[2] http://kafka.apache.org/

[3] http://storm-project.net/

[4] http://cassandra.apache.org/

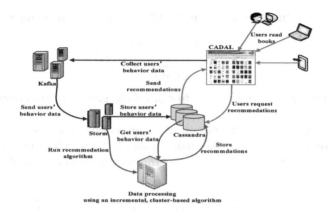

**Fig. 1.** The stream processing architecture of CADAL

we run recommendation algorithm to get data from the database and generate recommendations, then store them in the database. Finally, when users request recommendations, we fetch them from the database and show them to users.

An incremental algorithm will further enhance this stream processing architecture to be fully effective. The cluster-based algorithm we present later is a good match.

### 2.2   Cluster-Based Algorithm

**User Representation** In order to incrementally generate recommendations from logs of our website, we represent each user $u_i$ as an vector, where each dimension corresponds to one book. To be more exact, let $U$ and $B$ be the sets of users and books respectively. The $j$-$th$ element of the feature of a user $u_i \in U$ is

$$\vec{u_i}[j] = \begin{cases} 1 \text{ if user i read book j;} \\ 0 \text{ otherwise.} \end{cases} \tag{1}$$

where $b_j \in B$.

**Clustering.** In our method, a cluster $C$ is a set of users who share similar interests. The basic idea is that if two users read many same books, their interests are similar. Similar users should be in the same cluster and every cluster represents the unique tastes of its members. The centroid of a cluster is

$$\vec{c} = \left( \frac{\sum_{u_i \in C} \vec{u}_i}{|C|} \right) \tag{2}$$

where $|C|$ is the number of users in cluster $C$. Then we measure the similarity between a user and a cluster in cosine similarity [1], i.e.,

$$similarity(u, C) = \left( \frac{\sum_j u[j] \times c[j]}{\sqrt{\sum_j u[j]^2} \times \sqrt{\sum_j c[j]^2}} \right) \tag{3}$$

We adopt the diameter measure in [12] to evaluate the compactness of a cluster, i.e.,

$$D = \sqrt{\frac{\sum_{i=1}^{|C|} \sum_{j=1}^{|C|} (\vec{u_i} - \vec{u_j})^2}{|C|(|C| - 1)}} \tag{4}$$

We use a diameter parameter $D_{max}$ to control the granularity of clusters: $D_{max}$ is the max diameter of all clusters.

Thanks to the binary nature of our user representation, we do not need to examine and compute every user-user pairs in the cluster which is time-consuming, we do a little transform to Equation (4) in order to compute the diameter incrementally.

$$D_{C \cup u} = \sqrt{\frac{|C|(|C| - 1)D_C + |C| \sum_j |u[j] - c[j]|}{|C|(|C| + 1)}} \tag{5}$$

When in practice, we only need to store the numerator in Equation (4) as the compactness of clusters and update it for the convenience of computing the diameter.

Similarly, we can also update the centroid incrementally as shown in Equation (6).

$$\overrightarrow{c_{C \cup u}} = \left( \frac{|C|\vec{c}_C + \vec{u}}{|C| + 1} \right) \tag{6}$$

We now present our cluster-based algorithm as shown in Algorithm 1. This algorithm is efficient, scalable and unlike other popular clustering algorithms such as K-means, the number of clusters can be determined automatically by the algorithm itself.

Since the number of users could be very large, the number of clusters generated could be large as well. Thus, the potential bottleneck in our algorithm is the cost in finding the most similar cluster for users. However, the data from our website are quite sparse, since there are so many books in our website, and only a fraction of books is frequently browsed. In other words, the number of books shared by a user and a set of other users will not be very large, and we only need to examine the set of users that shared at least one book with the user $u$. Therefore, we adopt a data structure in [2] named dimension array to relieve this problem. Here is how dimension array, as shown in Figure 2, works. Each entry of the array corresponds to one dimension $d_i$ and links to a set of clusters $\Theta_i$, where each cluster $C \in \Theta_i$ contains at least one member $u_j$ such that $\vec{u_j}[i] \neq 0$. For instance, assume the non-zero dimensions of a user $u$ is $d_5$, $d_{10}$, $d_{15}$, in order to find the most similar cluster to $u$, we only need to examine the union set of cluster sets $\Theta_5$, $\Theta_{10}$, $\Theta_{15}$, which are linked by the $5th$, $10th$ and $15th$ entries of the dimension array, respectively. The most similar cluster to $u$ must be in this union.

Our approach only needs to examine the whole user set once. If users update their records i.e. reading some new books, we can redo clustering process for them to incrementally get new recommendations. Specifically, We create a set of

---

**Algorithm 1.** A cluster-based algorithm

---

**Input:** the set of users $U$ and the diameter threshold $D_{max}$;
**Output:** the set of clusters $\Theta$; dim_array[d] = $\emptyset$ for each dimension d;
1: **for** each user $u_i \in U$ **do**
2:     **if** $u_i \in \Theta$ **then**
3:        undo the clustering process on $u_i$
4:     **end if**
5:     $C$-Set = $\emptyset$;
6:     **for** each non-zero dimension d of $\vec{u_i}$ **do**
7:        $C$-Set $\cup=$ dim_array[d];
8:     **end for**
9:     $C = argmax_{C' \in C\text{-}Set} similarity(u_i, C')$;
10:    **if** diameter$(C \cup u_i) \leq D_{max}$ **then**
11:       $C \cup= u_i$; update the centroid and diameter of $C$;
12:    **else**
13:       $C$ = new cluster$(u_i)$; $\Theta \cup= C$;
14:    **end if**
15:    **for** each non-zero dimension d of $u_i$ **do**
16:       **if** $C \notin$ dim_array[d] **then**
17:          link $C$ to dim_array[d];
18:       **end if**
19:    **end for**
20: **end for**
21: **return** $\Theta$;

---

clusters as we examine the user set. For each user $u$, we first check out if he or she is a new user that has never been clustered, or just read some new books which means we need to re-cluster this user. If it is the later situation, we undo the clustering process on this user, which means change the data of cluster, centroid, dimension array, diameter etc. to the situation as if the clustering process has never been done to this user. Now this user is new to the algorithm either way, and we find the most similar cluster $C$ to $u$ among the clusters obtained for now. Then we test the diameter of $C \cup u$. If the diameter does not exceed the $D_{max}$ constraint, $u$ is assigned to $C$ and update $C$, centroid, diameter, etc. Otherwise, a new cluster only containing $u$ is created. Finally, we update the dimension array.

**Recommendations.** To be able to generate recommendations, we should first put some data into the algorithm to train our model and get some initial clusters. This is often executed off-line. After we trained our model and got some clusters, We can use this model to make recommendations. During the process of generating recommendations, the model itself is being constantly and incrementally updated in order to keep fitting data, which means there is no need to update the model off-line again. This is very efficient and suitable for real-time environment.

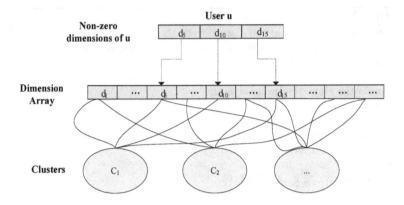

**Fig. 2.** The data structure for clustering

Recommendations are made to users according to the clusters they belong to. To be specific, each cluster has some users, and some entries of dimension array are linked to it, which means each cluster is linked with some books. We rank these books and recommend books that are ranked high to users of this cluster. While ranking can be done in a variety of ways, we rank books in the cluster based on the value of centroid of that cluster. Recall in Equation (2), centroid represents the tastes of users in this cluster, and the $j$-th dimension of the centroid is an indicator of how many members in the cluster have read the book $b_j$. It is reasonable to use centroid as the base of ranking function, since if so many users in the cluster love to read a book, then a user in this cluster is more likely to appreciate the book.

Our algorithm is efficient both in time and space, because unlike traditional memory-based CF method, we do not need to scan the whole datasets and to compute similarity between every user pairs every time when making recommendations for users. Our method generates cluster incrementally, consequently we do not need to store the whole datasets in memory and are more suitable to real-time environment. In addition to that, we only compute the similarity between users and clusters which is more efficient compared to computing every user pairs, since the number of clusters is smaller than that of users. Finally, as our approach incrementally learns users' preference and the number of clusters can be automatically determined instead of being fixed, our approach is also scalable.

## 3    Experiments

In this section, we first test our algorithm on MovieLens dataset, and comparing the accuracy and efficiency of our method to user-based CF method, one of the most popular traditional memory-based CF methods. Then we show the experimental results on CADAL user-chapter logs derived from our own website to demonstrate our method is effective and interpretable.

## 3.1  Experimental Design

The datasets we test our algorithm and measure its accuracy and efficiency are
MovieLens[5], one of the most popular datasets used by researchers and developers
in the field of CF.

The MovieLens datasets contain real data corresponding to movie ratings
captured on the website of the MovieLens movie recommender system[6]. We use
the MovieLens 1M dataset which contains 1,000,209 ratings of 3,952 movies
made by 6040 users. Ratings are made on a 5-star scale and each user has at
least 20 ratings.

Since our algorithm is designed for binary data, we need to preprocess the
MovieLens dataset as shown in Equation (7). For each rating, we denote $r_{orgin}$
as the original rating in the MovieLens dataset, and $r_{new}$ as the new rating after
we preprocess it.

$$r_{new} = \begin{cases} 1 \text{ if } r_{origin} \geq 3; \\ 0 \text{ otherwise.} \end{cases} \qquad (7)$$

We also use CADAL user-chapter logs to test our algorithm. Since the user-
chapter logs are generated from the click-through logs of our websites, it is
naturally in binary values. And this dataset contains 163,182 users with approximately 1,700,000 book chapters, the reason we recommend book chapters
instead of books is due to the digital lending mechanism CADAL adopts, which
is based on chapters of books [13].

We implemented our algorithm in C++ and used an Intel(R) Core(TM) i3-
2100 CPU(3.10GHz) with 3GB RAM to run our experiments on Ubuntu 10.04
system.

## 3.2  Evaluation Metric

Two basic metrics are utilized to evaluate the quality of our algorithm.

**Accuracy.** Since the top N items of the recommendation lists are usually paid
much more attention to, We focused on the top-N performance of the algorithm. While the majority of literature is focused on convenient error metrics
such RMSE and MAE, such classical error criteria do not really measure top-N
performance, they may serve as approximate indicators of the true top-N performance at most [3]. Direct evaluation of top-N performance must be accomplished
by means of alternative methodologies based on accuracy metrics. In this paper,
we adopt Hit Rate(HR) [4] as accuracy metric. We also use leave-one-out [6] to
evaluate our algorithm based on the accuracy metric. To be more specific, we
withhold an item and try to predict it using our algorithm and the remaining
items. If the withheld item is among the N recommended items, then we say
that a hit has occurred. we compute HR as follows:

$$HR = \frac{Number\ of\ hits}{L} \qquad (8)$$

---

[5] http://grouplens.org/node/73
[6] http://movielens.umn.edu

where $L$ is the number of items being withheld in the leave-one-out method. Noted that we withhold one item for every user.

**Efficiency.** Since the training process of our method can be done off-line which does not affect on-line performance, and user-based method does not have a training process. In order to show the efficiency of our approach, we compare the running time of making recommendations to users, i.e. prediction time, between our approach and user-based CF method, and use *speedup* which defined in Equation (9) as the key factor to demonstrate the superiority of the algorithm.

$$speedup = \frac{t_{UB}}{t_{CB\_Prediction}} \tag{9}$$

where $t_{CB\_Prediction}$ is the running time of prediction of our cluster-based method and $t_{UB}$ is the running time of prediction of user-based CF method.

### 3.3  Experimental Results

**HR.** We compare our method with user-based method while changing the number of top-N items recommended. Figure 3 shows the HR results of our experiment. This demonstrates that our method still maintains comparable accuracy, despite it generates recommendations incrementally and does not examine the whole datasets.

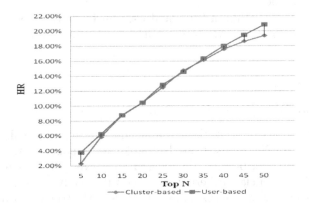

**Fig. 3.** HR results. The X axis represents the number of top-N items recommended

**Efficiency.** Compared with user-based method, our method does not need to examine the whole datasets and compute similarity between every user pairs when generating recommendations. We only compute similarity between users and clusters and incrementally generate recommendations. As a consequence, our method is theoretically more efficient than user-based method. The results of our experiments prove the efficiency of our method as shown in Table 1. If the datasets become larger, the merit of incremental method will be more apparent, consequently it is reasonable that the speedup value will be further improved.

**Table 1.** Results of Running Time Comparison

| Users | $t_{CB\_Train}$(sec) | $t_{CB\_Predict}$(sec) | $t_{UB}$(sec) | speedup |
|-------|----------------------|------------------------|---------------|---------|
| 500   | 96.39                | 6.38                   | 73.21         | 11.47   |
| 1000  | 96.39                | 12.59                  | 145.13        | 11.53   |
| 1500  | 96.39                | 18.71                  | 217.07        | 11.60   |
| 2000  | 96.39                | 25.13                  | 288.61        | 11.48   |

**Results on CADAL.** After showing the accuracy and efficiency on MovieLens datasets, now we turn to test our method on CADAL user-chapter logs to show its effectiveness and interpretability. Since the raw logs are quite noisy and we have not put our method on line to instantly get users' feedbacks, we only try to evaluate our results by examining the books linked to some clusters.

In some clusters, the books linked to them belong to a single topic (e.g. history, literature, politics, finance, art etc.), which indicates users in these clusters may be only interested in one type of books. There are also multiple topics in some other clusters which indicates users in these clusters have multiple tastes.

To further investigate the effectiveness and interpretability, we invite 10 people to judge the experiment results. We first measure the accuracy of a single clustering result, then evaluate the accuracy of multiple clustering results to measure the overall effectiveness. We adopt the judging rule as follows. For the first part, we randomly choose one cluster, randomly pick 10 books linked to that cluster $M_i$ times and show them to the i-th judge. For the second part, results of $N_i$ clusters are presented to the i-th judge. We randomly choose 10 books linked to each cluster and show them the same way as before to judges. In both parts, if the judge thinks these 10 books of a cluster are browsed by users sharing similar tastes, then we get 1 point from that judge. Suppose we get $P1_i$ and $P2_i$ points from the i-th judge respectively in the first part and the second. We calculate the accuracy of single clustering result and multiple results as follows:

$$ACC_{single} = \sum_{i=1}^{10} \frac{P1_i}{10 \times M_i} \tag{10}$$

$$ACC_{multiple} = \sum_{i=1}^{10} \frac{P2_i}{10 \times N_i} \tag{11}$$

The accuracy of the first part and the second is 64% and 58% respectively, which means the majority of judges considers that each cluster we generate does represent the taste shared by users in that cluster.

## 4    Conclusions

In this paper, we present an incremental, cluster-based algorithm on Stream Processing Architecture, which is scalable and suitable to real-time environment.

We evaluate our approach on MovieLens datasets and CADAL user-chapter logs. Our experimental results show our algorithm is efficient, while still maintains comparable accuracy and interpretability.

**Acknowledgments.** This work was supported by the China Academic Digital Associative Library Project, the Special Funds for Key Program of National Science and Technology (Grant No. 2010ZX01042-002-003), the Program for Key Innovative Research Team of Zhejiang Province (Grant No.2009R50009), the Program for Key Cultural Innovative Research Team of Zhejiang Province, the Fundamental Research Funds for the Central Universities, Zhejiang Provincial Natural Science Foundation of China (Grant No. LQ13F020001) and the Opening Project of State Key Laboratory of Digital Publishing Technology.

# References

1. Breese, J.S., Heckerman, D., Kadie, C.: Empirical analysis of predictive algorithms for collaborative filtering. In: UAI 1998, pp. 43–52 (1998)
2. Cao, H., Jiang, D., Pei, J., He, Q., Liao, Z., Chen, E., Li, H.: Context-aware query suggestion by mining click-through and session data. In: KDD 2008, pp. 875–883 (2008)
3. Cremonesi, P., Koren, Y., Turrin, R.: Performance of recommender algorithms on top-n recommendation tasks. In: RecSys 2010, pp. 39–46 (2010)
4. Deshpande, M., Karypis, G.: Item-based top-n recommendation algorithms. ACM Trans. Inf. Syst. 22(1), 143–177 (2004)
5. Giraud-Carrier, C.G.: A note on the utility of incremental learning. AI Commun. 13(4), 215–224 (2000)
6. Jamali, M., Ester, M.: Using a trust network to improve top-n recommendation. In: RecSys 2009, pp. 181–188 (2009)
7. Papagelis, M., Rousidis, I., Plexousakis, D., Theoharopoulos, E.: Incremental collaborative filtering for highly-scalable recommendation algorithms. In: Hacid, M.-S., Murray, N.V., Raś, Z.W., Tsumoto, S. (eds.) ISMIS 2005. LNCS (LNAI), vol. 3488, pp. 553–561. Springer, Heidelberg (2005)
8. Resnick, P., Iacovou, N., Suchak, M., Bergstrom, P., Riedl, J.: Grouplens: An open architecture for collaborative filtering of netnews. In: CSCW 1994, pp. 175–186 (1994)
9. Salakhutdinov, R., Mnih, A.: Probabilistic matrix factorization. In: NIPS 2007 (2007)
10. Yang, X., Zhang, Z., Wang, K.: Scalable collaborative filtering using incremental update and local link prediction. In: CIKM 2012, pp. 2371–2374 (2012)
11. Zhang, S., Wang, W., Ford, J., Makedon, F.: Learning from incomplete ratings using non-negative matrix factorization. In: SDM 2006 (2006)
12. Zhang, T., Ramakrishnan, R., Livny, M.: Birch: an efficient data clustering method for very large databases. In: SIGMOD 1996, pp. 103–114 (1996)
13. Zhang, Y., Wang, X., Yu, H., Li, R., Wei, B., Pan, J.: When personalization meets socialization: an icadal approach. In: JCDL 2011, pp. 459–460 (2011)

# Large-Scale Experiments for Mathematical Document Classification

Simon Barthel[1], Sascha Tönnies[2], and Wolf-Tilo Balke[1,2]

[1] IFIS TU Braunschweig, Mühlenpfordstraße 23, 38106 Braunschweig, Germany
[2] L3S Research Center, Appelstraße 9a, 30167 Hannover, Germany
{barthel,balke}@ifis.cs.tu-bs.de, toennies@l3s.de

**Abstract.** The ever increasing amount of digitally available information is curse and blessing at the same time. On the one hand, users have increasingly large amounts of information at their fingertips. On the other hand, the assessment and refinement of web search results becomes more and more tiresome and difficult for non-experts in a domain. Therefore, established digital libraries offer specialized collections with a certain degree of quality. This quality can largely be attributed to the great effort invested into semantic enrichment of the provided documents e.g. by annotating their documents with respect to a domain-specific taxonomy. This process is still done manually in many domains, e.g. chemistry (CAS), medicine (MeSH), or mathematics (MSC). But due to the growing amount of data, this manual task gets more and more time consuming and expensive. The only solution for this problem seems to employ automated classification algorithms, but from evaluations done in previous research, conclusions to a real world scenario are difficult to make. We therefore conducted a large scale feasibility study on a real world data set from one of the biggest mathematical digital libraries, i.e. Zentralblatt MATH, with special focus on its practical applicability.

**Keywords:** Text Classification, Mathematical Documents, Experiments.

## 1 Introduction

Digital libraries offer specialized document collections for many scientific domains combined with user interfaces and retrieval functionalities that are customized to the respective domain. The retrieval facilities of a digital library generally rely on two different types of metadata: classic bibliographic metadata (such as author, title, year of publication, and publisher) and semantic metadata (describing the content of a document). Today, especially semantic metadata is essential for the development of innovative methods for document retrieval, for instance explorative search, contextualization, personalization, and the creation of synergies between various digital libraries [1], [2].

There is a variety of possible semantic metadata annotations ranging from free tags over author keywords to terms from domain-specific taxonomies. In contrast to free tags (e.g., extracted from the Social Web) or keywords provided by authors, taxonomical metadata offers exceptional quality: it features a controlled vocabulary that is

S.R. Urs, J.-C. Na, and G. Buchanan (Eds.): ICADL 2013, LNCS 8279, pp. 83–92, 2013.
© Springer International Publishing Switzerland 2013

well understood by users in a domain, and is maintained and regularly updated by domain experts. While this quality is essential for libraries as controlled quality information providers, it comes at a price: not only is the maintenance of a taxonomy itself expensive, but the annotations of individual documents in a collection are too, since they usually are performed manually by domain experts.

Consider for instance the field of mathematics. There are two important digital libraries in this domain, Mathematical Reviews[1] in North America and Zentralblatt MATH[2] in Europe. Both provide abstracts and reviews covering the entire field of mathematics, e.g., for Zentralblatt MATH about 2,300 journals and serials world-wide, as well as books and conference proceedings. To offer the aforementioned assets for users (in contrast to general purpose web search engines), all provided documents are indeed manually annotated according to the Mathematics Subject Classification (MSC) taxonomy maintained by both organizations.

But is this effort in manual indexing sustainable? Currently, an exponential growth in the number of publications can be observed across all fields of science. Given the limited financial resources of libraries, this problem obviously cannot be handled by employing more domain experts for indexing tasks. Thus, the only solution is to provide more efficient (semi-)automatic indexing methods effectively reducing the manual indexing work while maintaining the resulting metadata quality. Fortunately, for the task of indexing the field of machine learning offers a multitude of automated text categorization methods which have already been applied to many text corpora with great success, see e.g. [3-7]. Indeed, it seems intuitive that text classification is key to being able to cope with the existing information flood. For instance, using MSC the approach in [8] achieved very good results with $F_1$ measures of 0.89. But looking closer at the experimental settings the experiments were performed in, they are hardly applicable to the workflow of a digital library because hard constraints to the incoming data were performed and full-texts were available. Moreover, it is also unclear what an $F_1$ measure of 0.89 really means in terms of quality for the applicability.

To provide additional perspective on these evaluations, we conducted a large-scale study on the feasibility of using different classification techniques for automatic indexing in practice. Motivated by the promising results in [8] we focused on mathematical documents according to the MSC taxonomy.

- Our document corpus taken from Zentralblatt MATH includes more than three million entries manually annotated with MSC classes and was chosen to ensure the applicability of our results to a real world scenario.
- We employed state-of-the-art text classification algorithms like support vector machines (SVM), Naïve Bayes classifiers, and C4.5 decision trees that were even specifically adapted to the domain, e.g. taking mathematical formulae into account for boosting classification performance.
- For the evaluation we do not only look at traditional $F_1$ measures or microaveraged break-even points, but also look behind these measures and evaluate what these numbers actually mean for practical application.

---

[1] http://www.ams.org/mr-database
[2] http://www.zentralblatt-math.org/zbmath/

Our contribution thus is threefold. First, we conduct a large-scale evaluation of text classifiers in a realistic taxonomy-based setting. We then provide an in-depth analysis of classification problems, and draw conclusions for today's digital libraries.

The rest of the paper is organized as follows: In section 2 we review related work presenting results for automated indexing based on bibliographic metadata. Section 3 introduces our experiments on the practical Zentralblatt MATH corpus. Section 4 addresses the applicability of automatic classifiers in a real-world scenario and explains the results in depth by additional experiments. Finally, section 5 closes with our conclusions for the practical application of text classification in digital libraries.

## 2    Related Work

Semi-automatic techniques for annotation of semantic metadata are covered by the field of tag recommendation. Tag recommendation are mainly based on two main approaches: co-occurences between tags [9], [10] and content-based tag recommendation [11]. A collaborative method for tag recommendation is presented in [10]. The authors used tag co-occurrences and tag aggregation methods to recommend Flickr tags. With this approach users can provide one or two initial tags, whereupon they receive recommendations for additional tags. On the other hand, content-based approaches as presented in [11] usually map the items to be tagged into a vector space, where either typical difference metrics between item vector and tag reference vectors are applied or a tag is recommended with respect to the output of a classifier which has been trained for that tag.

In [12] the author conducted experiments using bibliographic metadata of the Library of Congress and ranked Library of Congress class numbers for a given document. This was done by building reference vectors for each considered class and by ranking the classes for a new document according to the product of the document vector with each class reference vector. Reasonable results could be achieved by using the subject headings of a document. Here, the average rank for a relevant class was 1.36. However, as subject headings are normally already linked with a recommendation of a Library of Congress class number, this result is not particularly surprising. Furthermore, Library of Congress subject headings also belong to semantic metadata and have to be annotated manually. Without subject headings used in the ranking progress, the average rank of relevant classes raised up to 50.53. In [13] the authors performed a classification task for the ACM Computing Classification System. The eleven ACM categories could be predicted with a microaveraged $F_1$ measure of 60.81.

For the MSC the authors of [8] achieved a very good $F_1$ measure of 0.89. However, their experiments were applied in a setting which differs greatly from real world scenarios such as digital libraries. For instance, full texts were used, which are not generally available in the workflow of a digital library. Additionally, the whole corpus was filtered to only those documents with no secondary classes annotated. As the majority of documents have one main class and several secondary classes annotated, this constraint introduces a strong bias into the evaluation. Consequently, only 20 of the 63 top-level classes could be evaluated on the remaining corpus of 4,127 documents.

## 3    Experiments

In section 2 we presented related work with varying results for different text categorization tasks. From those results, conclusions for practical use can hardly be drawn. We therefore conducted a text classification task based on the data that is actually available in the workflow of a digital library and analyzed the results with respect to the practical usage. For our experiments we used a document corpus containing 2,051,392 documents covering the years from 1931 to 2013 delivered by the Zentralblatt MATH. The corpus contains titles, abstracts, authors, journals, and an unordered list of author keywords. To maintain applicability for a real world setting, we only applied a realistic and affordable data cleaning method. This included the application of a language guesser confining the corpus to English texts and the elimination of documents with missing abstracts or abstracts that only consist of one sentence. Statistical information about the corpus, including the distribution of documents over time, the distribution of categories over documents and the changes of the distribution of categories over time can be found at figshare[3].

As a ground truth, the documents are annotated manually with MSC classes by the technical editors of the Zentralblatt MATH. The MSC is a taxonomy used by many mathematic journals for semantic enrichment of their data. It is maintained and regularly updated by the two most important digital libraries in the area of mathematics, the Zentralblatt MATH and Mathematical Reviews. The last version of the MSC taxonomy (MSC2010) has three levels, containing 63 classes on the first level, 530 on the second and on 5202 on the third. An MSC class (e.g. 05D10 for Ramsey theory) is organized as follows: The first two digits determine the top level category (05 for combinatorics), followed by a character indicating the second level (D for extremal combinatorics) and two digits for the third level (10 for Ramsey theory). Each document has exactly one main class assigned and may have an arbitrary number of secondary categories assigned.

### 3.1    Text Classification

For document classification we evaluated Support Vector Machines, C4.5 decision trees as well as Naïve Bayes classifiers. For the document indexing we used a tokenizer that was adapted to our corpus and can distinguish formulae, references and plain text within the abstracts. We also analyzed the benefit of several standard text preparation, term reweighing and term selection methods like stemming, TF-IDF, latent semantic indexing, Euclidian normalization, and local term selection according to a feature scoring metric. Detailed explanations of these techniques are not in the scope of this paper, we refer to [14] for further details.

As proposed in [15], we focused on the three levels of the MSC individually, applying the same algorithms to each level in a hierarchical fashion with only minor adaptions.

For the training and evaluation of the second MSC level the corpus was projected to those documents that have the respective top class annotated. The same applies for level three. The classification error therefore sums up when a complete classification for all three levels has to be performed.

---

[3] http://dx.doi.org/10.6084/m9.figshare.796397

## 3.2    Formula Classification

In our mathematical corpus, formulae are the most important domain-specific feature. Since the naïve approach of treating formulae as simple text tokens had negligible impact on classification, we used a more sophisticated way to utilize formulae for classification.

In this experiment we used the formula search index described in [16]. In contrast to previous research we did not use this index to perform a search [17] [18], but to map formulae into a vector space. When a search query is performed on the index, multiple index nodes are visited. An index node can represent a complete formula, a sub formula, a terminal symbol or an abstract formula with no terminal symbols. Therefore, the nodes visited during the query evaluation yield a good semantic representation of a formula. When considering each index node as a dimension in a vector space, a formula can be mapped into that vector space by setting the coordinate of each index node to 1 if it was visited during the search query and to 0 otherwise.

One problem with this method is, that many formulae contained in abstracts are trivial (like e.g. $\lambda$) or not very complex and are therefore not adequate for formula classification. Therefore, the formula vector is merged with the vector obtained from a traditional bag-of-words approach on the plain text. This avoids the problem of finding an appropriate "complexity threshold" for formulae to consider them in formula classification and also increases the overall classification quality.

As many abstracts do not even contain a single formula, to verify the effectiveness of this approach we created a smaller collection of documents featuring formulae in their abstracts. The performance gain shown in Table 1 can therefore not be applied directly to the global performance but only serves as an argument for the general plausibility of this approach.

**Table 1.** Table of three best performing categories for formula classification in terms of $F_1$ measures.

| Top-level Category | only text | only formulae | combination |
|---|---|---|---|
| 34 (Ordinary differential equations) | 0.623 | 0.613 | 0.667 |
| 35 (Partial differential equations) | 0.674 | 0.609 | **0.734** |
| 11 (Number theory) | 0.664 | 0.531 | 0.667 |

We can see that even the relatively simple formulae mentioned in abstracts can be used to perform a classification based on formulae exclusively, or in a combined manner to improve the classification quality beyond that of pure text classification.

## 3.3    Results

In this section we present the results achieved by the machine learning algorithms mentioned above. For the training of the classifiers ultimately employed, we used titles concatenated with abstracts with no stemming applied. Formulae were ignored for bag-of-words indexing and were instead processed by the formula indexing method introduced in section 3.2. We then applied TF-IDF reweighting and Euclidean normalization on the document vectors and used these vectors to train Support Vector Machines. In the training process we used only those documents as positive examples which were tagged with the respective MSC class as main class. To prevent overfitting, the amount of positive and negative training examples were balanced to an equal number, where the negative examples were drawn equally distributed over all negative categories. By means of a tuning set, the threshold of the resulting classifiers were afterwards adapted to return an optimized $F_1$ measure.

The performance of the resulting classification system in terms of microaveraged $F_1$ measures are summarized in Table 2.

**Table 2.** Performance of the classification system in terms of microaveraged $F_1$ measures

|         | Top Level | Second Level | Third Level |
|---------|-----------|--------------|-------------|
| Top 10% | 0.815     | 0.898        | 0.919       |
| All     | 0.673     | 0.665        | 0.538       |

# 4    Classification Performance in a Real World Workflow of a Digital Library

Averaged results as shown at the end of the last chapter are commonly used to show the significance of the result of an experiment. They are often combined with microaveraged $F_1$ measures of the top $k$ best performing categories or examples for exceedingly favorable results. While for the evaluation of novel approaches for machine learning this manner of representation might be valid, for practical use cases it tends to be misleading. Let us therefore focus on the worst performing classifiers shown in Table 3.

**Table 3.** Performance of 5 worst categories in terms of the $F_1$ measure

| Top-level Category | $F_1$ measure |
|--------------------|---------------|
| 19 ($K$-theory)    | 0.182         |
| 12 (Field theory and polynomials) | 0.230 |
| 31 (Potential theory) | 0.240      |
| 08 (General algebraic systems) | 0.241 |
| 43 (Abstract harmonic analysis) | 0.242 |

Of course, in digital libraries, the annotations for each document have to be correct and complete to cater for effective subsequent searches. Since there are classifiers included in the classification system with performances as shown in Table 3, a fully automatic indexing is out of the question. Still, there are two possible ways to use the classification system.

One approach is to **tweak the precision** of each classifier to an expected precision of e.g. 0.95 by shifting the threshold for positive classifications appropriately. Consequently, classifiers as shown in Table 3 would then return poor recall values, meaning that these categories will hardly ever be annotated. Knowing that only 2.79% of all documents are annotated with more than three top level categories, we may consider a document to be annotated correctly if at least three high precision classifiers were triggered. After implementing and generalizing this approach for a hierarchical setting, we found that only about 1% of all documents could be automatically annotated with high precision MSC tags.

In the other approach the classifiers' thresholds are adjusted to **provide a good recall** of 0.95. These classifiers can then be used as tag recommendation service within the indexing workflow. In this setting, weak classifiers will be triggered far too often, invalidating the recommendation lists. A technical editor thus would have to work with recommendation lists containing a lot of irrelevant categories.

Both scenarios do not really contribute to the reduction of manual work for technical editors. In both cases the reason is not connected to the average performance of the classification system or the performance of the best classifiers but solely depends on the quality of the worst performing classifiers. For practical use, we therefore claim that the main focus must lie on the worst performing classifiers.

## 5    Confusion of Different Categories

To examine the extent of the problem we conducted further experiments with our MSC classifiers. In particular, we analyzed the confusion between all top level categories to determine whether a high degree of confusion between various categories might be the source of the problem. We defined a confusion matrix as

$$conf(c_1, c_2) = \frac{|\{\, d \mid Cons(d, c_1, c_2) \land Miss(d, c_1, c_2)\}|}{|\{d \mid Cons(d, c_1, c_2)\}|}$$

where *Cons* is used to specify the documents considered for the calculation of the confusion between $c_1$ and $c_2$. In our case all Documents are considered that have $c_1$ or $c_2$ annotated but not both $c_1$ and $c_2$. And *Miss* indicates a miss-classification of $d$ with respect to $c_1$ and $c_2$, meaning that $c_1$ or $c_2$ are missing or $c_1$ or $c_2$ have been mistakenly annotated. The resulting confusion matrix can be seen in Fig. 1.

We can see that there are quite a lot of categories with a confusion of 50% and higher. An explanation for this fact is that the information based on bag-of-words and formulae contained in title and abstract are not sufficient to separate the categories.

As a last experiment we analyzed the intra-class text similarity with Apache Lucene, one of the most popular full text indexing libraries. The Lucene full text index is used by many digital libraries as retrieval system and is therefore an important baseline to compare with. In the experiment we built a Lucene index with the given corpus and used every document for a "More like this" query. If textual content were a discriminating feature, documents in the result list should at least show the same main category as the query document. The result of this experiment can be seen in Fig. 2. Considering the top $k$ documents in the result list, the graph shows the percentage of documents which are annotated with the query documents main category.

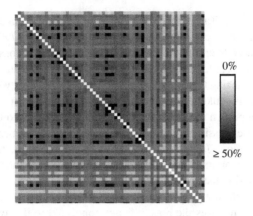

**Fig. 1.** Confusion between the top level classes of the MSC

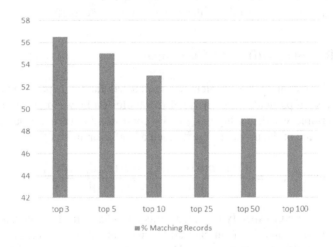

**Fig. 2.** Average matching of categories with Lucene "More like this" Queries

Fig. 2 shows two interesting points. On one hand, it shows that even for the top ranked documents according to the Lucene text similarity there is no confidence that the returned documents belong to the same category. On the other hand, the result show that even for rank 100 the confidence of 48% for receiving some relevant document is not significantly lower than on the ranks 1-3.

## 6    Conclusion

In this paper we studied the level of quality that state-of-the-art text categorization techniques can achieve for automated annotation of semantic metadata. With respect to microaveraged $F_1$ measures we can say that our results are comparable to current work in mathematical text classification. But we found out that for practical applications microaveraged $F_1$ measure may be misleading. As we have argued, for digital libraries the performance of a classification system is mainly dependent on the performance of the worst classifiers. This fact became obvious when we applied our MSC classifiers either for fully automatic indexing by tweaking the precision or for tag recommendation by boosting the recall. Both approaches resulted in a minimal reduction of manual work for technical editors.

Assuming that for every relevant classification task in digital libraries there are always bad performing classifiers involved, we can conclude that automated text classification alone cannot be used to reduce the manual work for indexing tasks in digital libraries. In our scenario this fact was true even though a notable amount of over two million documents were available for training and only the first level of the MSC were considered. In future work we plan to find out why this is the case and what can be done to solve the problem. First, we want to evaluate the inter-rater reliability for our classification task to see if humans can achieve a significantly higher categorization performance than automated classifiers, especially for those classes with high confusion. If this is the case, the question remains why humans are able to classify documents accurately while machines can't. Otherwise, if even human ratings are not consistent, it is not surprising that machines cannot perform significantly better. In this case it is also questionable if a strong annotation of taxonomy terms is sensible and if there is no need for alternative ways to enrich documents for the users of digital libraries.

We also want to extend our experiments to full text documents, which might – regarding formula classification – to some degree increase classification quality. In this case this means that digital libraries will need access to full text even if this full texts are not delivered as plain text but e.g. in the form of a feature vector. Otherwise, digital libraries can only restrict their scope and process less sources, lower the demands on delivered quality, or rely on different types of semantic metadata like free tags, author networks, or citation networks. Future work will show if using this kind of semantic metadata an adequate quality in retrieval and customization can be achieved.

**Acknowledgements.** Special thanks are extended to the German National Science Foundation (DFG) for supporting this study. We also wish to acknowledge the help provided by Corneliu-Claudiu Prodescu and Prof. Dr. Michael Kohlhase by applying the MathWebSearch index on the Zentralblatt MATH corpus. Moreover, we would like to express our appreciation to the Zentralblatt MATH for the provision of the corpus used in this study.

# References

1. Chirita, P.A., Nejdl, W., Paiu, R., Kohlschütter, C.: Using ODP metadata to personalize search. In: SIGIR 2005, Salvador, Brazil (2005)
2. Mirizzi, R., Ragone, A., Di Noia, T., Di Sciascio, E.: Semantic wonder cloud: exploratory search in DBpedia. In: Daniel, F., Facca, F.M. (eds.) ICWE 2010. LNCS, vol. 6385, pp. 138–149. Springer, Heidelberg (2010)

3. Homoceanu, S., Dechand, S., Balke, W.-T.: Review Driven Customer Segmentation for Improved E-Shopping Experience. ACM Web Science (2011)
4. Shen, D., Ruvini, J.-D., Sarwar, B.: Large-scale item categorization for e-commerce. In: CIKM 2012, Maui, Hawaii, USA (2012)
5. Cheng, W., Kasneci, G., Graepel, T., Stern, D., Herbrich, R.: Automated feature generation from structured knowledge. In: CIKM 2011, Glasgow, Scotland, UK (2011)
6. Dumais, S., Platt, J., Heckerman, D., Sahami, M.: Inductive learning algorithms and representations for text categorization. In: CIKM 1998, Bethesda, Maryland, USA (1998)
7. Cohen, W.W., Singer, Y.: Context-sensitive learning methods for text categorization. ACM Trans. Inf. Syst., pp. 141–173 (April 1999)
8. Řehůřek, R., Sojka, P.: Automated Classification and Categorization of Mathematical Knowledge. In: CICM 2008, pp. 543–557 (2008)
9. Song, Y., Zhuang, Z., Li, H., Zhao, Q., Li, J., Lee, W.-C., Giles, C.L.: Real-time automatic tag recommendation. In: SIGIR 2008 (2008)
10. Sigurbjörnsson, B., van Zwol, R.: Flickr tag recommendation based on collective knowledge. In: WWW 2008, Beijing, China (2008)
11. Byde, A., Wan, H., Cayzer, S.: Personalized Tag Recommendations via Tagging and Content-based Similarity Metrics. In: ICWSM 2007 (2007)
12. Larson, R.R.: Experiments in automatic library of congress classification. In: JASIS 1992, pp. 130–148 (1992)
13. Zhang, B., Gonçalves, M.A., Fan, W., Chen, Y., Fox, E.A., Calado, P., Cristo, M.: Combining structural and citation-based evidence for text classification. In: ICKM 2004 (2004)
14. Sebastiani, F.: Machine learning in automated text categorization. ACM Computing Surveys, 1–47 (2002)
15. Sun, A., Lim, E.-P.: Hierarchical text classification and evaluation. In: ICDM 2001 (2001)
16. Prodescu, C.C., Kohlhase, M.: Mathwebsearch 0.5-open formula search engine. In: Wissens-und Erfahrungsmanagement Conference Proceedings (2011)
17. Kohlhase, M., Matican, B.A., Prodescu, C.-C.: MathWebSearch 0.5: scaling an open formula search engine. In: CICM 2012, pp. 342–357 (2012)
18. Iancu, M., Kohlhase, M., Rabe, F., Urban, J.: The Mizar Mathematical Library in OMDoc: Translation and Applications. Journal of Automated Reasoning, 191–202 (2013)

# Ranking Vicarious Learners
# in Research Collaboration Networks

Andrea Tagarelli and Roberto Interdonato

DIMES - University of Calabria, Italy
{tagarelli,rinterdonato}@dimes.unical.it

**Abstract.** Despite being a topic of growing interest in social learning theory, vicarious learning has not been well-studied so far in digital library related tasks. In this paper, we address a novel ranking problem in research collaboration networks, which focuses on the role of vicarious learner. We introduce a topology-driven vicarious learning definition and propose the first centrality method for ranking vicarious learners. Results obtained on DBLP networks support the significance and uniqueness of the proposed approach.

## 1 Introduction

Research collaboration networks (RCNs) are being formed as prototypes of social networks on top of digital libraries. As for other major types of social networks, data management and mining research in RCNs has focused mainly on expert finding, community discovery, and relation (link) prediction (e.g., [3,6,11,13,14,10]). All these tasks have to be aware of the interactions underlying research collaboration, and in this respect, the discovery of hidden *expert-apprentice* or *advisor-advisee* relationships among researchers is particularly important. Mining such relationships can be useful for several reasons such as understanding how a research community is formed in a particular institutional context, how research themes evolve over time, predicting whether a researcher will likely influence a research community, and aiding an expert finding application to foster several experts on specific topics.

**Motivations and Challenges.** In this context, the current trend is to push the search for expert-apprentice relationships towards an expert-oriented investigation of co-authorships. By contrast, it seems that a study of roles as "non-expert" has been neglected in RCN mining research, despite the fact that a significant part of members in a RCN is more likely to be apprentice: after all, an apprenticeship or training status not only clearly holds for the initial stage of a researcher lifetime, but also naturally holds for any researcher w.r.t. any topic that at a particular time does not represent her/his main research interests.

A particularly challenging type of relationship to discover from the apprentice perspective concerns *vicarious learning*. In social learning theory, vicarious learning refers to the notion that people can learn through being given access to the learning experiences of others, and in general it is seen as a function of

S.R. Urs, J.-C. Na, and G. Buchanan (Eds.): ICADL 2013, LNCS 8279, pp. 93–102, 2013.
© Springer International Publishing Switzerland 2013

observing, modeling and replicating the learning behavior of others [1]. However, while vicarious learning can be seen as legitimate in any training stage, a question becomes whether in a publication context it can still be identified and measured in collaborations in which one might marginally contribute to the research activity (possibly materialized in a publication). The question is clearly tricky, since in reality it could be difficult even for human beings to judge who is vicariously learning by the track records related to a research community. Nevertheless, investigating the case of vicarious learners can offer us a chance to gain an insight into a research community that goes beyond the simple co-authorships. In particular, scoring RCN members based on their degree of vicarious learning should be seen as essential to determine the contingencies in the network under which different apprentice' behaviors occur; ultimately, it should aid devising both generic and ad-hoc strategies of eliciting more proactive participation in research activities, commitment to work in teams more collaboratively and trying to take influential actions, and building up strong collaborative subnetworks. Moreover, by analyzing the RCN over time, the changes in each apprentice's profile can be detected and several actions can be taken, for instance, to promote emerging researchers (e.g., with calls for tenure track positions).

**Contributions.** In this paper we address the novel problem of identifying and ranking vicarious learners in RCNs. We would like to point out that our usage of the term "vicarious learner" is intended to actually entail the meaning related to the more generic "advisee" and "apprentice"; however, as it will be clarified later, the term vicarious learner is chosen as preferred since it better fits the notion of knowledge gained in research collaboration.

To the best of our knowledge, we are the first to introduce the concept of vicarious learner into research on analysis and mining in RCNs. We provide a formal definition of vicarious learner and introduce a weighted directed network model to represent a vicarious-learner-oriented co-authorship network. Following a fully unsupervised learning approach, we propose the first centrality method in RCNs for ranking vicarious learners. For this purpose, we provide a specification of our ranking method based on PageRank, supported by the great potential that the popular Google's method has largely shown in co-authorship network analysis. We conducted experiments using DBLP as case in point, as both a static and a dynamic network. Moreover, we also resorted to ArnetMiner for purposes of ground-truth evaluation of the competing methods. Quantitative as well as qualitative results have indicated the significance and uniqueness of our ranking method, in contrast to traditional PageRank and baseline methods which might fail in ranking probable vicarious learners.

**Related Work.** As mentioned earlier, major attention in co-authorship network analysis has been paid to the discovery of author impact (e.g., [6,15,4]), and more recently focusing on expert search (e.g., [3,13]) and link prediction (e.g., [11]). Focusing on contexts closer to our study, [14] proposes a time-constrained probabilistic factor graph model to discover advisor-advisee relationships. Like in our case, the study exploits only information available on the network, with neither text annotations nor supervised information such as labeled relations (i.e., who is advisor of whom); however, the goal in [14] is to rank advisors for every author. [7] builds a linear regression model on Page-Rank scores to predict an improvement in productivity of the researchers. The method exploits mutual influence between each pair of co-authors, which significantly impacts on the ranking graph size, while it makes a straightforward adaptation of PageRank that only utilizes out-going links to score an author-node. Moreover, each author is initially assigned a weight that estimates the quality of her/his publication set based on an external, predefined rating scheme of the publication venues, which is clearly controversial by nature. In any case, the peculiarities of the respective models in both [14] and [7] make it improbable an adaptation to the problem of vicariously learner ranking.

## 2   The Proposed Model

**Modeling Vicarious-Learning-Oriented RCNs.** A common assumption in RCNs is that two researchers are regarded as connected to each other if they have co-authored a paper. Co-authorships in a RCN are naturally treated as symmetric relations, however a directed graph model would be more convenient when the target of investigation is on scoring influential researchers, or as in our setting, vicarious learners. Authors' interactions in a RCN are typically modeled as influence-oriented relationships, and in fact traditional ranking approaches, including PageRank based methods for RCN analysis (e.g., [15,4,9,8]), assume an influence graph model which implies that the more (or more relevant) incoming links a node has the more important it is; for instance, the more advisees a researcher supports the more authoritative or expert s/he might be. Clearly, as researchers might influence each other, both the incoming and outgoing links of a node should be taken into account. Moreover, vicarious learner behaviors build on the amount of information or benefit a node receives, therefore we believe that a convenient graph model is such that edges are drawn from experts to apprentices (except for cases of presumed equal relationships).

Our vicarious-learner-oriented RCN graph model assumes the availability only of basic information stored in a co-authorship network, at a given temporal window. Within this view, a reasonable solution is to look at each author's amount of publications to discriminate among the varying degrees of expertise/apprenticeship. Let us denote with $\mathcal{G}_t = \langle \mathcal{V}_t, \mathcal{E}_t, w_t \rangle$ a weighted directed graph representing a RCN at a discrete time interval $t$, with set of nodes (authors) $\mathcal{V}_t$, set of edges $\mathcal{E}_t$, and edge weighting function $w_t$. The semantics of any edge $(i, j)$ is that $j$ is likely most to benefit from the collaboration with $i$ at time $t$, and the edge weight, $w_t(i, j)$, expresses the strength of the benefit received by $j$ from $i$.

*Drawing edges.* A link $(i, j) \in \mathcal{E}_t$ is drawn from author $i$ to author $j$ if they are co-authors in some publication at time interval $t$, with author $i$ having a total number of publications (as calculated at time $t$ or earlier) greater than that of author $j$; in case of a tie, reciprocal edges are inserted between $i$ and $j$.

Clearly, author's academic achievements, citations and productivity indexes, such as h-index, might also be taken into account to uncover hidden expert-apprentice relationships; however, we do not follow that line since the above information is either not always available or easily derivable from a RCN (for some author or for any given time) or it may be too coarse. To corroborate our choice of simply using the amount of publication to estimate the expert/apprentice relationships, we indeed evaluated the impact of exploiting a criterion based on h-index. For this purpose, we used the co-authorship network derived from the whole DBLP dataset (cf. Table 1) as case in point, and we also retrieved the authors' h-indexes from an external source, ArnetMiner.[1] At first, we changed our defined edge drawing model by replacing an author's total number of publications with her/his h-index, but this actually led to a significant increase in the number of reciprocal edges (from 10% to 65% of the total number of edges). Then, we set an edge $(i, j)$ according to the comparison between the authors' h-indexes, and in case of a tie according to their number of publications: as a result, we surprisingly observed an overlap of 94% between this edge set and that based solely on number of publications; analogously, by inverting the two conditions for edge drawing (i.e., by amount of publication first, then by h-index), the overlap was about 99%.

*Weighting edges.* The number of co-authored publications between any two nodes can be regarded as an essential criterion for expressing the strength of collaboration; moreover, this simple criterion has the advantage of being readily available at any time interval. However, it should also be noted that an advisor has normally to divide her/his *attention* over all incoming stimuli that come from her/his advisees; consequently, the benefit each advisee might gain from her/his advisor could decrease as the number of advisees the advisor must support increases. Therefore, we weight the strength of $(i, j)$ not only as directly proportional to the evidence of collaboration in terms of publications but also as inversely proportional to the number of publications co-authored by the advisor $i$ with advisees other than $j$. Formally, at a time interval $t$:

$$w_t(i, j) = coPubs(i, j, t) \left( 1 - \frac{\sum_{k \in advisees(i,t) \setminus \{j\}} coPubs(i, k, t)}{\sum_{k \in advisees(i,t)} coPubs(i, k, t)} \right)$$

where $coPubs(i, j, t)$ is the number of publications co-authored by $i$ and $j$ at time $t$, and $advisees(i, t)$ denotes the set of $i$'s advisees (i.e., $i$'s out-neighbors) at time $t$.

**Ranking Vicarious Learners.** In order to capture the intuition that researchers influence each other in a RCN, both the incoming and outgoing links of a node will be taken into account in our notion of vicarious learning and, consequently, in our proposed ranking method. Within this view, the simplest non-trivial form of a measure of vicarious learner ranking would be given by the ratio of the in-degree to the out-degree of a node. However, this has clearly the

---

[1] http://arnetminer.org/ranks/author

disadvantage of giving many nodes the same or very close ranking scores and it totally ignores that both in-neighbors and out-neighbors might contribute to the status of a given node. Learning from our previous study on silent actors in online social networks [12], our key idea is hence to determine a node's status of vicarious learner according to the following criteria:

- to be inversely proportional to the node's out-degree, and
- to be proportional to the number of its in-neighbors and to their likelihood of being non-vicarious-learners (i.e., advisors or expert researchers), which is expressed by a relatively high out/in-degree.

The above set of criteria states that determining a vicarious learning status for a node not only relies on its in/out-degree ratio but also on the extent to which its in-neighbors are rather influential nodes (i.e., advisors or expert researchers) as well as its out-neighbors may in turn show a vicarious learning behavior.

To provide a complete specification of the above intuition, we resort to the renowned PageRank [2], which has been widely applied to various types of RCNs [15,4,9,8]. Remind that the PageRank vector is the unique solution of the iterative equation $\mathbf{r} = \alpha \mathbf{Sr} + (1 - \alpha)\mathbf{p}$, where $\mathbf{S}$ denotes the column-stochastic transition probability matrix, $\mathbf{p}$ is a vector whose non-negative components sum up to 1, typically defined as a vector of uniform scores, and $\alpha$ is a real-valued coefficient in $[0, 1]$, commonly set to 0.85, which acts as damping factor.

For any node $i \in \mathcal{V}_t$ in the RCN graph $\mathcal{G}_t = \langle \mathcal{V}_t, \mathcal{E}_t, w_t \rangle$, let $B_t(i)$ and $R_t(i)$ the set of $i$'s in-neighbors and the set of $i$'s out-neighbors at time interval $t$, respectively, and hence the sizes of $B_t(i)$ and $R_t(i)$ are respectively the in-degree and the out-degree of $i$. Upon the PageRank formula, our vicarious learner ranking method, named VLRank, is defined by the set of equations:

$$r_i = \alpha \left( \frac{1}{|R_t(i)|} \sum_{j \in B_t(i)} w_t(j, i) \frac{|R_t(j)|}{|B_t(j)|} r_j \right) + \frac{1 - \alpha}{|\mathcal{V}_t|}, \qquad \forall i \in \mathcal{V}_t$$

Note that to deal with sink nodes and avoid infinite in/out-degree ratios, we add-one smoothed both the in-degree and out-degree of a node. Moreover, like for the basic PageRank, we implemented a power-iteration method for an efficient computation of the ranking scores.

## 3   Experimental Evaluation

### 3.1   Assessment Methodology

*Data.* We used the DBLP XML data repository (dump updated at March 19, 2013[2]), from which we retrieved all types of publications and selected authors as well as editors—hereinafter we will simply refer to both as authors. We extracted information about the number of joint publications for each pair of co-authors,

---

[2] http://dblp.uni-trier.de/xml/

**Table 1.** Main characteristics of the DBLP datasets: comparison between the global network (updated at March 2013) and the last three terms of three years

| time interval | # nodes | # links | avg in-degree | avg path length | # source nodes # sink nodes | avg in/out-degree * | clustering coefficient |
|---|---|---|---|---|---|---|---|
| -2013 | 1,191,619 | 4,712,489 | 3.95 | 7.50 | 54,647; 533,101 | 1.75 | 0.18 |
| 2004-2006 | 341,282 | 957,922 | 2.81 | 7.61 | 32,511; 139,016 | 1.33 | 0.44 |
| 2007-2009 | 469,345 | 1,412,556 | 3.01 | 7.16 | 40,021; 188,166 | 1.41 | 0.32 |
| 2010-2013 | 582,206 | 1,926,184 | 3.31 | 6.82 | 45,916; 227,990 | 1.50 | 0.28 |

\* Sink nodes and source nodes are excluded.

and the total number of publications for every author, on a yearly basis. We devised two stages of evaluation: in the first one we used all the DBLP data in order to test the methods on a RCN as large as possible, while in the second stage we selected three subsets corresponding to the last three terms of approximately three years in order to assess the behavior of the methods in capturing the temporal evolution of the identified vicarious learners. Table 1 summarizes characteristics of the various datasets. It should be noted that the number of authors intuitively increases during the years, up to about 70% of increment from 2004-06 to 2010-13; moreover, the simultaneous increase in the average in-degree and decrease in the average path length confirms the growth in cooperation among researchers (both at intra- and inter-institutional level) that has occurred in recent years. Conversely, the decrease of the clustering coefficient would indicate that co-authors of one author are less likely to publish together, however this should be ascribed to an increasing number of peripheral nodes (i.e., newcomers, which obviously may have very few co-authorships) that both 2010-13 and 2007-09 have w.r.t. the corresponding earlier three-year term.

*Competitors and ground-truth evaluation.* We compared the proposed VLRank method w.r.t. the following competitors: the *in/out-degree* (henceforth InOut) distribution of the nodes in the network dataset, as a baseline, and a weighted version of PageRank, as a related ranking method. However, given the novelty of the problem addressed, we had to face the total lack of a gold-standard for vicarious learning. For this purpose, we followed two alternative approaches to the ground-truth evaluation of the ranking methods. In the first approach, for each of the selected DBLP datasets, we generated a *data-driven ranking* (henceforth DDRank) of a node by exploiting the different semantics of the strength of the relationships with in-neighbors, which likely model a vicarious learning modality, and the relationships with out-neighbors, which should instead express a higher likelihood of scholar advising modality. Formally, for each node $i \in \mathcal{V}_t$:

$$ r_i^* = \frac{1 + \sum_{j \in B_t(i)} w_t(j,i)}{1 + \sum_{j \in R_t(i)} w_t(i,j)} \exp(-nPubs(i,t)) $$

where weights on incoming (resp. outgoing) edges count the number of co-authored publications with an in-neighbor (resp. out-neighbor), and $nPubs(i,t)$ is the number of single-authored publications by author $i$ (at time $t$). In the second approach, we again exploited the academic statistics provided by ArnetMiner, and in particular the expert's *activity score* which is used to rank

**Table 2.** Comparative performance results: Kendall rank coefficient

| | -2013 | 2004-06 | 2007-09 | 2010-13 |
|---|---|---|---|---|
| VLRank vs. InOut | .153 | .249 | .259 | .256 |
| VLRank vs. DDRank | .284 | .283 | .295 | .298 |
| PageRank vs. InOut | -.097 | .182 | .177 | .177 |
| PageRank vs. DDRank | .133 | .246 | .246 | .255 |
| VLRank vs. AMRank | .115 | – | – | .148 |
| PageRank vs. AMRank | .043 | – | – | .083 |
| VLRank vs. PageRank | .422 | .424 | .410 | .407 |

the researchers based on the cumulated weighted impact factor of one's papers published in the last years.[3] We hence defined an ArnetMiner based ranking (henceforth AMRank) as follows:

$$r_i^* = \frac{1 + \sum_{j \in H^+(i)} AS(j)}{1 + \sum_{j \in H^-(i)} AS(j)}$$

where $H^+(i)$ (resp. $H^-(i)$) denotes the set of $i$'s co-authors who have h-index greater than (resp. lower than or equal to) the h-index of $i$, and $AS(j)$ denotes the ArnetMiner activity score for author $j$. Note that AMRank was not calculated for the subsets 2004-06 and 2007-09 since the activity scores are only available for the latest update of ArnetMiner.

*Assessment criteria.* In order to evaluate the performance of the ranking methods, we resorted to two well-known assessment criteria: *Kendall Rank correlation coefficient* and *Bpref*. The Kendall coefficient evaluates the similarity between two rankings, expressed as sets of ordered pairs, based on the number of inversions of pairs which would be needed to transform one ranking into the other. Formally: $Kendall(\mathcal{L}', \mathcal{L}'') = 1 - (2\Delta(\mathcal{P}(\mathcal{L}'), \mathcal{P}(\mathcal{L}'')))/(M(M-1))$ where $\mathcal{L}'$ and $\mathcal{L}''$ are the two rankings to be compared, $M = |\mathcal{L}'| = |\mathcal{L}''|$ and $\Delta(\mathcal{P}(\mathcal{L}'), \mathcal{P}(\mathcal{L}''))$ is the symmetric difference distance between the two rankings, calculated as number of unshared pairs between the two lists. Bpref evaluates the performance from a different view, i.e., the number of non-relevant candidates. It computes a preference relation of whether judged relevant candidates $R$ of a list $\mathcal{L}'$ are retrieved, i.e., they occur in a list $\mathcal{L}''$, ahead of judged irrelevant candidates $N$, and is formulated as $Bpref(R, N) = (1/|R|) \sum_r (1 - (\#\text{of } n \text{ ranked higher than } r)/|R|)$, where $r$ is a relevant retrieved candidate, and $n$ is a member of the first $|R|$ irrelevant retrieved candidates. In our setting, we distinguished two cases: when comparing w.r.t. the data-driven ranking, $N$ was defined as the set of nodes with data-driven ranking score below or equal to 1 (which should be regarded as an intuitive indicator of non-vicarious-learning), otherwise, i.e., comparison w.r.t. competing methods, as the bottom of the corresponding method's ranking having the same size as in the case of data-driven ranking. $R$ was selected as the set of nodes having top-$p\%$ score from the complement of $N$. Kendall and Bpref values are in the interval $[-1, 1]$ and $[0, 1]$, respectively, whereby values close to 1 correspond to better performance.

---

[3] http://arnetminer.org/AcademicStatistics

**Table 3.** Comparative performance results: Bpref

|  | -2013 | | | 2004-06 | | | 2007-09 | | | 2010-13 | | |
|---|---|---|---|---|---|---|---|---|---|---|---|---|
|  | $p=10$ | $p=25$ | $p=50$ | $p=10$ | $p=25$ | $p=50$ | $p=10$ | $p=25$ | $p=50$ | $p=10$ | $p=25$ | $p=50$ |
| VLRank vs. InOut | .336 | .584 | .664 | .362 | .561 | .702 | .409 | .583 | .713 | .415 | .580 | .714 |
| VLRank vs. DDRank | .687 | .784 | .744 | .605 | .701 | .706 | .644 | .726 | .717 | .667 | .730 | .720 |
| PageRank vs. InOut | .099 | .328 | .467 | .204 | .449 | .666 | .211 | .460 | .670 | .219 | .469 | .676 |
| PageRank vs. DDRank | .481 | .626 | .592 | .528 | .639 | .648 | .544 | .658 | .654 | .580 | .671 | .668 |
| VLRank vs. AMRank | .191 | .448 | .645 | – | – | – | – | – | – | .264 | .508 | .663 |
| PageRank vs. AMRank | .131 | .338 | .573 | – | – | – | – | – | – | .166 | .385 | .603 |
| VLRank vs. PageRank | .804 | .853 | .857 | .620 | .726 | .815 | .656 | .754 | .834 | .650 | .735 | .817 |

## 3.2 Results

Tables 2–3 provide performance results corresponding to the various DBLP networks. VLRank always obtained positive Kendall scores (Table 2) w.r.t. InOut, DDRank and AMRank, which tended to increase from 2004-06 to 2010-13, and were in general higher than in the largest dataset (-2013). More importantly, VLRank always achieved higher correlation with InOut, DDRank and AMRank than PageRank, with gains up to 21.7% for InOut, 11.8% for DDRank, and 6.5% for AMRank. Similar conclusions were drawn from Table 3, with VLRank always outperforming PageRank also in terms of Bpref, where the $p\%$ of relevant candidates for Bpref evaluation was set as $p = 10, 25, 50$. Bpref scores generally increased with $p$ when comparing VLRank and PageRank with InOut and AMRank, which indicates that in both cases the similarity between the rankings was lower (resp. higher) when comparing the head (resp. tail) of the lists. Interestingly, in contrast to the above results that would put in evidence the different behaviors of VLRank and PageRank (in favor of the former), the relative similarity between the corresponding rankings by VLRank and PageRank, for both Kendall and Bpref evaluations (last rows of the respective tables), prompted us to investigate this more in detail.

We therefore aimed to confirm the presumed higher reliability of the rankings produced by VLRank in capturing vicarious learners. For this analysis, we compared the top-100 ranked lists produced by VLRank and PageRank on the whole DBLP network (-2013). VLRank detected different situations in terms of total amount of publications produced in career, total number of co-authors, and average number of co-authors per publication. For instance, a few authors have produced little research in their short career and always within a research team, whose consistency of composition can vary from case to case. Other authors have shown a relatively long career and published several journal and conference papers together with many co-authors; for example, the 9th ranked author published 25 conference papers in the period 1999-2004 with an average of more than 10 co-authors per paper and a total of 17 co-authors. Overall, we can state that our VLRank detected and assigned highest scores to authors whose status can be tagged as vicarious learner with a certain objectivity. Conversely, PageRank did not behave as good as VLRank. The top-1 rank corresponded to an author with only one publication co-authored with other seven persons. Throughout the PageRank top-ranked list, we found authors with a potential

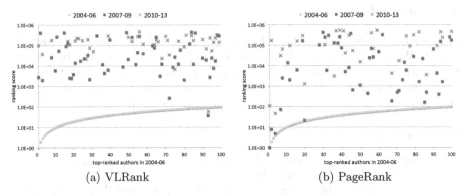

(a) VLRank    (b) PageRank

**Fig. 1.** Understanding the temporal evolution of vicarious learners

status as vicarious learner, however we also found a few other top-ranked authors exhibiting characteristics that do not look typical of a vicarious learner. For instance, the 2nd ranked author published more than 50 journal and conference papers, jointly with other colleagues but with different research teams in the career period (2004-12); an analogous situation was found for the 3rd ranked author who is involved in a team. In both cases, we easily found by looking at the authors' CVs in their homepages, that the authors should be instead considered as team leaders or at least active contributors. The case corresponding to the 6th ranked author is even more clearly close to a research team leader: 60 publications among journal and conference papers in nine years, usually co-authored with few other colleagues in very different groups.

We further investigated the behaviors of VLRank and PageRank by comparing, for each of the methods, the distribution of the top-ranked authors in the 2004-06 snapshot w.r.t. the subsequent terms of three-years. This was useful to gain an insight into the temporal evolution of the authors recognized as vicarious learners at a certain time interval (2004-06) by VLRank and PageRank, respectively. Looking at Figure 1(a), a large number of top-100 authors by VL-Rank in 2004-06 were also present in the subsequent periods (60% in 2007-09, 44% in 2010-13), but with much lower ranks (in the range of $10^2$-$10^5$): in effect, we then observed that such authors were effectively vicarious learners that later took on more expert roles; conversely, the authors present at 2004-06 but ranked higher later were effectively recognized as new cases of vicarious learners due to a drastic decrease in their individual productivity. PageRank (Figure 1(b)) seemed to be less able to effectively capture the temporal evolution of vicarious learners, since many of the top-100 authors in 2004-06 were still ranked high in 2007-09 (most of these cases were concentrated at the very top of the ranking). Upon investigation of such situations, we found in particular five authors within the top-20 in 2004-06 that were still ranked within the top-100 authors in 2007-2009, even though no case of vicarious learning could be clearly recognized among them, but rather a prolific collaboration among peers belonging to the same research team.

# 4 Conclusion

In this paper we have studied the new problem of ranking vicarious learners in a RCN. We developed a PageRank-style method that is able to effectively score the vicarious learning status of researchers in a collaboration network. Results obtained on DBLP co-authorship networks have shown that our method properly identifies and ranks vicarious learners who are not discovered by other methods.

# References

1. Bandura, A.: Social foundations of thought and action: A social cognitive theory. Prentice Hall, Englewood Cliffs (1986)
2. Brin, S., Page, L.: The anatomy of a large-scale hypertextual Web search engine. Computer Networks and ISDN Systems 30(1-7), 107–117 (1998)
3. Deng, H., Han, J., Lyu, M.R., King, I.: Modeling and exploiting heterogeneous bibliographic networks for expertise ranking. In: Proc. Int. Joint Conf. on Digital Libraries (JCDL), pp. 71–80 (2012)
4. Ding, Y., Yan, E., Frazho, A.R., Caverlee, J.: Pagerank for ranking authors in co-citation networks. Journal of the American Society for Information Science and Technology 60(11), 2229–2243 (2009)
5. Fagin, R., Kumar, R., Sivakumar, D.: Comparing Top k Lists. SIAM Journal on Discrete Mathematics 17(1), 134–160 (2003)
6. Das Gollapalli, S., Mitra, P., Lee Giles, C.: Ranking authors in digital libraries. In: Proc. Int. Joint Conf. on Digital Libraries (JCDL), pp. 251–254 (2011)
7. Li, X.-L., Foo, C.S., Tew, K.L., Ng, S.-K.: Searching for Rising Stars in Bibliography Networks. In: Zhou, X., Yokota, H., Deng, K., Liu, Q. (eds.) DASFAA 2009. LNCS, vol. 5463, pp. 288–292. Springer, Heidelberg (2009)
8. Liu, X., Bollen, J., Nelson, M.L., Van de Sompel, H.: Co-authorship networks in the digital library research community. Information Processing and Management 41, 1462–1480 (2005)
9. Ma, N., Guan, J., Zhao, Y.: Bringing PageRank to the citation analysis. Information Processing and Management 44(2), 800–810 (2008)
10. Sharma, M., Urs, S.R.: Network of Scholarship: Uncovering the Structure of Digital Library Author Community. In: Buchanan, G., Masoodian, M., Cunningham, S.J. (eds.) ICADL 2008. LNCS, vol. 5362, pp. 363–366. Springer, Heidelberg (2008)
11. Sun, Y., Barber, R., Gupta, M., Aggarwal, C.C., Han, J.: Co-author Relationship Prediction in Heterogeneous Bibliographic Networks. In: Proc. Int. Conf. on Advances in Social Networks Analysis and Mining (ASONAM), pp. 121–128 (2011)
12. Tagarelli, A., Interdonato, R.: "Who's out there?" Identifying and Ranking Lurkers in Social Networks. In: Proc. Int. Conf. on Advances in Social Networks Analysis and Mining (ASONAM), pp. 215–222 (2013)
13. Tsatsaronis, G., Varlamis, I., Torge, S., Reimann, M., Nørvrag, K., Schroeder, M., Zschunke, M.: How to Become a Group Leader? or Modeling Author Types Based on Graph Mining. In: Gradmann, S., Borri, F., Meghini, C., Schuldt, H. (eds.) TPDL 2011. LNCS, vol. 6966, pp. 15–26. Springer, Heidelberg (2011)
14. Wang, C., Han, J., Jia, Y., Tang, J., Zhang, D., Yu, Y., Guo, J.: Mining advisor-advisee relationships from research publication networks. In: Proc. ACM SIGKDD Int. Conf. on Knowledge Discovery and Data Mining (KDD), pp. 203–212 (2010)
15. Yan, E., Ding, Y.: Discovering author impact: A PageRank perspective. Information Processing and Management 47(1), 125–134 (2011)

# An Architecture for Community-Based Curation and Presentation of Complex Digital Objects

Klaus Rechert[1], Dragan Espenschied[2], Isgandar Valizada[1],
Thomas Liebetraut[1], Nick Russler[3], and Dirk von Suchodoletz[1]

[1] University of Freiburg,
Hermann-Herder Str. 10, 79104 Freiburg, Germany
[2] Karlsruhe University of Arts and Design,
Lorenzstr. 15, 76135 Karlsruhe, Germany
[3] RWTH Aachen,
Templergraben 55, 52056 Aachen, Germany

**Abstract.** Preservation of complex, non-linear digital objects such as digital art or ancient computer environments has been a domain reserved for experts until now. Digital culture, however, is a broader phenomenon. With the introduction of the so-called Web 2.0 digital culture became a mass culture. New methods of content creation, publishing and cooperation lead to new cultural achievements. Therefore, novel tools and strategies are required, both for preservation but in particular for curation and presentation.

We propose a scaleable architecture suitable to create a community driven platform for preservation and curation of complex digital objects. Further, we provide novel means for presenting preserved results including technical meta-data, and thus, allowing for public review and potentially further community induced improvements.

## 1 Introduction

Preservation of complex, non-linear digital objects such as digital art or ancient computer environments has been a domain reserved for experts until now. Digital culture, however, is a broader phenomenon. With the introduction of the so-called Web 2.0, digital culture became a mass culture.

For instance, a lot of digital art could and should be easily accessible, without too much emphasis on traditional aura and exclusivity. Like digital culture did in many areas, wide availability of tools and constant change in technology and theory made it an attractive entrance into the art world for newcomers and young artists. In the field of digital art, the general attitude of most participants is that anyone is always welcome to join in and spur the discourse. When it comes to longevity, however, it is quite difficult to find a suitable place for the resulting amount of artworks to survive in the swiftly changing technological landscape. This is an imbalance that needs to be tackled if digital art and digital culture as a whole should be able to create a notion of history: artists are having difficulties building a recognized body of work, institutions are having difficulties building

S.R. Urs, J.-C. Na, and G. Buchanan (Eds.): ICADL 2013, LNCS 8279, pp. 103–112, 2013.

a reputation. As a result, many mid-career artists will turn to more durable and therefore, sellable objects and formats [1].

A useful and quite promising approach to curate highly volatile digital art is recognizing it as mass culture, which in turn requires a mass-curation approach. In the domain of digital art there is no quasi standard on software used nor a uniform manifestation or appearance, since many artists have used software and tools in new, creative ways. This leads us to the assumption that a collection of digital artworks provides most likely the widest possible variety of complex digital artifacts of their time. Alike, preservation and presentation of digital art faces memory institutions with almost insolvable curation challenges. Since each artifact is unique there is no uniform approach, and thus, each object needs to be addressed separately. Pursuing a migration-based strategy then is either inadequate for presentation or inefficient w.r.t. the required development effort. Hence, due to its special appeal and diversity, digital art is not only able to expose structural and technical shortcomings of today's preservation strategies, but it also is an ideal use-case for a community-based curation model.

Therefore, we propose a scaleable architecture suitable for supporting technically and organizationally a community-driven platform for curation and presentation of complex digital objects. The proposed architecture focuses on making available emulation as a curation and presentation tool for a wide range of users. Institutions and individuals should be able to easily present preserved digital objects, including technical meta-data, and they should thus promote public display and review of the object's presentation but also allow the community to comment and potentially further improve the result.

## 2    Requirements

In theory it might be possible to reconstruct environments for almost any single digital artifact that re-enacts its performance exactly "as the artist intended" given suitable (financial) resources. In general, however, such an approach is either inefficient, i.e. too laborious for many artifacts, or it makes no sense because the artist's specifications cannot be met technically or logistically. Finally, the whole idea of individual technical restoration may not match the artifact's main performance features because it unfolds its impact in mass usage and distribution, and therefore has no "form" outside of practice.

Since there is no single way to render, view or use a digital artifact, it is futile to attempt to define one. Instead, making the largest possible amount of artworks accessible in combination with providing broadly generalized forms for their interaction and manipulation seems like the most worthwhile approach. The outcome is a reduced amount of rich simulated environments that enable the interaction of and with more artifacts. Hence a community-based approach with a scalable and user-friendly usage-model is required. Based on the aforementioned problem setting and use-case, we derive the following requirements for a scalable, emulation-based architecture, suitable for providing the technical backend for a community-based curation and presentation platform.

**Preparation:** We assume that the object to be rendered is already part of an archive or similar and already bears a basic set of meta-data, e.g. simple provenance data. In contrast to typical ingest procedures implemented at memory institutions the object preparation task is solely directed towards curation and re-enacting the object's usability.

Preparation in context of an emulation-based strategy focuses on providing a suitable rendering environment, i.e. choosing a technical platform consisting of operating system and emulator, a software stack and system configuration. In a second step the rendering environment has to be evaluated in context of a specific digital object. If the result is sufficient, meta-data is required, linking the digital object to the technical description of the rendering environment, and additionally, describing potential shortcomings and other content related performance observations. Content- and quality-related descriptions are useful to guide other users either to successful results or to difficult cases, requiring further work or expertise. Furthermore, the rendered object's significant features and their observed performance should be described, defining minimal expectations if compared to alternative rendering environments. Technical meta-data should describe the technical setup to allow an exact replication of the prepared environment.

**Presentation & Access Model:** With that goal of a simple presentation and access model, technical means are necessary to enable a wide variety of potential users to publish a rendered digital object. Hence, object owners should be able to present artifacts with minimal technical hurdles, for instance embed digital art in websites or blogs. For this, an interactive access method, ideally without additional software installation, to the emulated environment at the viewer's site is required. Furthermore, a decentralized and scaleable backend is necessary for dynamic allocation of computing resources to run requested rendering environments.

**Review & Improve:** The most essential feature for a community platform is to share experience and knowledge but also foster discussions. In this work we focus on aspects such as presentation as well as interaction with digital objects and their rendering environment and less on the general concept of building community pages. In a first step users should be able to review presentation results, i.e. review interrelation and interdependency between object and rendering environment. To improve or provide an alternative presentation, users need to (re-)build or adapt the rendering environment to match their ideas and concepts. For this, users require convenient access to virtualized or emulated environments without significant technical knowledge and skills, more specifically, a user-friendly framework to create, modify, and share rendering environments.

## 3   Architecture

Following the above defined requirements, we have developed an emulation-based architecture for curation and presentation of complex digital objects. Fig. 1 depicts its major components and general workflows. In our scenario, meta-data and objects are stored at the object owner's site, e.g. in a memory institution's repository. The objects are uploaded or accessed through dedicated interfaces on demand. Emulator images, i.e. bootable virtual disks containing the rendering environment, are published through a dedicated web-service interface, but are owned, maintained and published by the individual user.

For now, we assume that the preparation of rendering environments has been done previously. In this case the user has two options: firstly, they are able to publish a simple HTML-tag snippet on their web page, blog, etc., to present the chosen digital object in an interactive but user-friendly way. Secondly, the object may be published at a community site, enabling others to view, review and improve the object's presentation. In both cases the central component is the Emulation-as-a-Service provider exporting an embeddable HTML5 canvas, providing interactive emulator output. If user interaction is not desired by the object owner, the *interaction workflow description* (IWD) is able to provide "guided", view-only presentations, e.g. re-run captured interactions between user and rendering environment. The remainder of this section describes the aforementioned components in detail.

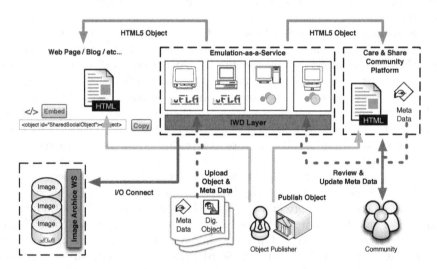

**Fig. 1.** General architecture of a community-based curation and presentation framework

### 3.1   A Unified Approach to Emulation

Up to now emulation has been seen as domain reserved for technical experts. Furthermore, emulation did not scale well due to the laborious preparation and technical setup procedures. For a successful community platform scalability and usability is essential. Therefore, as a first step a scaleable emulation service model is required: Emulation as a Service (EaaS).

The fundamental building block of an EaaS architecture are abstract *emulation components* to standardize deployment and to hide individual emulator complexity. Each emulation component encapsulates a specific emulator type as an abstract component with a unified set of software interfaces (API). This way, different classes of emulators become interoperable, e.g. could be interchanged or interconnected. Furthermore, single emulation components can be efficiently deployed in large-scale cluster or Cloud infrastructures. The control interface in combination with node- and user-management as well as emulation-related utilities represent a comprehensive EaaS API. Gateway nodes expose the EaaS's web-service API. These are take care of client authorization and authentication as well as for delegating resource requests to the service management entity. The service management entity is responsible for efficient hardware utilization, promoting or demoting machines on-demand. Fig. 2(a) illustrates the general EaaS architecture. Currently, emulation components for all major past and present desktop systems, e.g. PPC, M68k, Intel-based x86, etc., and major operation systems, e.g. OS/2, MS Windows, Mac OS 7 and newer, etc., are available for deployment. A detailed technical description of an EaaS framework and its workflows can be found in earlier work [2].

## 3.2  Scalable Emulation Services

For a scalable and cost-effective service model emulation components need only to be deployed when needed. For this, a framework for hardware- and software-deployment is required. For our purposes, we have chosen Canonical's Metal as a Service (MASS)[1] for hardware management, i.e. for creating emulation component machine instances on demand. If additional hardware resources are required, MASS is responsible for allocation and preparation of suitable machines and installation of a basic operating system (e.g. Ubuntu Linux) on that particular machine.

After a machine has been successfully prepared, in a second step the software deployment system Juju[2] starts the installation and configuration of the EaaS-framework. Juju is an orchestration management tool that requests installed machines from the underlying layer, in our scenario from MAAS. Then it deploys the requested service on that machine by running a (shell) script which installs and configures all needed services automatically. In this way, it is possible to scale a service by requesting additional instances through Juju, e.g. for short-term load peaks. If a node is no longer needed the node is marked as unused and powered down. Hence, the managed machine park saves energy or the node can be reused for other services.

A further benefit of having a flexible service orchestration tool like Juju is the possibility to use different environments at once. Thus, it is possible to allocate resources both from a local hardware pool managed with MAAS as well as from a commercial PaaS Cloud provider like Amazon EC2.

---

[1] Ubuntu Metal as a Service, http://maas.ubuntu.com, version 1.2+bzr1373
[2] Juju, http://juju.ubuntu.com, version 0.6.0.1+bzr618

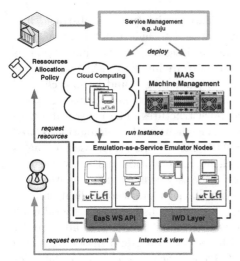

(a) Emulation-as-a-Service general architecture, major components and service-Model

(b) Evaluation of rendering performance

**Fig. 2.**

### 3.3    Management of Rendering Environments and Data Transport

Virtual disk images, i.e. emulated hard disks suitable to be run by an emulator, are the typical manifestation of a digital object's rendering environments. Depending on the environment and its technical demands, such disk images may reach a considerable file-size. Typical setups may range from a few hundreds of MBytes to several GBytes. Furthermore, the object's owner should be able to have complete control over her objects and decide whether users can create derivatives of her rendering environments. Most emulators also require writeable disk images to work properly but every user should be able to access the same, unchanged rendering environment. In the case of derivative works, it may even be desirable to save changes in the environment for later use. Through an architectural separation of image archive and emulation, the image archive can be deployed at the digital object owner's site. However, separating image archive and emulation component requires efficient network transport. Traditional file transport protocols are not appropriate, since copying large files over a network imposes high bandwidth requirements. Especially in cases of user-provided images, network utilization and potentially restricted bandwidth factors to be considered.

Our approach addresses these problems by defining a data storage interface that provides virtual disk images. A dedicated image archive web-service (IAWS) is used to do provisioning and management of those images and to provide uniform resource locators (URL) for the requested storage identifiers. These URLs are then resolved by the emulation component to attach a disk image to the emulator. The image archive retains control over the exported data stream and enforces the user's access policy. Since emulators directly operate on the exported disk image, write access has been implemented by using copy-on-write mechanisms provided by modern filesystems (e.g. Linux' btrfs [3] or Oracle's OCFS2 [4]), providing high-performance write access without loss of the image's original state at minimal data storage costs. Explicit environment derivatives are implemented as saved snapshots of modified disk images. These are then registered as a new rendering and are available for export.

For network transport we have chosen the network block device protocol [5] (NBD) which provides a very lightweight layer to access arbitrary blocks of a file via a network. In contrast to file copying or streaming protocols, requested chunks of the emulator images are only transferred when needed. Thus, the EaaS emulation component becomes operational immediately after initialization. Furthermore, less data transfer is needed for sparsely populated disk images or if not all of the environment's features are needed.

(a) Rendered original environment

(b) Digital object rendered in a prepared environment

**Fig. 3.** Functional access to digital art

### 3.4 Preparation, Curation and Access

A major part of the framework are workflows for object preparation, i.e to create or to modify system environments and to link a digital object to a specific rendering environment. While preparing a rendering environment through a guided process is optional, this however, results in technical meta-data with an exact description of the environments view-path and its configuration. This information then could be (re-)used to classify and index rendering environments, such that they provide a base for other objects and starting point for the creation

---

[3] BTrFS, http://btrfs.wiki.kernel.org/index.php/Main_Page, (6/5/2013)

[4] Oracle Cluster File System, http://oss.oracle.com/projects/ocfs2/, (6/5/13)

[5] Network Block Device, http://nbd.sourceforge.net/, (6/5/13)

of new derivatives. For instance, Fig. 3(b) shows a rendered CD-ROM from the Transmediale Archive in a prepared emulated environment. A detailed description on the workflow and meta-data generated can be found in earlier work [3]. In some cases however, there is no isolated artifact available, instead the object is connected to its rendering environment or the environment itself qualifies as a valuable object, e.g. an image of the hard-disk of a famous person. In this case, only the emulation component is configured to run the environment. For instance, Fig. 3(a) shows an emulated version of a hard-disk image taken from an original Apple Macintosh computer held by the Flusser Archive in Berlin, Germany.

In both cases, the user has to make available the virtual disk image and if required additional objects. The preparation workflow allows the user to run the environment by means of a suitable emulation component. Furthermore, the user is able to evaluate the performance of the environment and object. Fig. 2(b) shows the UI for the art domain. Rendering of digital art and evaluation of their performance have been evaluated using a large collection of CD-ROM art[4]. The Outcome of this workflow is technical meta-data describing the runtime configuration of the chosen setup. This file can be published and used to replicate exactly the same environment by invoking an emulation component, given a publicly available image archive. The meta-data is available as JSON and XML, but also as embeddable HTML-tag rendering the output as an interactive HTML5 canvas.

To present an artifact by exposing only a certain feature, it can be published in a view-only mode and simultaneously execute a number of automated interactions by using the interaction workflow description (IWD) layer (cf. Fig. 2(a)). IWD is designed as an abstract user-machine interaction description system to capture and replay user-machine interactions (e.g. keystrokes, mouse movement, etc.) in a platform- and system-independent way [5]. IWD allows for a full reproduction of the user's actions, i.e. reproduce and demonstrate specific workflows but also allows to automate the replication of rendering environment, i.e. automate captured installation and configuration tasks. In contrast to a video capture the system can hand over control to the user and take it away if required.

## 4     Related Work

Geoffrey Brown and colleagues have also addressed the problem of preserving CD-ROMs as well as providing access by using an emulation-based strategy [6,7]. To enable several institutions to make use of and potentially contribute to the collection, the CD-ROMs are served through a distributed filesystem. Further, they require some client preparation regarding emulator setup. Compared to local provisioning of a complex service stack as also proposed in KEEP [8,9], a networked approach reduces technical and organizational hurdles at the client's side significantly. In contrast, we present a versatile server-based infrastructure providing functional access to a wide range of emulators and operating systems without any requirements regarding the user's client environment beside a standard modern web browser. Instead of adapting a large software package including proprietary software components to various, fast changing end-user devices, EaaS emulation components run in a well controlled, maintained environment.

Guttenbrunner et al. provide a generic framework qualifying emulator performance [10]. Furthermore, there is a lively discussion on authentic simulation of individual technical components such as CRT screen simulation [11,12]. With respect to specific technical aforementioned work is able to scientifically quantify the performance of a certain system setup. The goal of of our work is is to enable a wide community to use emulation as a tool in digital preservation. Hence, a quantification of technical performance features is less relevant for a community driven curation platform. Furthermore, by using an emulation-as-a-service architecture model, new emulators and technology can be integrated with reasonable effort, being then available for any already present digital artifact. The quantification of the performance of a digital artifact in a specific rendering environment is a different matter, due to their partly subjective experience.

## 5    Discussion and Outlook

To create the possibility for artifacts to reach cultural and historical significance in the first place, fidelity and ease of access need to be balanced. What "ease of access" means depends on technology and usage patterns available at the time of access. In general, the least expert knowledge is needed to interact with an artifact, the better. We have presented an emulation-based architecture and implementation reducing significantly technical hurdles for curation and presentation of digital art, by using shareable and interactive HTML5 access to complex digital objects in combination with a scaleable backend and service model. Additionally the required curation workflows are provided.

The highest grade of accessibility is the possibility for general users to be confronted with an artifact and interact with it in their usual context. The accessibility of a re-enactment can quite easily be asserted, fidelity, though, is an open-ended scale. Highly synchronous sound effects using web technologies is challenging and needs further work. Artifacts that either rely on certain subtleties of their environment that are hard or impossible to cover via emulation or staging, or that requirie a context too large to re-create or stage, are certainly losing some of their quality. The most problematic issue, however, is a non-technical one: intellectual property rights on software and operating systems. While most of the ancient software components are today commercially totally irrelevant, digital art most probably increases its cultural value with time progressing. But without a relevant user group and public awareness these issues won't be solved soon with the consequence of not only loosing access to many artifacts but also loosing knowledge on their appropriate presentation and usage.

While the architecture and technology have been discussed using a digital art use-case, the proposed community approach is not limited to this domain. One can find various hobby communities curating for instance OS/2 drivers and software, game related communities etc. The proposed architecture not only provides a more efficient curation tool but also allows these communities to present a piece of computer history to a wider audience in a more useful and meaningful way.

# References

1. Watz, M.: The futility of media art in a contemporary art world, `http://www.scribd.com/doc/110282792/20121015-LISA-The-Futility-of-Media-Art-in-a-Contemporary-Art-World` (October 2012)
2. Rechert, K., Valizada, I., von Suchodoletz, D., Latocha, J.: bwFLA – A Functional Approach to Digital Preservation. PIK – Praxis der Informationsverarbeitung und Kommunikation 35(4), 259–267 (2012)
3. Rechert, K., Valizada, I., von Suchodoletz, D.: Future-proof preservation of complex software environments. In: Proceedings of the 9th International Conference on Preservation of Digital Objects (iPRES 2012), pp. 179–183. University of Toronto Faculty of Information (2012)
4. Espenschied, D., Rechert, K., von Suchodoletz, D., Valizada, I., Russler, N.: Large-scale curation and presentation of cd-rom art. In: iPRES 2013 (to appear, 2013)
5. von Suchodoletz, D., Rechert, K., Welte, R., van den Dobbelsteen, M., Roberts, B., van der Hoeven, J., Schroder, J.: Automation of flexible migration workflows. International Journal of Digital Curation 2(2) (2010)
6. Woods, K., Brown, G.: Assisted emulation for legacy executables. International Journal of Digital Curation 5(1) (2010)
7. Brown, G.: Developing virtual cd-rom collections: The voyager company publications. International Journal of Digital Curation 7(2), 3–22 (2012)
8. Pinchbeck, D., Anderson, D., Delve, J., Alemu, G., Ciuffreda, A., Lange, A.: Emulation as a strategy for the preservation of games: the keep project. In: DiGRA 2009 – Breaking New Ground: Innovation in Games, Play, Practice and Theory (2009)
9. Lohman, B., Kiers, B., Michel, D., van der Hoeven, J.: Emulation as a business solution: The emulation framework. In: 8th International Conference on Preservation of Digital Objects (iPRES 2011), pp. 425–428. National Library Board Singapore and Nanyang Technology University (2011)
10. Guttenbrunner, M., Rauber, A.: A measurement framework for evaluating emulators for digital preservation. ACM Trans. Inf. Syst. 30(2), 14:1–14:28 (2012)
11. Scott, J.: What a wonder is a terrible monitor (2012), `http://ascii.textfiles.com/archives/3786`
12. Guttenbrunner, M., Rauber, A.: Re-awakening the philips videopac: From an old tape to a vintage feeling on a modern screen. In: Proceedings of the 8th International Conference on Preservation of Digital Objects (iPres 2011), pp. 250–251 (2011), Posterpresentation: iPres 2011 - 8th International Conference on Preservation of Digital Objects

# Migrating Researcher from Local to Global: Using ORCID to Develop the TLIS VIVO with CLISA and Scopus

Chao-chen Chen, Mike W. Ko, and Vincent Tsung-yeh Lee

Graduate Institute of Library and Information Studies,
National Taiwan Normal University, Taipei, Taiwan
cc4073@ntnu.edu.tw
{mikgtk,bigyes}@gmail.com

**Abstract.** This paper presents a prototype of TLIS VIVO, a researcher networking system of the Library and Information Science field based in Taiwan, by using ORCID, VIVO, and Linked Open Data technologies. It extends VIVO with the author identifier system ORCID, and integrates data thus harvested from *Chinese Library & Information Science Abstracts* (CLISA), and Scopus. The study demonstrates a practical approach to increase the visibility, collaboration of local and global researchers.

**Keywords:** VIVO, Research Networking, ORCID, Library & Information Science, Open Linked Data.

## 1 Introduction

Contemporary research is regarded as growingly complicated. It is team-based, interdisciplinary, and cross-institutional cooperation. The universities involved always aim for openness which is the most important trend of scholarly communication in the digital age. To eliminate academic segregation set by disciplines and institutions, scholars need to turn to the Web for better discovery and communication at a distance, instead of in proximity. Interdisciplinary and international e-Science cooperation needs to tackle the problem of distributed data in different formats and subject-specific terms. This leads to the Semantic Web which strives for standardized knowledge representation so that data can be linked and integrated in a more meaningful way. The Linked Open Data project is a result of the Semantic Web technology. On the other hand, VIVO can be seen as an application of the technology in the academic sector [3]. Sometimes it may seem a difficult task for scholars to maintain his/her VIVO profile, especially on the part of publication list. To coordinate local and international publications with ease in a standard open format for the Internet is the problem this study tries to deal with.

## 2 Purpose of Research

Modeled on the NTNU VIVO experience and spirit [2], this study tries to build up a cooperative open scholar network of data and research. Focusing on local Library and

S.R. Urs, J.-C. Na, and G. Buchanan (Eds.): ICADL 2013, LNCS 8279, pp. 113–116, 2013.
© Springer International Publishing Switzerland 2013

Information Science (LIS) scholars, it employs open source technology for a Taiwan LIS (TLIS) VIVO. For local Chinese articles, they would be covered by *Chinese Library and Information Science Abstracts* (CLISA), while English articles by Scopus. With these sources, 95% or more of local LIS publications can be discovered. By using the global author identifier Open Research and Contributor ID (ORCID), resources can be integrated with the issue of name disambiguation settled. VIVO and ORCID are interoperable [6]. This provide a working basis for the study.

## 3     Implementation of the Prototype

The process can show that it is feasible to link related data of resources to the subject-specific TLIS VIVO.

### 3.1     CLISA and Scopus to ORCID

Transliteration would cause repetition and ambiguity for both Chinese and English names of Chinese researchers. To reference the situation, for example, two-thirds of the six million authors in MEDLINE share a last name and first initial with at least one other author, and just one ambiguous name can involve up to eight persons on average [7]. ORCID can solve this problem by providing a central registry of unique identifiers for researchers, as well as its capability for Chinese character encoding and multiple name input [5].

Importing data from Scopus to ORCID is straight forward. With the name fields in both sources  mapped, the author can first identify personal Scopus Author profile, select the appropriate items, then export them into the ORCID system.

For CLISA, this study uses a dedicated data harvester which, after parsing, distinguishes the data  fields, then makes use of the identifier attribute for Author to single out the field value. With an ORCID API, each CLISA record can be transcribed to the ORCID Messages Schema XML format. The POST command of cURL can export CLISA data to ORCID, and the PUT command updates the related data.\

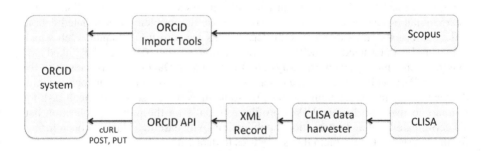

**Fig. 1.** Workflow of exporting data from Scopus, CLISA to ORCID

## 3.2    ORCID to TLIS VIVO

Through the use of ORCID API, and GET command of cURL, three ORCID data formats are obtained: Profile, Bio, Works, all in ORCID Messages Schema XML.

Technically, such XML formats cannot be directly imported into TLIS VIVO because VIVO uses RDF triplestore format to store records, with every data entry composed in the form of subject-predicate-object, as required by different ontologies and the publication requirement of Linked Data. For this study, the XML exported from ORCID is parsed to map the corresponding CSV (comma-separated values) file. According to VIVO's *Data Ingest Guide* [1], a local ontology and workspace model is created, then the CSV file is converted to RDF and the tabular data mapped onto ontology. Next, SPARQL query is used to construct the ingested entities.

The diagram below shows the following processes: To complete the process of ORCID data conversion, they are loaded to a Web repository. For vocabularies, popular ontologies such as BIBO, FOAF, and SKOS are used. Furthermore, to make TLIS VIVO a node in the LOD Cloud Diagram, the following requirements need to be met: access of the entire dataset via RDF crawling, an RDF dump or a SPARQL endpoint.

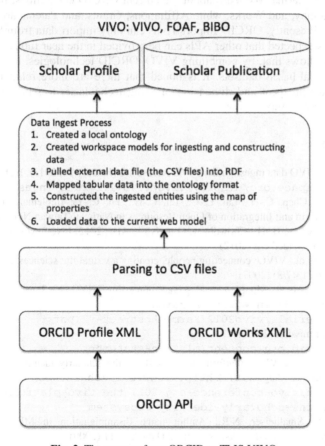

**Fig. 2.** The process from ORCID to TLIS VIVO

Throughout the implementation, there were challenges. One needs to have knowledge of Semantic Web technologies, including RDF and ontologies, and programming skills such as SPARQL. Incidentally, Thorisson [6] says getting data out and into VIVO triplestores is a challenge. Knoblock et al. [4] also remark that "mapping existing legacy data to the VIVO ontology and generating the corresponding RDF data that can then be loaded into VIVO can be very challenging", which led to the devleopment of Karma, an open-source information integration tool that allows a user to quickly map legacy data sources into RDF for loading into VIVO.

## 4    Conclusion

Our study provides a practical approach in building a prototype of TLIS VIVO. We use ORCID to integrate the inflow of data located in CLISA and Scopus. With VIVO featuring Linked Data, TLIS VIVO can serve the purpose of enhancing the visibility, discovery and collaboration of local LIS scholars.

During the study process, we exploit other people's efforts, such as the data integration tool Karma. We learn about the current ORCID capabilities, for instance, Profile, Biography, and Works, while Affiliations, Grants, and Patents are still under development. Presently, ORCID Import Tools can only import data from Scopus and CrossRef. It is expected that other APIs can be provided in the near future.

This study shows that, by combining VIVO, ORCID technologies, it can integrate local- and global-based datasets. It is hoped that there are more related studies to show a greater prospect and dimension of using technologies to serve LIS and other subject fields for discovery and use.

## References

1. Blake, Jim: VIVO data ingest guide. VIVO release 1.2 (January 26, 2013), https://wiki.duraspace.org/display/VIVO/VIVO+1.2+Data+Ingest+Guide
2. Chen, C.-C., Chen, C.-H., Lai, C.-C., Lu, C.-H., Yu, C.-Y.: Implementation of Open Scholar Platform and Integration of Open Resources in National Taiwan Normal University (NTNU). In: Chen, H.-H., Chowdhury, G. (eds.) ICADL 2012. LNCS, vol. 7634, pp. 344–346. Springer, Heidelberg (2012)
3. Devare, M., et al.: VIVO: connecting people, creating a virtual life sciences community. D-Lib Magazine 13(7/8) (2007)
4. Knoblock, C.A., et al.: Mapping existing data sources into VIVO (2012), http://isi.edu/integration/karma/other-materials/vivo2012/Karma-Abstract-v2.pdf
5. ORCID. Our mission (2013), http://orcid.org/content/mission-statement
6. Thorisson, G.: The VIVO platform and ORCID in the scholarly identity ecosystem. In: VIVO Conference (August 2011), http://www.slideshare.net/gthorisson/vivo-conference-aug-2011-the-vivo-platform-and-orcid-in-the-scholarly-identity-ecosystem
7. Torvik, V.I., Smalheiser, N.R.: Author name disambiguation in MEDLINE. ACM Transactions on Knowledge Discovery from Data 3(3), 11 (2009)

# The Common Man: An Examination of Content Creation and Information Dissemination on Twitter during the 2012 New Delhi Gang-Rape Protest

Saifuddin Ahmed and Kokil Jaidka

Wee Kim Wee School of Communication and Information,
Nanyang Technological University, Singapore
{saif0002,koki0001}@e.ntu.edu.sg

**Abstract.** Twitter has become a critical force in generating and disseminating information pertaining to news events, public and media action, especially in situations such as protests, where public activism and media coverage form a symbiotic relationship. This study identifies different types of users or the "key actors", e.g., traditional media organizations, new media organizations, non-government organizations and individual users who posted on Twitter in the period before, during and after the mass protests pertaining to a gang-rape incident in the Indian capital city of New Delhi in December 2012. The study especially focuses on the role of ordinary citizens or The Common Man in creating and disseminating information. Our results show that individual users contributed to more than half of the information dissemination, and the common man played an active part in creating and facilitating this information flow. Our findings can be leveraged by digital libraries for customizing the library experience for individual users as well as virtual communities according to the new dynamic paradigms of information creation and consumption.

**Keywords:** Social media, online communities, twitter, news communities.

## 1 Introduction

At the dawn of the twenty-first century, the harbinger of social revolution was the Internet, which transformed the globe into a digital world with an exploding networked population rising from mere thousands to billions in a span of twenty years. The need to index and archive digital content led to the conceptualization of digital libraries – a sociotechnological system connecting information, documents, people, and practises [1]. Until very recently, digital library research has mainly focused on building and managing collections of multimedia content. However, the recent advancements in technology and communication have led to a need to revise and redefine the role of digital libraries in different online or offline social contexts. A popular activity online is the creation and dissemination of user-generated content, also known as *social media,* on websites such as Twitter. Twitter's application as a collaborative gossip and news publishing tool makes it an ideal medium for studying the relative roles played by user groups in creating and disseminating information, and as

S.R. Urs, J.-C. Na, and G. Buchanan (Eds.): ICADL 2013, LNCS 8279, pp. 117–126, 2013.
© Springer International Publishing Switzerland 2013

a communication platform for mass communication or interpersonal conversations. The importance of users in specialized roles, or "actors", amplifies during time-sensitive or crises situations such as natural disasters, political emergencies, and protests or social movements. Studies on actors in social movements have established that journalists, activists and ordinary citizens [2][3] are key influencers in propagating information. This study follows in the tracks of previous studies which analyzed the role of ordinary citizens or The Common Man in the social media space [2][3][4][5][6]. The common man is the average digital library user, who is today as much an active participant as a consumer of information. It has been found that the common man acts as 99% of all propagators for information on Twitter [4]. It has also been found that despite exerting average, or less-than-average influence, the common man still presents an optimal, cost–effective vehicle for information dissemination [6]. Furthermore, in the case of social movements, he rises up to the occasion and co-constructs news in social media through interactions with journalists and activists, as witnessed in the 2012 protests in Egypt and Tunisia [2]. The present work builds on these earlier contributions in three key respects. First, it presents a case study of an anti-gangrape protest in India, a country with one of the lowest Internet penetrations in the world at only 11.4% and 66 million social media users [7]. For the first time in India's nascent information communication technologies (ICTs) environment, Twitter was extensively used during major protests, allowing a small but growing part of the Indian public to transform India's public sphere. Secondly, it recognizes the emerging role of new actors, such as new media sources and politicians, in colouring Twitter conversations, and compares them against other known actors in the context of a mass protest. Thirdly, it extends the ideas for measuring influence discussed in [2] to characterize the information flow and usage patterns of actors through their posting of original, reflected or mixed content.

Our study is relevant for digital libraries in order to identify the processes and user roles in the context of an "information ground", the phenomenon of people coming together to share information informally and serendipitously [8]. Unless digital libraries embrace the emerging social aspects of the information creating, seeking and sharing processes, they face the danger of being relegated to "passive warehouses" [8][9][10]. However, in social movements such as the 2012 protests in Egypt and Tunisia, social media platforms such as Twitter emerged as a key tool for informing, mobilizing and connecting the populace when communication or information is officially censored. Our study addresses three main research gaps in social media – firstly, the need to recognize Twitter's role as the "online press", a moniker for Twitter's ever-ticking, evolving timeline of developing events - comprising streaming newsflashes, conversations, views, reactions and resolutions. During the Delhi gangrape protest, Twitter transformed into an information resource for timely and accurate news updates, live coverage of events at the protest venues, a portal to reach out to their family and friends and to connect with activists to plan the next course of action.

Secondly, digital libraries need to recognize the evolving role of users as active participants rather than passive consumers in the content generation process – they post, upload, seek or retweet to contribute to the spread of news and information.

The significance of their contribution is reflected in the way traditional media such as newspapers and television channels used the content posted by protesters on Twitter to describe the ground realities in their news coverage. Finally, our study identifies virtual communities of users who share a common context, social structure, culture, context or agenda amongst themselves and discusses the potential for digital libraries of engaging online communities as users. Motivated by these research gaps, this study addresses the following research questions:

1.  What was the trend of Twitter usage and the most active phase during the Delhi gangrape incident?
2.  Who were the major actors contributing in information dissemination on Twitter?
3.  What was the role of the common man in this information dissemination?
4.  What was the nature of tweet content in this information dissemination and what were the roles of different actors in the information flow?

## 2    Background

On 16th December 2012 a 23 year old physiotherapy student was gang raped and physically tortured along with her male friend by five men in New Delhi, India. Soon news spread in the online sphere and the incident was reported by the national media and this wide attention led to small protests mostly by students in New Delhi. On 20th December, as the Indian parliament discussed the atrocity, the state government called upon Rapid Action Forces to disengage small protests. This resulted in extreme public reaction, including on Twitter, with a buzzing demand for larger protests for justice. Consequently, with the help of social media, massive public protests were organized at India Gate on 22nd and 23rd December which met with resistance from the police, who resorted to tear gas, water cannons and physical violence. The protest gained mass attention in India and abroad as the public and the protestors were largely successful in scripting India's largest social movement yet – especially one where social media played a drastic role.

## 3    Method

### 3.1    Data Collection

We used Topsy (http://www.topsy.com/), an archive of the public Twitter stream to download tweets posted from 17th December, 2012 to 25th December, 2012. We used a Java program to query the Application Programming Interface (API), Otterapi (http://code.google.com/p/otterapi/) in the Eclipse IDE environment by referring to the trending hashtags for the gang rape incident:

*DELHI OR gangrape OR rape OR #delhigangrape OR #delhiprotest OR #delhi-*
*protests OR #indiagate OR #stopthsisshame&maxtime= 1356460199&mintime=*
*1355682600&order=date&lang=en*

The Topsy archive identified and granted public access to only 62,437 as "significant" or non-spam and non-repetitive tweets. For these 62,437 tweets, we collected information about the tweet's text, its timestamp, username, type of tweet (tweet, link, image or video), hits, trackbacks, embedded links and mentions in tab-delimited format. Only English language tweets were analyzed in this study as we did not have resources to analyze tweets in native language, which in any case, were marginal (less than five per cent of the overall).

## 3.2    Social Network Analysis

To better understand the characteristics of the social community formed around the #delhigangrape, we first conducted a social network analysis of the time phases from the news outbreak on Twitter until the day of the last major protest in Delhi. Accordingly, we divided the data into three phases – pre-protest days, protest days, and post-protest days. The details of each phase are as presented:

1. Pre-protest: A total of 20,366 tweets between the period 17th December, 2012 and 21st December, 2012.
2. Protest: A total of 25,207 tweets for the major protest days, 22nd and 23rd December, 2012.
3. Post-protest: A total of 16,900 tweets for post-protest days, 24th and 25th December, 2012.

We used NodeXL to analyze formed network of three phases and visualize them. Analyzing the communities for each phase were based on the following relationships: "Replies To", "Mentions", "Followers" and "Tweets that are not replies to or mentions". Figure 2 shows the social network statistics and the SNA layout for each phase. For social network graph rendering, the Harel-Koren Fast multiscale layout was used to cluster nodes which were closely associated with each other. At this stage, the approach followed was at the macro-level to analyze the generated network, focusing on the characteristics of the entire network and its evolution during the three time phases. This was followed by the micro-level content analysis of individual users, described in the following paragraphs.

## 3.3    Social Media Analytics: Coding Categories

For the micro-level content analysis, the unit of analysis was one tweet and the coding was done in three stages. The first stage involved classifying actors behind each tweet into one of the following categories:

1. Traditional media organizations (TMOs): This comprises traditional mainstream mass media organizations that are present in the offline sphere through television, newspapers or radio, as well as in the online sphere through websites or social networking accounts (e.g., @ibnliverealtime and @httweets).
2. New media organizations (NMOs): This comprises news websites and news blogs that only exist online (e.g., @firstpostin).

3. Individuals: This comprises all individuals who tweet independent of any organizations (e.g., @alok_bhatt,@sakshikumar). (This category is further broken down in
the next section)
4. Non-governmental organizations (NGOs): This comprises NGOs that work for social causes and are present online (e.g., @justiceforwomen)
5. Others: This comprises actors that do not fit in any of the above mentioned categories (e.g., @techiteblog).

Once the main actors behind tweets were identified, we conducted a second level of
coding for the Individuals category to identify its sub-types:

1. Activists: This comprises individuals who identified themselves as activists and
continually posted about activism issues (e.g., @sakshikumar).
2. Politician: This comprises individuals who are primarily related to political environment within India (e.g., @shashitharoor).
3. Journalist: This comprises individuals who were employed by either any TMO or
NMO (e.g., @BDutt).
4. Celebrity: This comprises individuals who belonged to a celebrity status in India
outside of politics and media, usually related to (but not limited to) movies and
sports (e.g., @faroutakhtar).
5. Blogger: This comprises individuals who regularly posted about different issues on
their blogs and identified themselves as 'Bloggers' (e.g., @dubash).
6. Common man: This comprises ordinary citizens who belonged to the common
public and did not fit into any of the categories above ( e.g., @khalidkhan787).
7. Others: This included individuals who did not fit in any of the categories mentioned above. (e.g., @trendingtweet).

At the final level of coding, we differentiated between the content posted by individuals belonging to the activists, journalists and the common man categories. Each tweet
was classified as one of the following three categories:

1. Original: This category comprises original tweet content posted by the author (e.g.,
@prasanto "Tip to protestors: carry polythene bags to wrap your mobile phones in,
to avoid police water cannons destroying them. #Delhi #GangRape"
2. Reflected: This category comprises tweet content which was a re-tweet from a different source including TMO, NMO, NGO, activists, politicians, celebrities, bloggers or others (as defined above) (e.g., @raghubabs "RT @ibnlivePolitics: Delhi
gangrape: Protesters meet Sonia and Rahul, say demonstrations will continue
http://t.co/MXf7kbah").
3. Mixed: This category comprises tweet content which was a mix (e.g., @iagarwal5
"WOW..Shame on them!! RT: @IBNLiveRealtime: Delhi gangrape: Police lob
tear gas shells on protesters").

A coding team consisting of four members was employed to code the tweets for the
above mentioned categories. Each user's category was determined by analyzing their
stored Twitter profile, mentioned links and latest tweets. Disagreements were resolved at the end, through discussion and mutual consensus between the coders.

The Cohen's kappa values indicating reliability for the stages of coding were: for main actor types: 0.88; for sub-actor individual category: 0.76; for tweet content (original, reflected, mixed): 0.94.

## 4    Results and Discussion

Figure 1 presents the frequency distribution of tweets for the entire observational period. There were a total of 62,473 tweets with 20,366 for the pre-protest, 25,207 for the protest and 16,900 for the post-protest phase. The timeline shows an increase in frequency in the protest phase with the peak of the timeline on 23rd December, 2012 – the second day of the protest. When we compare the means for the three phases, we find that the average frequency over the protest days' was remarkably higher than the overall mean, while the average mean for the pre-protest phase was the lowest The standard deviation of values over local means increased linearly with time as represented by the long dashes-and-dot line at the bottom of the graph.

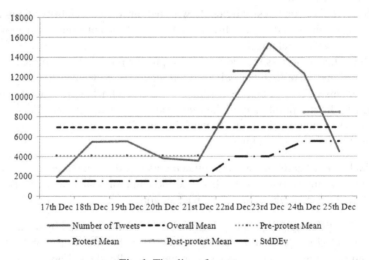

**Fig. 1.** Timeline of tweets

Figure 2 presents the social network statistics and the social network layout for each phase. The table shows the highest gain in new authors as compared to the other phases. The numbers for graph density and average degree are highest for the protest phase. However, the sparsity of the network and the hub-spoke structures in the graphs point to a power law distribution of the average degree, which can extrapolate to infinite variance in the author-to-author network connections. The numbers for betweenness and closeness centrality provide a clearer picture of interaction during the time periods because they reflect decentralized interaction during the protest phase as compared to the relatively localized interaction in the pre-protest and post-protest phases. This is also evident in the graphs, where the widespread interaction among users during protest phase is easily distinguishable from the relative entrenchment of interaction in the pre- and post-protest period.

| SOCIAL NETWORK ANALYSIS | Pre-protest | Protest | Post-protest |
|---|---|---|---|
| Authors | 6032 | 9821 | 6470 |
| New Author for this Phase | 6032 | 8145 | 2862 |
| Repeating Author From Last Phase | | 1676 | 3608 |
| Graph Density | 0.0068 | 0.055 | 0.0072 |
| Average Degree | 1.698 | 2.058 | 1.855 |
| Betweenness Centrality | 1080.474 | 5404.42 | 2516.478 |
| Closeness Centrality | 0.359 | 0.183 | 0.263 |
| Eigenvector Centrality | 0.077 | 0.042 | 0.013 |

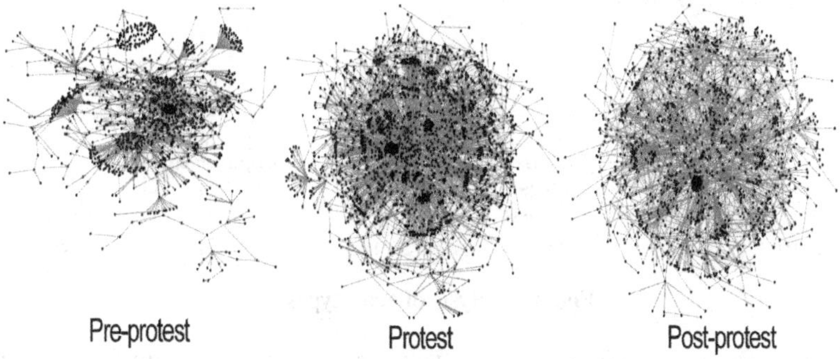

Pre-protest          Protest          Post-protest

**Fig. 2.** SNA statistics and layout for the three time phases

At the second stage of our analysis, we examined the actors participating in the on-line Twitter protest. Consistent with the previous analysis, we used tweets as the unit of analyses. Figure 3 reveals that individuals were the most dominant actors over all phases because they generated the most tweets, over all the three time phases– pre-protest (46.45%, n= 9,459), protest (55.23%, n= 13,923) and post-protest (50.21%, n= 8,485) with the highest participation during the protest phase. TMOs were the second most common actors. They were most active in the pre-protest phase (28.89%, n= 5,883 of overall tweets, n= 20,366). Unexpectedly, their participation decreased dur-ing the protest phase (21.26%, n= 5,358). This may not reflect a decrease in participa-tion since the number of tweets is almost consistent, but a higher overall participation in the protest phase, because of which TMOs accounted for a smaller proportion of the total. Their lack of participation may also reflect the nascence of their information technology services and social media presence and their preferment of offline news, suited to a country like India with low internet penetration. In their absence, individ-ual users took on the baton of citizen journalism, accounting for more than half of the content created and shared during the protest. Individuals may have been more suc-cessful simply because there were more individual twitter accounts, giving them an influential advantage. Another likely reason is that individuals are unaligned with any organizational agenda, thus are more liberal in generating and spreading information with political ramifications during major news events. NMOs did not show a notable change in tweeting frequency pattern over the three phases (7.20%, 8.37% and 7.50% for three phases respectively) while non-governmental organizations marginally in-creased tweeting in the protest phase.

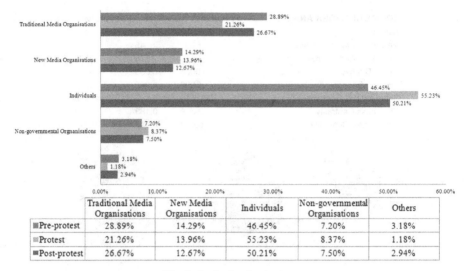

| | Traditional Media Organisations | New Media Organisations | Individuals | Non-governmental Organisations | Others |
|---|---|---|---|---|---|
| ■Pre-protest | 28.89% | 14.29% | 46.45% | 7.20% | 3.18% |
| ■Protest | 21.26% | 13.96% | 55.23% | 8.37% | 1.18% |
| ■Post-protest | 26.67% | 12.67% | 50.21% | 7.50% | 2.94% |

**Fig. 3.** Analysis of actor types

Figure 4 shows the results from the analysis of the sub-types within the individual actors' category. The common man category were the most active in all three phases - pre-protest (28.42%, n= 2,688 of overall, n= 94,59), protest (42.12%, n= 5,865 of overall, n= 13,923) and post-protest phases (38.02%, n= 3,226 of overall, n= 8,485). The common man category was followed by activists and journalists. They also show the highest jump in frequency (13.70%) from the pre-protest (28.42%) to protest phase (42.12%). In comparison, journalists reflected a minor increase in participation (4.99%) from protest to post-protest phases. Similar to TMOs at the organizational level, at the individual level too, journalists practised objectivity typical of their profession, limiting their interaction with other users and hardly contributing any tweets of their own, choosing instead to observe and retweet information.

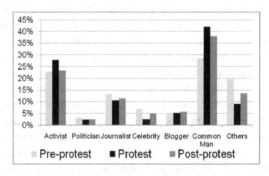

**Fig. 4.** Individual sub-actors

At the next level of analysis, we investigated the tweet content and the influence of actors in the information flow during these phases. We focused on three main sub-categories: activists, journalists and the common man. Figure 5 reflects a marked shift in the content of tweets posted by the common man category during the three phases There is a change of balance from reflected content (62.43%, n= 1,678 of the overall, n= 2,688) during the pre-protest phase, to original content during the protest phase (57.19%, n= 3,354 of the overall, n= 5865) and back to reflected content (43.15%, n= 1392 of the overall, n= 3,226) during post-protest phase. Mixed tweets are in about the same proportion in the pre- (20.16%, n= 542) and post-protest (22%, n= 710) phases, but they are overshadowed by original tweets in the protest phase (10.88%, n= 638). Tweets by journalists are predominantly reflected in the three phases of pre-protest (65.56%, n = 832 of the overall, n = 1,269), protest (56.22%, n = 835 of the overall, n = 1,435) and post-protest (58.81%, n = 574 of the overall, n = 976).

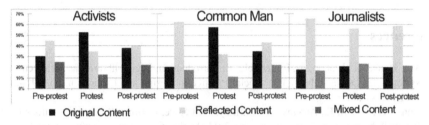

**Fig. 5.** Individual sub-actors

On the other hand, there is a prominent shift in the tweeting pattern of activists over the three time phases. In the pre-protest phase, the tweets posted by activists are mostly reflected (44.85%, n = 972 of the overall, n = 2167), with smaller proportions of original (30.42%, n= 659) or mixed content (24.73%, n= 536). This changes during the protest phase, when more than half of their tweets (52.47%, n= 2,038 of the overall, n= 3,884) are original in nature and there are fewer reflected (34.53%, n= 1,341) and mixed tweets (13.00%, n= 505). In the post-protest phase, their tweets are a balance between original (37.90%, n= 752 of the overall, n= 1,984), reflected (39.97%, n= 793) and mixed tweets (22.13%, n= 439). Evidently, the common man and the activist categories were the ones to commandeer the online social movement for the Delhi gangrape protest through original posts and retweets.

## 5    Conclusion

Our study investigated the Indian online Delhi gangrape protest on Twitter in 2012 and it has contributed in leading to an understanding of the influence of the common man and 140 characters of his authorship. Firstly, our findings show that traditional news and media organizations remained detached from the evolving social scenario and played only a marginal role in creating and disseminating information. On the other hand, the common man and activists unleashed a wave of citizen journalism through their posts and retweets which were unabashedly emotional about their cause, unswervingly critical of the government, unafraid of standing up for their rights and united in their goal of spreading their message and mobilizing more support. We recommend that social media should be recognized as a new online press, and recorded in annals and archives to represent a true picture of society in the twenty-first century.

Secondly, we have shown that in the Delhi gangrape, different users had different roles, but all users became content generators – individual users generated more than half of all tweets. We suggest that digital libraries could observe the information behaviour patterns for social media users and tailor their digital library experience to be a more interactive, helpful one.

Thirdly, our study identified how a virtual community peaked and abated in its common goal to protest a criminal incident. It is suggested that digital libraries should embrace social technologies and facilitate social information behaviour, such as collaborative information seeking, content creation and content curation.

# References

1. Van House, N., Bishop, A., Buttenfield, B.: Introduction: Digital libraries as sociotechnical systems. In: Digital Library Use: Social Practice in Design and Evaluation, pp. 191–216. MIT Press (2003)
2. Lotan, G., Graeff, E., Ananny, M., Gaffney, D., Pearce, I., Boyd, D.: The revolutions were tweeted: Information flows during the 2011 Tunisian and Egyptian revolutions. Int. J. Comm. 5, 1375–1405 (2011)
3. Hu, M., Liu, S., Wei, F., Wu, Y., Stasko, J., Ma, K.L.: Breaking news on twitter. In: Proceedings of the 2012 ACM Annual Conference on Human Factors in Computing Systems, pp. 2751–2754. ACM (2012)
4. Wu, S., Hofman, J., Mason, W., Watts, D.: Who says what to whom on twitter. In: Proceedings of the 20th International Conference on World Wide Web, pp. 705–714. ACM (2011)
5. Cha, M., Benevenuto, F., Haddadi, H., Gummadi, K.: The world of connections and information flow in twitter. IEEE Transactions on Systems, Man and Cybernetics Part A: Systems and Humans 42(4), 991–998 (2012)
6. Bakshy, E., Hofman, J., Mason, W., Watts, D.: Everyone's an influencer: quantifying influence on twitter. In: Proceedings of the Fourth ACM International Conference on Web Search and Data Mining, pp. 65–74. ACM (2011)
7. Zee Research Group: India's Internet journey a study in contrasts (2013), http://zeenews.india.com/exclusive/indias-internet-journey-a-study-in-contrasts_6306.html (retrieved)
8. Fisher, K., Durrance, J., Hinton, M.: Information grounds and the use of need-based services by immigrants in Queens, New York: A context-based, outcome evaluation approach. J. American Soc. Inf. Sci. Tech. 55(8), 754–766 (2004)
9. Ackerman, M.: Providing social interaction in the digital library. In: Proceedings of the Digital Libraries Workshop, Springer, Heidelberg (1994), http://www.jcdl.org/archived-conf-sites/dl94/position/ackerman.html (retrieved June 23, 2013)
10. Brewer, A., Ding, W., Hahn, K., Komolodi, A.: The role of intermediary services in emerging virtual libraries. In: Proceedings of the ACM International Conference on Digital Libraries, pp. 29–35 (1996)

# Social Media as Online Information Grounds: A Preliminary Conceptual Framework

Bhuva Narayan[1], Bazilah A. Talip[2], Jason Watson[2], and Sylvia Edwards[2]

[1] Communication Studies, University of Technology Sydney
bhuva.narayan@uts.edu.au
[2] School of Information Systems, Queensland University of Technology
{bazilah.atalip@student,ja.watson@,s.edwards@}qut.edu.au

**Abstract.** Researchers are increasingly grappling with ways of theorizing social media and its use. This review essay proposes that the theory of Information Grounds (IG) may provide a valuable lens for understanding how social media fosters collaboration and social engagement among information professionals. The paper presents literature that helps us understand how social media can be seen as IG, and maps the characteristics of social media to the seven propositions of IG theory. This work is part of a wider study investigating the ways in which Information Technology (IT) professionals experience social media.

**Keywords:** Social media use, information professionals, IT professionals, information grounds theory, collaboration, social networking, Twitter study.

## 1 Introduction

This paper is a review essay that is part of a larger study that uses the theory of information grounds (IG) to explore how Information Technology (IT) professionals use online social networks when compared to face-to-face networks. IG are social settings where information, people, and place come together to create information flow within a physical environment [2]. This research uses the IG framework as a lens for understanding how social media (SM) fosters collaboration and social engagement among Information Technology (IT) professionals, which includes Digital Library professionals and researchers. It attempts also to understand how users within SM actually experience it as a place (a place to be in, a place to go to, a place to gather, or a place to be seen in) – or *information grounds* – and use it for professional purposes such as information sharing, networking, dissemination of their work, public communications, or for collaboration. This is vital for digital library professionals to understand how their users are getting and sharing information.

## 2 Information Grounds Theory

Karen Pettigrew first proposed the theory of information grounds in 1998 wherein she proposed that wherever people come together at a physical space informally for one

S.R. Urs, J.-C. Na, and G. Buchanan (Eds.): ICADL 2013, LNCS 8279, pp. 127–131, 2013.

purpose, there is a space created spontaneously where information exchange and sharing takes place [2], and that "information grounds are synergistic environment[s] temporarily created when people come together for a singular purpose but from whose behaviour emerges a social atmosphere that fosters the spontaneous and serendipitous sharing of information" [2] Pettigrew's theory of Information Grounds was built upon Granovetter's theory of "The Strength of Weak Ties" [4] which suggests that any individual's network comprises weak ties (acquaintances) and strong ties (close family, friends), but that weak ties are more useful sources of new information because strong ties usually possess the same information as the individual. In terms of social networks, this theory can be interpreted in the following manner – broad and diverse networks with weak ties are a richer source of new information than narrow and homogenous networks with just strong connections. IG theory can also be connected to the theory of Third Place [5]; Ray Oldenburg, an urban sociologist proposed the concept of the "third place" or so-called "hangouts at the heart of the community". Soukup [6] proposed that computer-mediated communication is highly suitable for being considered a "third place" in the contemporary world. However, the social engagement within the online spaces does not usually provide deep emotional support, although they expose individuals to a diversity of worldviews [7]. Although rooted in Granovetter's [4] and Oldenburg's ideas [5], Counts and Fisher [1] propose seven propositions of IG where they focus on the information sharing aspect. They are:

- Information Grounds (IG) can occur anywhere, in any type of temporal setting.
- People meet at IGs for a primary purpose other than information sharing.
- Information Grounds attended by various communities play different roles in information flow.
- Social interaction is a primary activity at Information Grounds.
- Individuals participate in formal and informal information sharing.
- People use information obtained at information grounds in alternative ways.
- Many sub-contexts exist within information grounds and are based on people's perspectives.

Many researchers agree that information grounds can be virtual and digital [3, 9] but Pilerot [10] found that there is no existing framework demonstrating the connection of people, place, and information in information sharing and seeking activities. Such a study has potential to offer us some new knowledge into digital and social media communication within both everyday and professional contexts.

## 3     Social Media as Information Grounds

Traditional physical information grounds such as office tea rooms, hair salons and cafés facilitate people to come together physically for reasons other than information exchange, but information exchange happens nevertheless, albeit in a dynamic and unplanned manner, although it is restricted to the physical space and time and hence to the number of participants that can be part of the communication [2, 3]. Instead, social media platforms foster temporary virtual spaces and enable information grounds that can be accessed anytime, anywhere, and is not restricted to the number of participants [1]. The openness, transparency, and availability of social media has also helped users share, disseminate, and find information in online spaces [11]. This element agrees with proposition #1 of Counts and Fisher [1] that "information grounds can occur anywhere, in any type of temporal setting and are predicated on the presence of individuals".

Mobile social media applications have also overcome the limitations of mobile-device-based services, which were previously limited to targeted communications and direct marketing [1] and did not aid information discovery. Now, with increased mobile connectivity and also geo-location services integrated with social media, serendipitous information discovery is more common within social networks and this accords well with IG propositions #2, #4, and #6.

Morris and Unsworth [12] found that social media technologies have also helped academics develop social spaces and communicate with fellow academics and students anytime and anywhere [13]. Thomas and Thomas [14] state that many academics prefer to engage in social media because it encourages their students to actively participate and collaborate in discussions in a social manner, but where they can also share educational information. Social media plays a similar role as physical spaces for communication and collaboration purposes, and online environment is local, unique, and accessible, which has transformed traditional social network connections in developing a community of experts [15]. Social media tools match proposition #2 in that "people gather at information grounds for a primary, instrumental purpose other than information sharing" and is relevant to proposition #4 in that "social interaction is a primary activity at information grounds such that information is a by-product". These findings show that virtual spaces can be similar to information grounds, but there is no research that maps this similarity (or the differences) through empirical research. Additionally, virtual spaces may have additional dimensions of facilitating communication that could be revealed in this study.

Social media also enables professionals to develop a hub for a specific target audience to disseminate information for serendipitous discovery by others [16]. Fisher, et al., [3] also found that offline interactions have significantly influenced the social interaction within the online spaces, where the offline and online relationships overlap. This element relates to proposition #5 as "Individuals participate in formal and informal information sharing and information flow appears in many directions" and as well as proposition #7 that "many sub-contexts exist within information grounds and these are based on people's perspectives and physical factors". Social media platforms are unique and focal, which enable users to foster collaboration, develop communities of practice, and serendipitously discover useful information through both strong and weak ties.

# 4    Implications for Digital Libraries

This work is part of a wider study of how IT professionals experience social media for professional purposes, and is using online observations of IT professionals on Twitter and interviewing them in order to map out the connections between IG and social media. IT professionals, along with information science and digital library experts (who often work together on digital library projects) are often involved in designing and building digital libraries. With social media becoming more and more prolific and prevalent in our society it is important for us to understand social media use on a conceptual level, for just like many other online interfaces, digital libraries too can flourish and become more integrated within communities if they can become information grounds where people and information meet in cyberspace.

## 5    Conclusion

The key gap in our understanding of the social media phenomenon is how it functions as a place despite being in cyberspace, along with an understanding of how it is experienced by its participants. This paper proposes that *information grounds* theory is a viable conceptual framework for understanding how social media can be perceived as place. The *information grounds* theory is a well-understood and validated theory that is built upon research in physical spaces. It proposes the people-information-place triad, which fits in with what online social media facilitates. This calls for empirical research to understand and theorize this phenomenon in a scholarly manner.

## References

[1]   Counts, S., Fisher, K.E.: Mobile social networking as information: A case study. Library & Information Science Research 32, 98–115 (2010)

[2]   Pettigrew, K.E.: The role of community health nurses in providing information and referral to the elderly: A study based on social network theory, Disertation. University of Ontorio, London (unpublished)

[3]   Fisher, K.E., Landry, C.F., Naumer, C.: Social spaces, casual interactions, meaningful exchanges: 'information ground' characteristics based on the collage student experience. Information Research 12(2), 1–12 (2007),
http://informationr.net/ir/12-2/paper291.html (May 18, 2012)

[4]   Granovetter, M.S.: The Strength of Weak Ties. American Journal of Sociology 78, 1360–1380 (1973)

[5]   Oldenburg, R.: The Great Good Place: Cafes, Coffee Shops, Community Centers, Beauty Parlors, General Stores, Bars, Hangouts, and How They Get You Through the Day. Paragon House, New York (1989)

[6]   Soukup, C.: Computer-mediated communication as a virtual third place: building Oldenburg's great good places on the world wide web. New Media & Society 8, 421–440 (2006)

[7]   Steinkuehler, C.A., Williams, D.: Where Everybody Knows Your (Screen) Name: Online Games as "Third Places". Journal of Computer-Mediated Communication 11, 885–909 (2006)

[8]   Fisher, K.E.: Information Grounds. In: Fisher, K.E., Erdelez, S., McKechnie, L.E.F. (eds.) Theories of Information Behavior, pp. 185–190. ASIST Monograph Series, New Jersey (2005)

[9]   Savolainen, R.: Small world and information grounds as contexts of information seeking and sharing. Library & Information Science Research 31, 38–45 (2009)

[10]  Pilerot, O.: LIS research on information sharing activities – people, places, or information. Journal of Documentation 68, 1–35 (2012)

[11]    Campbell, K., Ellis, M., Adebonojo, L.: Developing a writing group for librarians: the benefits of successful collaboration. Library Management 33, 14–21 (2012)
[12]    Morris, V.I., Unsworth, K.: "Morphing distance education into social media communities of practice," presented at the 2nd DGI Conference: Social Media & Web Science - The Web as a Living Space, Düsseldorf, Germany (2012)
[13]    Gu, F., Widen-Wulff: Scholarly communication and possible changes in the context of social media: A Finnish case study. The Electronic Library 29 (2011)
[14]    Thomas, M., Thomas, H.: Using new social media and web 2.0 technologies in business school teaching and learning. Journal of Management Development 31, 358–367 (2012)
[15]    Skågeby, J.R.: The irony of serendipity: disruptions in social information behaviour. Library Hi Tech. 30, 321–334 (2012)
[16]    Kreitzberg, A.P.: Building a Web 2.0-Friendly Culture: Success on the Web is About People, not Technology. People and Strategy 32, 40–45 (2009)
[17]    Hughes, A.L., Palen, L.: Twitter Adoption and Use in Mass Convergence and Emergency Events. In: 6th International ISCRAM Conference, Gothenburg, Sweden (2009)

# Influence Diffusion Detection Using Blogger's Influence Style

Luke Kien-Weng Tan, Jin-Cheon Na, and Yin-Leng Theng

Wee Kim Wee School of Communication and Information
Nanyang Technological University, Singapore
{w080078,tjcna,tyltheng}@ntu.edu.sg

**Abstract.** Previous studies on detecting blogosphere influence diffusion had used blog features such as in-degree and sentiment links. The approaches in most of these studies assumed that influence increases with the number of links and largely ignored the possible effect of bloggers' influence style on the diffusion of influence between linked bloggers where influence could be further described through the engagement style, persuasion style, and the persona of the bloggers. In this paper, we propose an Influence Diffusion Detection Model – Influence Style (IDDM-IS) that includes the use of bloggers' influence styles to detect influence diffusion through the blogosphere. Our study analyzed 107 bloggers with varying influence styles to detect the influence diffusion path. The results showed performance for IDDM-IS to be better than the in-degree and sentiment-values baseline approaches. In addition, IDDM-IS could provide a fine-grained description of the influence diffusion paths using the bloggers' influence styles.

**Keywords:** Influence diffusion detection, influence style profiling, blogger influence.

## 1    Introduction

Blog postings are readily available sources of opinions and sentiments that in turn could influence the opinions of the blogs' readers. This is evident from blog sites having effect on their readers' purchase decisions (e.g., www.engadget.com), political viewpoints (e.g., www.huffingtonpost.com), and others. The importance of understanding the influence propagation phenomenon has led to increasing influence analysis research in the blogosphere digital space. Previous studies had attempted to detect influence in blogs' social network where methods used include analyzing blog features such as the number of in-links and out-links [1, 2], similarity comparison through content analysis [12], and more recently sentiment analysis to detect positive and negative sentiments links [3, 10]. However, these studies focused on a single notion of the influence of blogs in detecting influence, that is, the existence of influence between blogs with hypertext links, but not on details in the manner or style in which blogs exert influence. Influential bloggers are not restricted to a limited description of influence and may differ in influence styles, and our previous work [13] had studied into the influence styles of blog sites through further describing the blog sites' engagement style, persuasion style, and persona style.

S.R. Urs, J.-C. Na, and G. Buchanan (Eds.): ICADL 2013, LNCS 8279, pp. 132–142, 2013.
© Springer International Publishing Switzerland 2013

| Skype scores an iOS update with improved calling UI and some bug fixes *by Terrence O'Brien posted Mar 7th, 2013 at 5:31 PM* | Skype for iPhone and iPad updated with improved calling interface, general improvements *Written by: MARK GURMAN, March 7, 2013 / 9:10 am* |
|---|---|
| Not every update from the Microsoft-owned VoIP service needs to be high-profile. Every so often a *nice subtle* tweak is all it takes to add a *lovely layer of polish* to an already *beloved* app. Both the iPad and iPhone versions of Skype were *bumped* to version 4.6 today. There are, of course, a number of bug fixes included in the update. But the *most immediately* visible change is to the UI for actually placing calls. The new look is *a bit cleaner* and more modern, though *not very* different functionally. There's also a new way to mark conversations as read with "just a few taps." Though, if you ask us "a few" is *probably still too many*. *Hit up* the iTunes app store now for your update and check out the source for a complete changelog. | Today, Skype has updated both its iPhone/iPod touch and iPad applications with an improved calling user-interface. Additionally, the company has added a new *handy* feature to mark all recent text-based conversations as read in a *quicker* fashion. The updates also include general fixes and improvements. Earlier today, we highlighted updates to Path, Fantastical, and a few others apps. |
| Retrieved from http://www.engadget.com/2013/03/07/skype-scores-an-ios-update/ on 1st May 2013. | Retrieved from http://9to5mac.com/2013/03/07/skype-for-iphone-and-ipad-updated-with-improved-calling-interface-general-improvements/ on 1st May 2013. |

**Fig. 1.** Blog post showing subjective persuasion influence syle

**Fig. 2.** Blog post showing objective persuasion influence style

In this study, we propose to improve influence detection performance through the identified traits of bloggers' influence style. For example, identifying whether bloggers are contributors or just passive sharers, or whether bloggers express ideas in an objective or subjective manner, or whether bloggers' posts are received positively or negatively by the readers. To illustrate persuasion as an influence style, the blog post in Figure 1 exerts influence in a subjective manner seen from the numerous subjective words and phrases as compared to Figure 2's blog post which contains minimal subjective expressions indicating a more objective influence style. Previous studies [1, 2] using simple links features could only attempt to detect the presence of influence between the linked blogs, while our study further identified the influence styles of bloggers to better understand the influence exerted by the bloggers in detecting influence diffusion. These additional influence style features could better fit the characteristics of the influence exerted by the bloggers and hence improve the performance of our influence diffusion detection model. In this paper, we aim to detect influence diffusion between bloggers using the influence styles of bloggers. We further describe the influence between bloggers as consisting of three possible styles, mainly engagement style, persuasion style, and the persona of the blog sites, and incorporate the influence styles as features in our Influence Diffusion Detection Model – Influence Style (IDDM-IS) based on the Independent Cascade approach [6]. We evaluated IDDM-IS against the in-degree and sentiment-values baseline methods, and the results show IDDM-IS's performance to be better than the baseline approaches.

The layout of this paper is as follows. First, we provide the related work, followed by a description of the proposed model on how we derive the bloggers' influence styles and compute the influence probability scores. This is followed by the model's evaluation and results, and finally the conclusion.

## 2    Related Work

Previous studies [9, 15] had measured the personality of bloggers in relation to predicting blogging. Costa and McCrae [5] evaluated personality based on clinical studies through five key traits: *neuroticism, extra-version, agreeableness, openness to experience*, and *conscientiousness*. Neuroticism represents an individual's tendency to experience distress. Extraversion is the dimension underlying a broad group of traits, including sociability, activity, and the tendency to experience positive emotions. Agreeableness is a dimension of interpersonal behavior where high agreeableness individuals are trusting, sympathetic, and cooperative. Openness to Experience refers to traits that describes individuals as imaginative and sensitive to art and beauty and have a rich emotional life. Conscientiousness is a dimension that contrasts scrupulous, well-organized, and diligent people with lax and disorganized individuals. Guadagno et al. [9] measured the personality of bloggers based on the five key traits by [5] to predict blogging. Their studies indicated that people who are high in openness to new experience and high in neuroticism are likely to be bloggers. The results indicated that personality factors impacted the likelihood of being a blogger and have implications for understanding who blogs. Similarly, Yarkoni [15] analyzed blogger personality on word use in their blog postings to study the association between personality and language of bloggers. However, these studies had manually measured bloggers' characteristic and personality with regards to their propensity to blog, and did not relate the characteristic and personality of bloggers to their influence styles. Moreover, the five key personality traits by [5] are not directly applicable for measuring influence style. In our work, we study bloggers' traits in relation to their influence style, which could determine their propensity to influence bloggers.

The use of graph-based blog features to detect influence in the blogosphere had been studied in previous work [1, 2]. These studies utilized positive interactions (e.g., agreement and trust) between individuals, and ignored the negative relationships and conformity of people. More recent studies include the consideration for both positive and negative links in the analysis of influence. Leskovec et al. [10] adapted a framework of trust and distrust in an attempt to infer the attitude of one user toward another using the observed positive and negative relations. Cai et al. [3] defined social influence through positive and negative social relationships. The study was inspired by the idea of persona in sociology studies where influence is the approvals gained from other reliable people. In our study, we used the graph-based blog features in-degree and sentiment value between linked bloggers approach as baseline comparison to the IDDM-IS. Gruhl et al. [8] measured the blog features metrics and further applied the metrics on diffusion models such as Threshold model [7] and Cascade model [6] to detect influence within social networks. Lim et al. [11] used the independent cascade model to explain information diffusion in blog network, where the diffusion probability assigned to each edge between a pair of bloggers in the blog network was derived from the number of posts, comments, trackbacks, and scraps. However, these studies had focused on a single notion of the influence of bloggers in detecting influence, that is, the existence of influence between the linked blog posts, and had not studied in details the influence types and styles of the bloggers.

# 3     Influence Diffusion Detection Model – Influence Style

## 3.1     Influence Styles Detection

In our proposed Influence Diffusion Detection Model – Influence Style (IDDM-IS), influence is described in terms of Engagement style, Persuasion style, and Persona style of the bloggers. Engagement style indicates the blogger's level of engagement and consists of the Listening-Participating (LP) type, Board-Focused (BF) type, Creating-Sharing (CS) type, and the Consistent-Casual (CC) type. Persuasion style is defined as the level of subjectivity expressed by the blogger, and Persona style describes the level of agreement towards the blogger. The influence styles were extracted through analyzing the target blogger's in-link posts and out-link posts as shown in Figure 3.

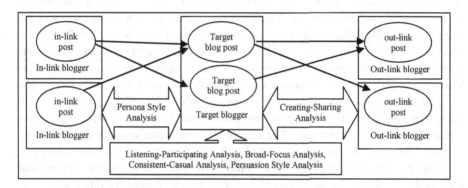

**Fig. 3.** Engagement Style Analysis (Listening-Participating (LP), Creating-Sharing (CS), Broad-Focus (BF), Consistent-Casual (CC)), Persuasion (PES) Style Analysis, and Persona (PER) Style Analysis.

In order to measure the degree of influence style, the *Listening-Participating (LP)* score, *Creating-Sharing (CS) score*, *Broad-Focus (BF) score*, *Consistent-Casual (CC)* score, *Persuasion Style* score, and the *Persona Style* score were computed respectively from the influence concept given in [13]. We measure the *LP-Score* by the number of blog post titles that contain the target topic and related feature terms. The count value was then normalized by the total number of posts for each respective blogger to give the *LP-Score*. In this study, we limit the target topic scope to only

Apple related product postings in detecting the influence diffusion path. A high percentage of target topic or related feature postings would indicate that the blogger is of Participating type, and conversely, a low percentage shows a Listening type. The *BF-Score* is measured by the number of unique target topics and their related features found in the blog post titles and normalized by the total number of target topics in the network. A wide range of topics and their related features discussed would indicate a Broad type, while a limited number of topics and their related features discussed refer to a Focused type. The *Creating-Sharing type* is evaluated through analyzing the similarity between the target blog posts content and it's out-link blog posts content based on the Jaccard coefficient: $J(A_{linking\ blog\ post}, B_{linked\ blog\ post}) = |A \cap B|/|A \cup B|$, defined as the size of the intersection divided by the size of the union of the two (A and B) bloggers' linked posts content. A high similarity value would mean that the blogger shares most of the out-link blog post content. On the other hand, the target blog post contains more original content if the similarity value is low. The *CS-score* is given as (1 minus Jaccard coefficient value) to reflect the propensity to influence for bloggers who are creative and original in their content. The *Consistent-Casual* type is determined by the number of target blog postings in a near-term (within 1 month), mid-term (within 2 to 3 months), and long-term (beyond 3 months) duration linked by the in-link posts within the analyzed time period. The *CC-Score* is computed by assigning a nil score for near-term posts, a score of 0.5 for mid-term posts, and a score of 1.0 for long-term posts. The assigned scores are summed and normalized over the number of posts for each blogger. This gives consideration for the consistency of the blogger to harness links for its mid and long term postings. We detect *Persuasion Style* by analyzing the subjectivity expressed by the bloggers in their blog posts through counting the number of subjective terms in the target blog posts. This is done by matching the subjectivity terms from [14] with the target blog posts terms. The matched number of subjectivity terms is then normalized by dividing with the length of the blog post. The *PES-Score* is derived from taking the average subjectivity scores of the blogger's total postings. The degree of compliance towards the blogger is measured based on the persona of the blogger. *Positive persona* describes bloggers with high positive influence, where their links from others often indicate approval and agreement. *Negative persona* represents bloggers with high negative influence, where their links from others usually express disagreement or distrust. The bloggers' persona were identified by detecting the sentiments expressed between the in-link and target blog posts based on the natural language processing approach used in [13] with the *PER-Score* for each blogger given as the ratio of number of similar sentiments posts over total number of posts for each blogger. Sentiment analysis was performed at phrase level on identified features where the aspects and features (e.g., screen and pixels are features of the display aspect) were extracted from Apple products related websites (e.g., www.apple.com). An overview of the influence styles score measurement is shown in Table 1.

**Table 1.** Overview of influence styles score measurement

| Influence Style Score | Influence Style Score Measurement |
|---|---|
| Listening-Participating Score | Count number of postings on target topics by blog site and normalize the value by the total number of posts for each respective blogger. |
| Creating-Sharing Score | Measure content similarity (Jaccard coefficient) between target blog posts and out-link blog posts and compute (1-Jaccard coefficient). |
| Broad-Focused Score | Count number of unique target topics within blog posts titles and normalize the value by the total number of target topics in the network. |
| Consistent-Casual Score | Assign a nil value for near-term posts, value of 0.5 for mid-term posts, and value of 1.0 for long-term posts. Sum the assigned values and normalize over the number of posts for each blogger. |
| Persuasion Score | Count number of subjective terms within each blogger's posts and normalize the value by dividing with the blog posts' length. Take average score based on blogger's total posts. |
| Persona Score | Ratio of similar sentiments posts over total number of posts for each blogger. |

## 3.2    Influence Diffusion Detection

Our study aims to introduce the concept of influence styles to improve performance of influence diffusion detection at blogger level in the blogosphere based on the *Independent Cascade* (IC) approach [6]. The objective of our study is to show the use of influence styles in detecting influence diffusion that is initiated from and along a single targeted blogger path and is not measured through multiple influence path. Hence, the use of the Linear Threshold model [7] is inappropriate for our study. The bloggers' network is defined as a directed network (or equivalently graph) $G = (V, E)$, where $V$ is the set of nodes (referred as bloggers) and $E$ a set of links, where each link is denoted by $e = (v, w) \in E$ and $v \neq w$, meaning there exists a directed link from a node v to a node w. For each directed link, a real value $\kappa_{v,w}$ with $0 < \kappa_{v,w} < 1$ is specified as the diffusion probability through link $(v, w)$. In the IC model, diffusion process proceeds from a given initial active set $D(t=0)$ in the following way. When a node $v(\in D(t))$ first becomes active at time-step $t$, it is given a single chance to activate each currently inactive child node w, and the attempt succeeds with probability $\kappa_{v,w}$. If v succeeds, then w becomes active at time-step $t+1$, i.e., $w(\in D(t+1))$. If multiple parent nodes of w first become active at time-step $t$, then their activation attempts are sequenced in an arbitrary order, but all the attempts are performed at time-step $t$. Whether or not v succeeds, v will not make any further attempts to activate w in subsequent rounds. The diffusion process starts with an initial activated set of nodes, and then continues until no further activation is possible. We attempt to derive the influence diffusion probability of each link through introducing the *Influence Style Function ($F_{IS}$)* of a blogger given as:

$$F_{IS} = \left\{ \left[ W_{LP} \times \sum_i^n \frac{LP_{i-score} - LP_{min\,score}}{LP_{max\,score} - LP_{min\,score}} \right] + \left[ W_{BF} \times \sum_i^n \frac{BF_{i-score} - BF_{min\,score}}{BF_{max\,score} - BF_{min\,score}} \right] + \right.$$
$$\left[ W_{SC} \times \sum_i^n \frac{CS_{i-score} - CS_{min\,score}}{CS_{max\,score} - CS_{min\,score}} \right] + \left[ W_{CC} \times \sum_i^n \frac{CC_{i-score} - CC_{min\,score}}{CC_{max\,score} - CC_{min\,score}} \right] +$$
$$\left. \left[ W_{PES} \times \sum_i^n \frac{PES_{i-score} - PES_{min\,score}}{PES_{max\,score} - PES_{min\,score}} \right] + \left[ W_{PER} \times \sum_i^n \frac{PER_{i-score} - PER_{min\,score}}{PER_{max\,score} - PER_{min\,score}} \right] \right\} / 6$$

$$- (1)$$

The normalizing constant (Feature Style$_{max\ score}$ – Feature Style$_{min\ score}$) ensures the posterior adds up to 1, and is computed by summing up the numerator over all possible values of each links weight score. In this study, we assumed a simple approach by taking all weight ($W$) values to be 1 in the model evaluation. Future studies would attempt to identify optimal weight values to improve performance. The Influence Style Function ($F_{IS}$) is then normalized by taking average of the six influence style scores. We compute the influence diffusion probability from blogger A to the respective linked blogger B as: $\kappa_{A,B}$=*Prob(Blogger A to influence)* x *Prob(Blogger B is influenced)*. The probability of Blogger A to influence is inferred through the ($F_{IS}$) score of the influencing Blogger (A), while the probability of Blogger B is influenced is derived from the similar sentiment values expressed when Blogger B is linked to Blogger A. Hence,

$\kappa_{A,B}$=*F$_{IS}$(A) x {number of similar sentiment posts$_{A,\ B}$/number of linked posts$_{A,\ B}$}* - (2)

, where $F_{IS}(A)$ is the normalized influence style function score of Blogger A, while *{number of similar sentiment posts$_{A,\ B}$/number of linked posts$_{A,\ B}$}* is the normalized similar sentiment value between Blogger A and Blogger B. To illustrate how influence style is used to detect influence in our approach, Figure 4 shows an influence network of an influential Blogger A with its influence link to Blogger B indicated in the diagram. Figure 5 shows the influence style scores for Blogger A ($F_{IS}(A)$) and the normalized similar sentiment value between Blogger A and Blogger B ($\Omega_{A,\ B}$=0.75), with the computed influence diffusion probability of Blogger A towards Blogger B given as ($\kappa_{A,B}$= $F_{IS}(A)$(=0.73) * $\Omega_{A,B}$ (=0.75) = 0.55). Blogger B will be activated if ($\kappa_{A,B}$=0.55) is greater than an arbitrary random number (referred as the IC weight value), which we determine for optimal performance of the IDDM-IS model to be equal 0.025 through extensive experiments. From equation (2), the influence diffusion probability ($\kappa_{A,B}$) is derived from the ability of Blogger A to influence and the degree to which Blogger B is influenced. The IDDM-IS model attempts to relate influence diffusion probability to influence diffusion by comparing influence diffusion probability against the IC weight as an influence threshold value.

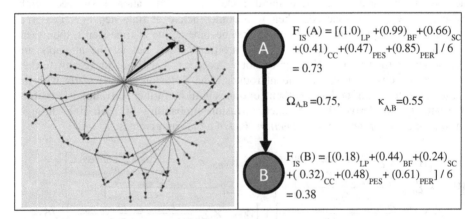

**Fig. 4.** Influence network diagram (with Blogger A and Blogger B as indicated)

**Fig. 5.** Scores for linked Blogger A and Blogger B

# 4    Model Evaluation and Results

We identified seven influential blog sites (www.9to5mac.com, www.macrumors.com, www.tuaw.com, www.engadgets.com, www.techcrunch.com, www.slashgear.com, and www.theverge.com) from Technorati.com based on their high Technorati Authority values. The "search for more reactions" feature found in Technorati.com was used to extract the in-link posts to the target blog site. A total of 107 bloggers with 9107 in-link posts, 8879 target posts, and 19317 out-link posts were extracted from the blog sites from 11 Feb 2013 to 5 April 2013. The in-degree weight defined as the number of in-links over the total number of out-links for a blogger, as well as the similar sentiment value between two linked bloggers were used in the baseline comparison with the IDDM-IS. A node is activated when the in-degree weight of the influencing blogger is higher than that of the influenced blogger. In the second baseline approach, nodes were activated when the linked bloggers expressed similar sentiment values on common topics, identified based on the number of similar sentiment links being greater than the number of non-similar sentiment links. In addition, the similar sentiment values between linked bloggers were also used as the diffusion probability values in the Sentiments-Independent Cascade model, where extensive testing showed optimal performance is achieved when the IC weight value for the Sentiments-Independent Cascade model equals 0.05. In the evaluation testing, the linked network path of an influential blogger consisting of 514 linked blog posts were manually classified as influence or non-influence, with the two coders' Cohen's kappa index [4] computed to be 0.68. Conflicting tags by the coders were reviewed and then manually re-classified and used as the answer keys. We measured the performance of the models in detecting influence diffusion using the F1-score measure given as F1=(2•Precision•Recall)/ (Precision+Recall).

**Table 2.** Evaluation testing results

|           | In-Degree | Sentiments-Only | Sentiments-Independent Cascade | IDDM-IS |
|-----------|-----------|-----------------|--------------------------------|---------|
| Precision | 0.626     | 0.719           | 0.725                          | 0.732   |
| Recall    | 0.347     | 0.562           | 0.637                          | 0.785   |
| F-Measure | 0.447     | 0.631           | 0.678                          | 0.757   |

**Table 3.** T-test results of respective influence styles

| Influence Styles         | p     | μ(yes) | μ(no) |
|--------------------------|-------|--------|-------|
| Listening-Participating  | 0.001 | 0.308  | 0.166 |
| Broad-Focus              | 0.013 | 0.590  | 0.494 |
| Creating-Sharing         | 0.000 | 0.493  | 0.415 |
| Consistent-Casual        | **0.182** | 0.414  | 0.439 |
| Subjectivity             | 0.013 | 0.488  | 0.514 |
| Persona                  | 0.002 | 0.792  | 0.762 |

From Table 2, it can be seen that the IDDM-IS (F-measure=0.757) performed better than the In-Degree (F-measure=0.447), Sentiment-only (F-measures=0.631), and Sentiment-Independent Cascade (F-measure=0.678) baseline approaches. The poor performance in the In-Degree (ID) approach could be because links to a blogger's post may not indicate influence, but could also express dissimilar sentiments or are just referencing the linked blogger's posts. This is seen in Figure 6 where the linking blog post made reference to the linked blog post, and expressed negative sentiments on the target topics, while the linked blog post is slightly positive on the target topics. Both the sentiment value approaches performed better than the ID approach as similar sentiment expression on common topics between linked bloggers provide clearer indication of influence. The higher performance of Sentiment-Independent Cascade versus Sentiment-Only shows the capability of independent cascade method in modelling influence diffusion as compared to using only the sentiment values between linked bloggers. The IDDM-IS performed well as compared to the baseline methods in detecting influence diffusion within a blogger network. This could be because the IDDM-IS relates closely to influence diffusion by further considering the bloggers' influence styles, where each of the influence style characteristic could have provided clearer indication of the blogger's propensity to influence.

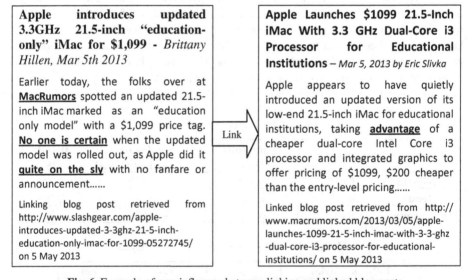

**Fig. 6.** Example of non-influence between linking and linked blog posts

For example in Figure 5, Blogger A who has an influence style that is more participating, broad, creating, consistent, and positive in persona was able to influence Blogger B, who is only similar to Blogger A in persuasion style. We further analyze the relation between each of the influence styles scores and the ability of the blogger to influence to determine the significant influence styles that could detect influence diffusion. From the independent sample t-test results shown in Table 3, we could see that the influence styles, except for Consistent-Casual (CC) style are significantly different (p<=0.05) in their $\mu(yes)$ mean score and $\mu(no)$ mean score, indicating their ability to detect influence. It is noted the Influence Style Function ($F_{IS}$)'s assumption that subjective persuasion style would be more influential differs from the results. Based on these preliminary findings, we would attempt to determine the optimal weight values of the Influence Style Function ($F_{IS}$) in future work. The difference in mean scores for CC style was deemed to be insignificant (p>0.05), which means both influential and non-influential bloggers have similar consistency in their blog posts' links, inferring that CC style could not differentiate between influence or not and could be omitted from the Influence Style Function computation. From the results, we could also see that influential bloggers tend to be participating, broad, creative, objective, and have positive persona. In addition to detecting influence diffusion within the blogger network, IDDM-IS further describes the manner and style in which influence is diffused through the network path by providing the bloggers' influence styles. We could plot the influence styles of each blogger along the influence path to visualize the pattern of influence styles in the influence flow. For example, if the bloggers in the influence path are of the focused type, we could infer that the influence diffusion is focused on specific topics, where the information could be applied for companies marketing their products through the blogosphere. It is noted that bloggers' influence styles are not static and would change over time. Hence, the effectiveness of IDDM-IS is specific to the period of analysis. The IDDM-IS is also dependent on the performance of the sentiment analysis approach. Any performance changes to the sentiment analysis would inadvertently affect the results of IDDM-IS.

## 5    Conclusion

Previous studies that used graph-based blog features to detect influence in the blogosphere had assumed that influence exists between linked blogs, and had not considered the manner and style in which influence was diffused in the network. Our study proposed the IDDM-IS model that further describe influence in terms of bloggers' influence style. The IDDM-IS relates closely to the influence styles of the bloggers and performed well compared to the in-degree and sentiment values baseline approaches. In addition to detecting influence diffusion in a blogger network, the IDDM-IS describes the influence style of each blogger in the influence path, providing a fine-grained description of the manner in which influence is diffused.

## References

1. Adar, E., Adamic, L.A.: Tracking Information Epidemics in Blogspace. In: Conference on Web Intelligence, pp. 207–214 (2005)
2. Agarwal, N., Liu, H.: Modeling and Data Mining in Blogosphere. Morgan & Claypool (2009)

3. Cai, K.K., Bao, S.H., Yang, Z., Tang, J., Ma, R., Zhang, L., Su, Z.: OOLAM: An Opinion Oriented Link Analysis Model for Influence Persona Discovery. In: Web Search and Data Mining, pp. 645–654 (2011)
4. Cohen, J.A.: Coefficient of Agreement for Nominal Scales. Educational and Psychological Measurement 20(1), 37–46 (1960)
5. Costa Jr., P.T., McCrae, R.R.: Normal personality assessment in clinical practice: The NEO Personality Inventory. Psychological Assessment 4, 5–3 (1992)
6. Goldenberg, J., Libai, B., Muller, E.: Talk of the Network: A Complex Systems Look at the Underlying Process of Word-of-Mouth. Marketing Letters 12(3), 211–223 (2001)
7. Granovetter, M.: Threshold models of collective behavior. American Journal of Sociology 83(6), 1420–1443 (1978)
8. Gruhl, D., Guha, R., Liben-Nowell, D., Tomkins, A.: Information diffusion through blogspace. In: Proceedings of the 13th International Conference on World Wide Web, pp. 491–501 (2004)
9. Guadagno, R.E., Okdie, B.M., Eno, C.A.: Who blogs? Personality predictors of blogging. Computers in Human Behavior 24(5) (2008)
10. Leskovec, J., Huttenlocher, D., Kleinberg, J.: Predicting Positive and Negative Links in Online Social Networks. In: World Wide Web, pp. 641–650 (2010)
11. Lim, S.-H., Kim, S.-W., Kim, S., Park, S.: Construction of a blog network based on information diffusion. In: Proceedings of the 2011 ACM Symposium on Applied Computing, pp. 937–941 (2011)
12. Matsumura, N., Yamamoto, H., Tomozawa, D.: Finding Influencers and Consumer Insights in the Blogosphere. In: International Conference on Weblogs and Social Media AAAI, pp. 76–83 (2008)
13. Tan, L.K.W., Na, J.-C., Theng, Y.-L., Chang, K.Y.: Blog Site Profiling through Influence Style Detection. In: International Conference on Asian Digital Libraries ACM, pp. 329–332 (2012)
14. Wilson, T., Wiebe, J., Hoffmann, P.: Recognizing Contextual Polarity in Phrase-Level Sentiment Analysis. In: Human Language Technology Conference on Empirical Methods in Natural Language Processing ACL, pp. 347–354 (2005)
15. Yarkoni, T.: Personality in 100,000 words: A large-scale analysis of personality and word use among bloggers. Journal of Research in Personality (2010)

# Use of Short Message Service (SMS) to Maximize the Library Usage: A Tale of Two Libraries

K. John Paul Anbu[1] and Sridevi Jetty[2]

[1] University of Swaziland, Swaziland
anbuj@uniswa.sz
[2] Bundelkhand University, Jhansi, UP, India
sridevi.jhs@gmail.com

**Abstract.** This paper is a case study of a semi-automated Content Alert System using mobile SMS alerts, implemented at two university libraries; The university of Swaziland, Swaziland, Southern Africa and Bundelkhand University Library in India. The project ran in two phases; first a content alert system was tried and tested at the University of Swaziland with the help of Emerald Publishers and a prototype was developed on its completion. The second phase used the prototype to create a similar content alert service with a larger heterogeneous user group and incorporated a number of publishers on a larger scale. This paper is a record of the project details, methods used and the findings of the projects.

**Keywords:** Short Message Service, SMS, Mobile Computing, Mobile library applications.

## 1 Introduction

We are living at a time where communication technologies are used extensively by students and staff at universities for accessing and disseminating information. Yoo-Seong Song and Jong-Moon Lee's (2012) study of mobile device ownership among international business students show that close to 82% students owned smartphones. Olatokun observed in 2006 that "Mobile phones have become an inseparable part of everyday life". The real impetus for the mobile devices started with the arrival of web 2.0 applications especially the active participation of the user towards the web which has pushed the growth of mobile devices in academic institutions. There is no wonder that libraries which play an integral part in today's information society also strive to make use of this opportunity by exploiting the advantages of the technology and provide innovative services to its patrons.

## 2 Libraries and Mobile Technology

Over the past decade a number of SMS projects for teaching and learning were reported in various literatures. Walsh (2009) refers to a number of small-scale and pilot

S.R. Urs, J.-C. Na, and G. Buchanan (Eds.): ICADL 2013, LNCS 8279, pp. 143–146, 2013.
© Springer International Publishing Switzerland 2013

projects in mobile learning but most of them remain as experimental projects and have not yet been brought to the mainstream learning environment. Thinking specifically for libraries, Simon So observes that libraries can better reach out and serve students by sending and receiving SMS-based library information (So, S. 2009). One example of its use in libraries is a SMS based alert service offered by the Hong Kong Institute of Education (HKIED, 2012). Kroski (2012) refers to Library SMS Notification used at the University of Illinois at Urbana-Champaign which offers students the opportunity to be notified by text messaging when librarian research specialists offer in-depth reference service. Hill and Sherman (2007) reports extended text messaging reference which can text SMS messages to and receive answers from librarians at Southeastern Louisiana University. AltaRama's Reference by SMS and Mosio's Text a Librarian are notable commercial SMS reference tools.

## 3     Project Background

In 2009 a project was attempted at the University of Swaziland to experiment whether SMS technology can be effectively used to engage the library users into using library services, especially the electronic resources and whether it is possible to effectively market the library services through SMS technology. The project consisted of creating a SMS platform to send SMS messages to a group of selected students on a number of compiled SMS messages, mostly of Table of Contents, article alerts, quotations and library alerts and send them to the students as SMS. On transmission the usage of the electronic resources were monitored and a prototype was created. Realizing that the pilot project was limited in a number of aspects a similar attempt was made at Bundelkhand University, in the heartland of India, where the authors have made an attempt to see whether a slightly modified version of the project with specific alert messages which are normally received from the publishers can be effectively sent to library patrons on an SMS based SDI simulation method.

## 4     Methodology

### 4.1     Web Enabled SMS Platform

For sending seamless SMS messages it is important to have a web enabled SMS gateway so that it is easy to maintain and administer as it can send SMS from desktop computer itself. Most of the SMS service providers provide such an interface and a number of open sources and propriety software are also available. In both the projects two separate web enabled SMS platforms were experimented. In the initial case Emerald's Intouch portal which makes use of Elgg, an open source software was used and in the second phase a commercial SMS vendor was used.

### 4.2     User Profile

The important component of SMS based alert service is the creation and maintenance of the user profile. This is the place which acts as an intermediate between the information and recipient. All the relevant information about the users are stored in this profile, which can be a database or table. A user profile consists of information about the user and his information needs. A prototype of a user profile for mobile based SDI service consists of the userid, contact number, keywords or subject and the frequency of information.

### 4.3    Assimilation of Content Alerts

The key ingredient to the whole project is the alerts. In the case of the first project a straightforward table of content alerts from Emerald Management Database was generated. The expansion of the second project involved a heterogeneous user group drawn out of different faculties. For this an SDI simulation method was used to ascertain the subject requirements of every user. Accordingly the user subject keywords from each users profile were picked. All the databases subscribed by the university were used to assimilate the content by soliciting email based content alerts using the keywords supplied by the staff.

### 4.4    Transmission of the Content

On successful assimilation of alerts the final step is to transmit them as SMS messages to the users. The SMS gateway was used to transmit those messages from the portal which also acts as a permanent record of all the activities which will help to determine the usage and all the other administrative statistics. Once again the first phase of the project was simple because all the alerts were transmitted to all the users. In the case of the second project, each content alert was cross-checked against each users and accordingly the specific alert was sent to each user.

## 5    Findings

On completion of the project a reviews were conducted to see the impact of the services. In the case of the first project with the University of Swaziland it was very easy to ascertain the results as the alerts were sent to a specific set of users and the alerts were picked from the Emerald Database. The results showed that the number of downloads and the number of sessions the users engaged with the database increased dramatically. The Full Text downloads were increased by almost 150% compared to that of the previous two months. On a year to year comparison the growth rate again showed an impressive 150%. In the second project the total number of downloads and access to databases were analyzed. Once again the results showed that there was tremendous increase in the usage. A comparison of year to year downloads for five main databases showed that there was a marked difference compared to the previous year. In the case of American Chemical Society, the increase is close to a staggering 5 times more than that of the previous year, while the other databases also showed similar increase in the download.

## 6    Conclusion

With all the advancements happening in the ICT and in the Satellite communication system there is no doubt that mobile applications are influencing major changes in libraries. While the modern gadgets and applications seem to be much versatile, age old services like SMS which is cost effective and at the same time effective and timely can be used to cater to the basic needs of the information seekers. The underlying principle of the next generation of library services is to link – people, technology and information in the context and environment which they are comfortable with.

## References

1. Hill, J.B., Madarash Hill, C., Sherman, D.: Text messaging in an academic library: integrating SMS into digital reference. The Reference Librarian 47(1), 17–29 (2007)
2. HKIED, Library SMS alert service. Hong Kong Institute of Education (2012), https://libsms.ied.edu.hk (retrieved on September 6, 2012)
3. Kroski, E.: On the Move with the Mobile Web: Libraries and Mobile Technologies. Library Technology Reports. American Library Association, pp. 1–48 (2012), http://eprints.rclis.org/bitstream/10760/12463/1/mobile_web_ltr.pdf (accessed on September 6, 2012)
4. So, S.: The Development of a SMS based Teaching and Learning System. Journal of Educational Technology Development and Exchange 2(1), 113–124 (2009)
5. Song, Y., Lee, J.: Mobile device ownership among international business students: a road to the ubiquitous library. T Reference Services Review 40(4), 574–588 (2012)
6. Walsh, A.: Text messaging (SMS) and libraries. Library Hi Tech News (8), 9–11 (2009)

# Playing Human Computation Games for Mobile Information Sharing: The Influence of Personality and Perceived Information Quality

Ei Pa Pa Pe-Than, Dion Hoe-Lian Goh, and Chei Sian Lee

Wee Kim Wee School of Communication and Information,
Nanyang Technological University, Singapore
{ei1,ashlgoh,leecs}@ntu.edu.sg

**Abstract.** Applications that use gaming elements to harness human intelligence to tackle computational tasks are increasing in popularity and may be termed as Human Computation Games (HCGs). Recently, HCGs have been utilized to offer a more engaging experience for mobile information sharing. Yet, there is a lack of research that examines individuals' personality and behaviors related to HCGs. This understanding may be important in identifying HCG features that suit different personality orientations. Thus, this study aims to investigate the influence of individuals' personality and perceptions of information quality on intention to play HCG for mobile information sharing. In a study of 205 participants, results revealed that personality traits of extraversion and openness, as well as perceived information accuracy and relevancy were significant in predicting intention to play. Implications of our work are also discussed.

**Keywords:** Human computation game, mobile multiplayer game, mobile information sharing, personality, information quality.

## 1    Introduction

The increased popularity of information sharing applications creates an opportunity for digital libraries to harness human intelligence to improve their services and user experience. Further, the rapid adoption of smart mobile devices has expanded the landscape of information sharing by facilitating the seeking and sharing of information on the go. In essence, mobile information sharing applications allow individuals to express themselves whenever they are, and to encounter diverse types of information which may be helpful for them. These applications yield benefits for the creation of digital libraries that employ crowdsourcing for collection development, for instance, getting users to generate tags for digital photographs and annotations for georeferenced content [14]. Despites these benefits, the voluntary nature of sharing information may limit a more widespread adoption of such applications [11]. Thus, these applications need to employ effective motivational strategies to reach a larger user base.

S.R. Urs, J.-C. Na, and G. Buchanan (Eds.): ICADL 2013, LNCS 8279, pp. 147–156, 2013.

In this regard, mobile information sharing applications have recently begun utilizing gaming concept to encourage participation [5]. The paradigm of harnessing human intelligence through games is known as human computation game (HCG) [18]. In a HCG, players perform specified information-based tasks and generate information as a byproduct of gameplay. Although games serve as a motivator to foster users' participation [5], research has shown that some HCGs have the potential to better maintain players' attention than others [18]. Thus, there is a need for research to investigate the factors affecting individuals' intention to play HCGs.

Individuals' intention to play games is of considerable interest because both researchers and designers can greatly benefit from understanding their driving forces. In particular, personality represents the experiential aspect of an individual that drives the way an individual thinks, behaves, and approaches a particular situation [9]. It has been identified as a salient factor predicting users' behaviors and attitudes towards pure entertainment games [16]. Although influential, research on how individuals' personality influences their intention to play HCGs has been lacking.

In addition, research on pleasure-oriented information systems has shown that individuals' continued usage is strongly influenced by their perceived quality of information encountered [13]. As HCGs create opportunities for players to consume outputs generated besides providing entertainment [11], their perceived quality of information may impact intention to play. However, research has yet to fully explore this phenomenon. Driven by these research gaps, the present study aims to examine the influence of individuals' personality traits and perceived of information quality on their intention to play, using our developed mobile information sharing HCG, called *SPLASH*.

## 2    Background Literature

### 2.1    Related Work on Mobile Information Sharing

A number of digital libraries supporting user-generated content have emerged over the past years. One example is *G-Portal* [14] which hosts user-generated geospatial content, such as Web pages and annotations. Next, *PhotoGeo* [1] is a digital library that holds a collection of geo-referenced, user-generated photos, and supports automatic annotation of these photos to facilitate retrieval.

Recently, gaming elements have been utilized in information sharing context to promote better user experience and engagement. *Metadata Games* [3] is one example in which players contribute tags for archival media such as images, videos and audio recordings. Next, in *MobiMissions* [4], content sharing is accomplished by means of creating and responding missions, defined by a series of photographs and text annotations associated with specific locations. The *CityExplorer* [15] is another example where players conquer a city segment by placing as many markers as possible on that segment, achieved through contributing photos of the locations of their chosen categories such as food and café.

To date, most of the studies on mobile information sharing HCGs are centered on their design and implementation perspective. A few studies have focused on users' perceptions and motivations with these games. However, the roles of personality and perceived information quality in HCG context have yet to be fully explored.

## 2.2   Personality, Gaming, and Social Media Research

The use of personality serves as a functional and efficient approach to understanding media usage behaviors of individuals [8]. In recent studies, the Big-Five personality model is employed to assess personality orientations [6]. This model approaches personality as traits, and determines an individual's personality along five bipolar dimensions:   extraversion, agreeableness, conscientiousness, neuroticism, and openness [9]. Research has shown that the Big-Five personality traits impacted the generic and specific use of social media [7], as well as individuals' game genre preferences and in-game behaviors [6]. This study thus aims to investigate how individuals' personality determines their intention to play HCGs using the Big-Five model.

First, extraversion refers to the extent to which individuals are sociable, outgoing, active, assertive, and enthusiastic [9]. Thus, extraverts enjoy social activities or prefer activities that involve large group of people. Extraverts were also found to enjoy group and social activities while playing games [6] and sharing information with others online [7]. Second, agreeableness represents the extent to which an individual expresses tendencies towards altruism, friendliness, cooperativeness, modesty, and trust [9]. As agreeable people are willing to help others, they were found to cooperate with other players in games [6]. However, they were less likely to be involved in online information exchange [17].

Third, conscientiousness reflects the degree to which an individual is careful, efficient, responsible, self-disciplined, thorough, and has a high will to achieve [9]. Research has shown that conscientious people were found to use online for informational activities, rather than leisure activities [7]. Fourth, neuroticism refers to the extent of an individual's tendency to express negative emotions such as anxiety, sadness, nervousness, and embarrassment [9]. Prior research has suggested that neurotic people were more likely to use information sharing applications with rich forms of social interaction [7] and spend a long duration of time playing games [17]. Finally, openness represents the extent of an individual's willingness to explore and accept new ideas and experiences, and is characterized by traits such as curiosity, imaginativeness, artistic, and having broad interests [9]. Individuals who rated high on openness were found to enjoy exploring different aspects of game worlds [6].

The above studies underline how personality plays an important role in both gaming and information sharing. A HCG utilizes gaming elements to promote user experience and engagement. It also facilitates interaction among players by means of information sharing and the expression of one's ideas and exploration of information contributed by others. Thus, we deem that individuals' personality may influence their intention to play, and present the following hypotheses:

H1: *Personality traits of a) extraversion, b) agreeableness, c) conscientiousness, d) neuroticism, and e) openness are positively related to intention to play a HCG for mobile information sharing.*

### 2.3     Perceived Information Quality

Information quality has been considered as an important factor determining the success of information-oriented applications [13]. Research has shown that perceived information quality significantly affects users' attitudes and sustained usage of online information sharing applications [10]. Individuals may use HCGs to discover information besides seeking enjoyment [21], thus perceived information quality may influence their intention to play. This study aims to evaluate the impact of perceived information quality on intention to play HCG for mobile information sharing through accuracy, completeness, relevancy, and timeliness dimensions which are recognized as the most important quality dimensions in online context [13].

First, accuracy is defined as the correctness of information, and composed of attributes such as correctness, reliability, and believability [13]. Past studies have identified the significant impact of perceived information accuracy on users' attitudes towards online knowledge sharing [10]. Second, completeness represents sufficient breadth of scope and depth of detail of information relevant to users [13]. It was found to influence users' behaviors in searching online information [12].

Third, relevancy is defined as the extent to which users perceive information to be applicable, relevant, usable, and helpful enough for the task at hand [13]. While seeking information online, users have expressed concerns for information relevancy [12]. In the mobile information sharing context, users may expect to discover information relative to their current locations, and successful discovery may impact their attitudes. Finally, timeliness is an important quality dimension in real-time environments, and represents the degree to which content is up-to-date or current [13]. Research has shown that information timeliness has an impact on users' satisfaction [12].

These studies highlight the importance of the abovementioned quality dimensions in the online context. As information is the central aspect of mobile information sharing HCGs, we deem that players who perceive higher levels of information accuracy, completeness, relevancy, and timeliness are more likely to continue playing these games. Hence, the following hypotheses are proposed:

H2: *Perceived information quality in terms of a) accuracy, b) completeness, c) relevancy, and d) timeliness are positively associated with intention to play a HCG for mobile information sharing.*

### 2.4     *SPLASH*: The Mobile HCG Used for the Study

*SPLASH* (Seek, **PLA**y, **SH**are) is an Android-based mobile HCG that allows players to create, share, and access location-based content. Content is in the form location-based information known as "comments" comprising titles, tags, descriptions, media (e.g. photos) and ratings (Figure 1a). In *SPLASH*, "places" represent an arbitrary geographic area visualized as "mushroom houses" on the map (Figure 1b). Such places may also be further divided into "units" with each unit holding its own set of comments. For example, a shopping mall may be considered as a place and a store inside represent a unit.

*SPLASH* adopts a pet-based game genre in which players "feed" location-based information to virtual pets (see Figure 1c) which stay inside the units of mushroom houses. The appearances of a pet and mushroom house change according to four attributes of information – amount (size), quality (pet's color and house's wall color), recency (pet's age and house's roof color), and sentiment (pet's mood and house's weather). Figure 1e and 1f show the different appearances pet and mushroom house respectively.

To foster socializing, *SPLASH* provides virtual rooms which are pets' apartments (Figure 1d). Players may visit and decorate these rooms with items purchased from the game store, such as mini-game arcade machine. There is also a comment board enabling players to contribute comments while socializing. Finally, players can represent themselves with customizable avatars.

*SPLASH*'s reward system includes in-game currency (gold), leaderboards and awards. Players earn gold by viewing, creating, and rating comments, as well as playing mini-games inside virtual rooms. Awards are won by completing specified missions (e.g. creating a certain number of comments). Leaderboards show the top players in the game such as those with the most gold.

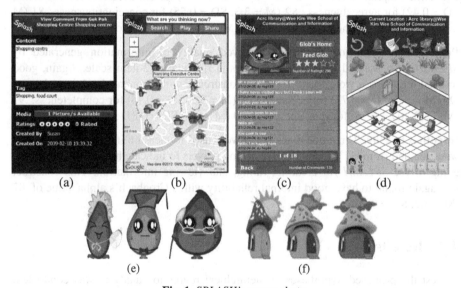

**Fig. 1.** *SPLASH*'s screen shots

## 3    Methodology

Our study was conducted on 205 undergraduate and graduate students from a local university with ages from 19 to 41 with an average of 26 years. The sample consisted of 58% females and 42% males. Here, 50.7% of participants used location check-in features of social networking applications while 42.4% shared information about locations. Further, the majority of participants (67.3%) were players of online games.

First, participants were introduced to *SPLASH* and its features. Next, they were each provided with a HTC Desire mobile phone preloaded with *SPLASH* and were asked to familiarize themselves with the game. The actual study then began, and participants were asked to perform a series of tasks including information viewing, creating, and rating, visiting virtual rooms, customizing their avatars, and viewing leaderboards. Finally, a paper-based survey was administered, which captured participants' personality traits, perceived information quality, and intention to play, along with other demographic data. Participation was voluntary and anonymous. The entire study took approximately 40 minutes to complete, and participants were also paid a modest incentive of $5 for their effort.

The two independent variables used in our study were personality traits and perceived information quality, while the dependent variable was intention to play. Scales for these variables are described below. Questions were measured on a 5-point Likert scale ranging from 1 (strongly disagree) to 5 (strongly agree).

**Personality Traits.** The Big-Five personality traits were assessed using the 44-item Big Five Inventory [9]. All five personality traits had good internal reliabilities with Cronbach's alpha values of .92 (M = 3.5, SD = 0.70) for extraversion, .78 (M = 3.9, SD = 0.42) for agreeableness, .82 (M = 3.3, SD = 0.55) for conscientiousness, .81 (M = 3.0, SD = 0.58) for neuroticism, and .85 (M = 3.5, SD = 0.52) for openness.

**Perceived Information Quality.** Perceived quality of information generated by *SPLASH* was assessed with four constructs [13] using a 12-item scale. Again, good internal reliabilities were found for these constructs, with Cronbach's alpha values of .96 (M = 3.4, SD = 0.77) for accuracy, .96 (M = 3.2, SD = 0.78) for completeness, .91 (M = 3.3, SD = 0.75) for relevancy, and 1.0 (M = 3.6, SD = 0.81) for timeliness.

**Intention to Play.** Three questions items were used to measure intention to play, and were adapted from [11]. Items involve asking players to indicate how likely they were going to use *SPLASH* for creating, rating, and viewing information. This construct was again found to have good internal reliability with a Cronbach's alpha value of .87 (M = 3.2, SD = 0.96).

## 4     Results

To test the proposed hypotheses, a hierarchical regression analysis was conducted. The Big-Five personality traits were entered into the first block, and the four perceived information quality constructs were added into the second. The results shown in Table 1 revealed that the model was significant, and accounted for 34% of the variance in intention to play.

With regards to the Big-Five personality traits, extraversion was significant in predicting intention to play *SPLASH* ($\beta$ = 0.20), and hence hypothesis 1a was supported. This indicates that players who scored high on extraversion are more likely to play *SPLASH* than those who scored low on this trait. Contrary to expectations, openness was found to have a significant negative effect on intention to play ($\beta$ = −0.16), indicating that the more the individual wants to express oneself more openly, the less likely he/she will play *SPLASH*. Therefore, hypothesis 1e was not supported. There were no significant associations between agreeableness, conscientiousness and neuroticism, and intention to play, and thus hypotheses 1b, 1c, and 1d were not supported. This indicates that individuals' altruistic and neurotic tendencies, and goal-oriented behaviors did not influence their intention to play *SPLASH*.

Regarding the information quality dimensions, perceived information accuracy ($\beta$ = .18) and relevancy ($\beta$ = .39) were found to be significantly positively associated with intention to play *SPLASH*. Thus, hypotheses 2a and 2c were supported. This suggests that the more accurate information is observed in *SPLASH*, the more likely the player will continue playing it. As well, the higher the perceived relevance of information is, the more likely the player will play *SPLASH*. However, perceived completeness and timeliness of information did not exhibit a significant influence on intention to play, indicating that players are not concerned about, or do not expect to obtain, complete and timely information during *SPLASH* play. Therefore, hypotheses 2b and 2d were not supported.

**Table 1.** Hierarchical regression analysis with Big-Five personality and perceived information quality as predictors of intention to play, N = 205

| Dependent variable = Intention to play | | |
|---|---|---|
| **Independent variables** | **Standardized $\beta$** | **t-values** |
| **Big-Five Personality** | | |
| Extraversion | .20 | 2.6** |
| Agreeableness | .12 | 1.5 |
| Conscientiousness | .01 | .08 |
| Neuroticism | −.01 | −.05 |
| Openness | −.16 | −2.1* |
| Adjusted $R^2$ | **.03*** | |
| **Perceived Information Quality** | | |
| Accuracy | .18 | 2.4** |
| Completeness | .12 | 1.4 |
| Relevancy | .39 | 4.6*** |
| Timeliness | −.03 | −.30 |
| Changes in adjusted $R^2$ | **.32** | |
| Final Adjusted $^2$ | **.34*** | |

* p < .05, ** p < 0.01, *** p < 0.001

## 5    Discussion and Conclusion

This study examines how individuals' personality and perceived information quality affect their intentions to play a HCG for mobile information sharing. Our results suggest that the personality traits of extraversion and openness, as well as perceived information accuracy and relevancy have statistically significant effects on intention to play. As HCGs have been increasingly adopted in the digital libraries context in recent years, we anticipate that this study will provide insights into what can be done to increase users' intention to play such games.

First, the finding for the personality trait of extraversion indicates that HCGs for information sharing serve as an effective medium for extraverted individuals to interact with others because sharing and rating information facilitates interaction. While previous studies argued that extraverted people enjoy games that support social interactions [7], this study provides a more nuanced perspective that the fulfillment of the social need in HCGs determines their intention to play. Thus, this finding suggests the importance of incorporating mechanisms, such as team-based challenges, into HCGs. Here, *SPLASH*'s objective of developing pets by means of sharing and rating information facilitates a sense of cooperation among players.

Unexpectedly, our results suggest that people with high levels of openness are less likely to play mobile information sharing HCGs, which is inconsistent with previous studies [7, 17]. One possible explanation could be the lack of features in *SPLASH* that explicitly ask players to discover information about specific locations and reward them for successful discovery. *SPLASH*'s pets only express happy and sad emotions based on positivity and negativity of information fed, which may not be sufficient to satisfy people who rated high on openness because they may enjoy games that support more varied emotional expressions, such as *The Sims* [6]. To address this issue, features that facilitate deep emotional expressions such as extremely happy/sad, and exploration of game worlds through narratives should be integrated into HCGs.

Interestingly, agreeableness was found to be non-significant, suggesting that altruistic and helpfulness tendencies do not influence intention to play HCG for mobile information sharing. This is noteworthy because agreeable people are community-oriented and willing to help others [9], which could be achieved in HCGs that are built upon the collaborative effort of players. One possible explanation could be the lack of features in *SPLASH* that notify players as recognition of their contributions. Thus, HCGs should incorporate features that enhance players' perceived helpfulness to others, such as sending virtual gifts as a return of their help.

Likewise, the relationship between conscientiousness and intention to play was not significant. Although conscientious people were found to have preferences for online informational activities [7], they are less likely to devote excessive amounts of time to playing mobile games [8], which may probably contribute to this result. Therefore, HCGs should include features that enable players to set easily achievable short-term goals such as completing specified daily activities and racking up experience points.

Similarly, neuroticism did not influence intention to play. As neurotic people are not inclined to cooperate with others in games [8], it could be speculated that *SPLASH*'s approach of gameplay, where cooperation among players is essential to evolve the pets, may contribute to this result. For instance, to keep the pets happy, players need to contribute more positive information. However, future work is still needed to validate this finding.

Another interesting finding is that perceived information relevancy was found to have a significant positive influence on intention to play. One plausible explanation is that players encounter information that is relevant to them during gameplay, and the chance of encountering this information further determines their intention to play.

This finding therefore highlights the importance of mechanisms in HCGs that promote relevancy of outputs. Examples include personalization, and reward and punishment strategies to encourage the contribution of relevant information. Here, *SPLASH*'s browsing feature facilitates players to discover a new place of interest, or new content that might be useful for them, thereby fueling their intention to play.

Next, the significance of perceived information accuracy suggests that players who observed information to be accurate are more likely to play HCG. Thus, HCGs should employ mechanisms to enhance information accuracy. Examples include comparison with other sources of information, and error detection. *SPLASH*'s visualization features facilitate information accuracy assessment, which is determined based on the ratings given to that information collectively. That is, the higher the rating is, the more accurate the information is and the brighter the color of the pet will be.

Finally, the non-significance of perceived information completeness and timeliness suggests that players are not concerned about these issues while playing HCGs, which is inconsistent with previous studies [10, 12]. Speculatively, it is possible that *SPLASH* attracts more of opinion and social content in which the completeness measure is not important [2], thus diminishing the roles played by completeness of information on intention to play. With regards to timeliness, the mobility of *SPLASH* encourages players to share information about current events, causing the currency of information to be understated, resulting in its non-influence on intention to play.

Our findings have implications for both research and practice. From a research perspective, our study contributes to a more thorough understanding of antecedents of intention to play HCGs. More importantly, we found that individuals who rated high on extraversion and low on openness are the most promising group of HCG players. Also, information accuracy and relevancy were found to be important for HCG players. From a practical standpoint, our results can help designers to enhance HCG design features that appeal to a larger user base. One, understanding players' personalities may help designers identify appropriate features that suit different personality orientations. Two, the importance of information quality underlines the need to design HCG features that yield good quality information and allow players to assess information quality efficiently. Taken together, the findings of this study could be beneficial to digital libraries and other information repositories hosting location-based content that may wish to employ games to encourage users' participation.

As with other survey research, there are some limitations in our work. First, the findings were obtained from one study that focused on mobile information sharing area using a single HCG genre. Thus, caution must be taken when interpreting our results. Second, this study did not explore the effects of moderating variables on our constructs. Future research should incorporate potential moderators such as perceived enjoyment and usefulness into our proposed model. Finally, our participants were graduate and undergraduate students, and thus replicating the study with a diverse group of population would be beneficial to validate the present findings.

# References

1. de Figueirêdo, H.F., Lacerda, Y.A., de Paiva, A.C., Casanova, M.A., de Souza Baptista, C.: PhotoGeo: a photo digital library with spatial-temporal support and self-annotation. Multimedia Tools and Applications 59, 279–305 (2012)

2. Fichman, P.: A comparative assessment of answer quality on four question answering sites. Journal of Information Science 37, 476–486 (2011)
3. Flanagan, M., Punjasthitkul, S., Seidman, M., Kaufman, G.: Citizen Archivists at Play: Game Design for Gathering Metadata for Cultural Heritage Institutions. In: Proceedings of DiGRA 2013: DeFragging Game Studies (2013)
4. Grant, L., Daanen, H., Benford, S., Hampshire, A., Drozd, A., Greenhalgh, C.: MobiMissions: the game of missions for mobile phones. In: ACM SIGGRAPH Educators Program, p. 12. AMC Press, New York (2007)
5. Goh, D.H., Ang, R.P., Lee, C.S., Chua, A.Y.K.: Fight or unite: Investigating game genres for image tagging. Journal of the American Society for Information Science and Technology 62, 1311–1324 (2011)
6. Griebel, T.: Self-Portrayal in a Simulated Life: Projecting personality and values in The Sims 2. International Journal of Computer Game Research 6 (2006)
7. Hughes, D.J., Rowe, M., Batey, M., Lee, A.: A tale of two sites: Twitter vs. Facebook and the personality predictors of social media usage. Computers in Human Behavior 28, 561–569 (2011)
8. Jeng, S.-P., Teng, C.-I.: Personality and motivations for playing online games. Social Behavior and Personality: an International Journal 36, 1053–1060 (2008)
9. John, O.P., Robins, R.W., Pervin, L.A.: Handbook of personality: Theory and research. Guilford Press, New York (2008)
10. Kim, B., Han, I.: The role of trust belief and its antecedents in a community-driven knowledge environment. Journal of the American Society for Information Science and Technology 60, 1012–1026 (2009)
11. Lee, C.S., Goh, D.H.-L., Chua, A.Y.K., Ang, R.P.: Indagator: Investigating perceived gratifications of an application that blends mobile content sharing with gameplay. Journal of the American Society for Information Science and Technology 61, 1244–1257 (2010)
12. Lee, Y.J., Park, J., Widdows, R.: Exploring antecedents of consumer satisfaction and repeated search behavior on e-health information. Journal of Health Communicatio 14, 160–173 (2009)
13. Lee, Y.W., Strong, D.M., Kahn, B.K., Wang, R.Y.: AIMQ: A methodology for information quality assessment. Information & Management 40, 133–146 (2002)
14. Lim, E.P., Goh, D.H., Liu, Z., Ng, W.K., Khoo, C., Higgins, S.E.: G-Portal: A map-based digital library for distributed geospatial and georeferenced resources. In: 2nd ACM+IEEE Joint Conference on Digital Libraries, pp. 351–358. ACM Press, New York (2002)
15. Matyas, S., Matyas, C., Schlieder, C., Kiefer, P., Mitarai, H., Kamata, M.: Designing location-based mobile games with a purpose: collecting geospatial data with CityExplorer. In: International Conference on Advances in Computer Entertainment Technology, pp. 244–247. ACM Press, New York (2008)
16. Park, J., Song, Y., Teng, C.-I.: Exploring the links between personality traits and motivations to play online games. Cyberpsychology, Behavior, and Social Networking 14, 747–751 (2011)
17. Ryan, T., Xenos, S.: Who uses Facebook? An investigation into the relationship between the Big Five, shyness, narcissism, loneliness, and Facebook usage. Computers in Human Behavior 27, 658–1664 (2011)
18. von Ahn, L., Dabbish, L.: Designing games with a purpose. Communications of the ACM 52, 58–67 (2008)

# The Metadata Schema Design and Utility Architecture for Thai Lanna Inscription Collection

Churee Techawut[1], Papangkorn Inkeaw[1],
Jeerayut Chaijaruwanich[1], and Trongjai Hutangkura[2]

[1] Department of Computer Science, Faculty of Science, Chiang Mai University, Thailand
churee.t@cmu.ac.th, jeerayut.c@cmu.ac.th
[2] Princess Maha Chakri Sirindhorn Anthropology Centre, Bangkok, Thailand
trongjai.h@sac.or.th

**Abstract.** Digitization has been applied to the Thai Lanna script, or so-called the Fakkham script. Two major requirements to create a digital collection of the Thai Lanna inscriptions is to preserve them in the digital format and to infer for the engraving period of each inscriptions supporting the linguists and historians to interpret the contents within an appropriate context. The digital inscription images can be processed by the image processing techniques to create an important output, a set of each character images. It does not only use for a data set training in a preservation process, but also indicate the evolution of ancient characters, character relationships and stories in the historical times. This paper presents two key issues. First, the creation of metadata schema for the output describing Thai Lanna inscriptions and storing a set of character images by reusing and extending the metadata schema from Thai Lanna archives. Second, the architecture of utilization showing the contributions of our metadata schema design that serves as the foundation of the architecture.

**Keywords:** Metadata Schema, Digital Character Image, Thai Lanna Inscription.

## 1 Introduction

Generally, ancient texts in inscriptions are transliterated and translated into modern scripts and languages by paleographers. In some cases, paleographers might encounter problems of unclear characters and texts. Therefore, application of digital technology might fulfill their need of solving the problems. With modern technology, both character images and inscription information are valuable for their studies. In Northern Thailand, the Lanna Kingdom (ca. 13th - 16th centuries) used two types of scripts, namely Tham Lanna script and Thai Lanna script [1] (widely used between the 14th and 18th centuries).

Based on the work of Inkeaw [2], the Thai Lanna script was chose as a case study on application of digitization to paleography, and the image processing techniques are applied for semi-automatic collection of Thai Lanna character images. The webpage for viewing each digital character images from Thai Lanna inscription collection is shown in Fig. 1. This work has a basic metadata schema to describe the collection. In order to collect the inscription details and the digital character (shortened to DC)

S.R. Urs, J.-C. Na, and G. Buchanan (Eds.): ICADL 2013, LNCS 8279, pp. 157–160, 2013.
© Springer International Publishing Switzerland 2013

images extracted from the digital inscription (shortened to DI) images, the new metadata schema must be redefined for common use and sharing.

This paper firstly presents the metadata schema design of the Thai Lanna inscriptions based on the metadata schema of the Thai Lanna archives [3]. It is extended from Functional Requirements for Bibliographic Records (FRBR) model [4] by adding some entities for describing and collecting the character images. Finally, the paper presents the architecture of utilization focusing on the contributions of our metadata schema design that serves as the foundation of the architecture.

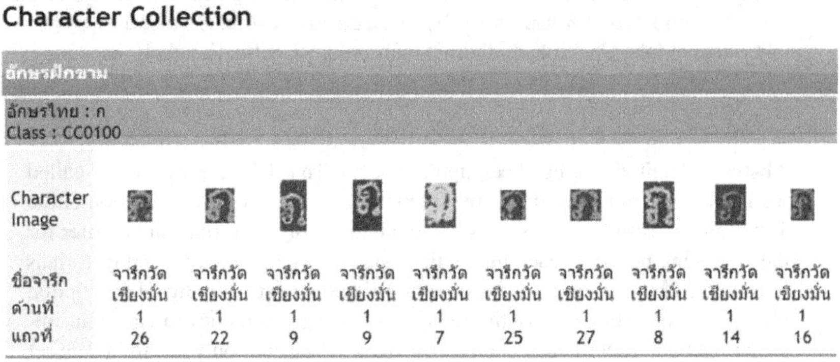

**Character Collection**

**Fig. 1.** The application screenshot for viewing each DC images

## 2    Metadata Schema Design

The metadata schema must be designed to support three statements of requirement specification as follows: 1) Provide some basic information of the inscriptions and the persons who created, funded and contributed them. 2) Provide some information of the DI images, publishers and copies of image. 3) Provide some details of the DC images and their relations with the digital source image.

The metadata schema of Thai Lanna archive, originally developed from FRBR model, is corresponding to the inscription metadata. It is reused and extended some entities for describing and collecting the DC images.

Fig. 2 shows the conceptual model of the metadata schema. The basic information of the inscriptions is described in both Inscription and Expression entities. The information of the DI images and its copies are described in Manifestation and Copy entities. However, the new Epigraph entity is added, and used to describe the DC images. Some attributes for each entity are added for supporting our major requirements and some further applications. The attributes which describe inscription information are studied from [5].

The following schemas show attributes of each entity. Attributes shown in italics are newly added to describe the Thai Lanna inscriptions. It does not appear in Thai Lanna archives metadata.

- Inscription (title, abstract, identifier)
- Expression (created date, *funded date*, language, note, *material, size of material*, identifier)

- Manifestation (format, digitized date, source, provenance, rights holder, *side*, identifier)
- Copy (URI, *side*, identifier)
- Epigraph (character, *Thai alphabet*, character URI, *side*, *line*, *column*, identifier)
- Agent (name, family name, given name, type of agent, organization name, address, identifier)

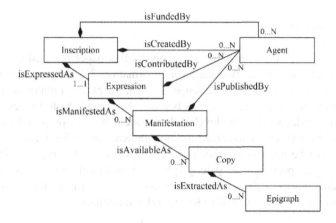

**Fig. 2.** Metadata schema for Thai Lanna inscriptions based on Thai Lanna archives

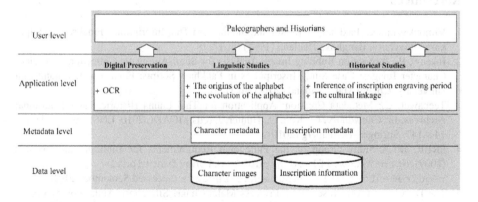

**Fig. 3.** The utilization level architecture of Thai Lanna inscription collection

## 3    Utilization of Thai Lanna Inscription Collection

Fig. 3 shows the utilization architecture of the Thai Lanna inscription collection. The first application is for the digital preservation. The optical character recognition (OCR) [6] helps to preserve the inscriptions in the digital format. Many character images are used for training a learnable model. The second application is for the paleographic studies. The metadata supports paleographers find the origin and evolution of the Thai alphabets. The DC images are used to connect and explain relationship of the alphabets. The third application is for historical studies. The inference of inscription engraving period [7] can support historians to interpret the contents within an appropriate context. In additions, study of cultural linkage also requires character images of various cultures and civilizations for comparing writing pattern in order to reveal their cultural connection.

# 4    Conclusion

The Thai Lanna inscription metadata proposed in this paper is based on Thai Lanna archive metadata. It can describe the basic information, DI images, and DC images. It can support user's search within a scope of requirements. It is important to have the Epigragh entity in the metadata schema, because it can describe to the level of digital character images deeper than the level of digital archives. The proposed metadata can be deployed and further implemented for any applications of digitization to paleography. It can also be applied to other types of characters. The major utilizations are focused on digital preservation, paleographic and historical studies. The digitization and data management of the Thai Lanna inscription is worth for the studying of the evolution of alphabet that can link to several related cultures.

# References

1. Vimonkasam, K.: Fakkham Scripts found in Northern Thai Inscriptions: Final report, Silpakorn University, Bangkok, Thailand (1981) (in Thai)
2. Inkeaw, P.: Inscription Rubbing Image Analysis for Semi-Automatic Collection of Ancient Character Images: Case Study Inscriptions in Fakkham Scripts: Final report, Chiang Mai University, Chiang Mai, Thailand (2013) (in Thai)
3. Techawut, C.: Metadata Creation: Application for Thai Lanna Historical and Traditional Archives. In: Chowdhury, G., Koo, C., Hunter, J. (eds.) ICADL 2010. LNCS, vol. 6102, pp. 144–147. Springer, Heidelberg (2010)
4. FRBR. IFLA Study Group on the Functional Requirements for Bibliographic Records (2009), http://www.ifla.org/publications/functional-requirements-for-bibliographic-records (accessed September 2012)
5. The Database of Thai Inscription. Princess Maha Chakri Sirindhorn Anthropology Center (2006), http://www.sac.or.th/databases/inscriptions (accessed September 2012)
6. Mara, H., Hering, J., Kromker, S.: GPU Based Optical Character Transcription for Ancient Inscription Recognition. In: 15th International Conference on Virtual Systems and Multimedia, VSMM 2009, September 9-12 (2009)
7. Gangamma, B., Murthy, K.S., Punitha, P.: Curvelet Transform based approach for prediction of epigraphical scripts era. In: 2012 IEEE International Conference on Computational Intelligence & Computing Research (ICCIC), December 18-20 (2012)

# RefConcile – Automated Online
# Reconciliation of Bibliographic References

Guido Sautter [1], Klemens Böhm[1], and David King [2]

[1] Karlsruhe Institute of Technology (KIT), Am Fasanengarten 5, 76128 Karlsruhe, Germany
[2] The Open University, Walton Hall, Milton Keynes MK7 6AA, UK
{guido.sautter,klemens.boehm}@kit.edu, David.King@open.ac.uk

**Abstract.** Comprehensive bibliographies often rely on community contributions. In such settings, de-duplication is mandatory for the bibliography to be
useful. Ideally, de-duplication works online, i.e., when adding new references,
so the bibliography remains duplicate-free at all times. While de-duplication is
well researched, generic approaches do not achieve the result quality required
for automated reconciliation. To overcome this problem, we propose a new
duplicate detection and reconciliation technique called RefConcile. Aiming
specifically at bibliographic references, it uses dedicated blocking and matching
techniques tailored to this type of data. Our evaluation based on a large real-
world collection of bibliographic references shows that RefConcile scales well,
and that it detects and reconciles duplicates highly accurately.

**Keywords:** Bibliographic References, Data Cleansing, Record Linkage.

## 1 Introduction

Compiling bibliographies covering entire scientific domains is challenging. An
additional challenge for bibliography platforms that rely on a user community for the
addition of new data is a tradeoff between comprehensiveness and data quality. This
is because, to maintain data quality, and to keep the rate of duplicates low in
particular, many platforms include interactive duplicate detection procedures in the
data upload process, i.e., no full automation. An example of such a platform is
ZooBank [24]. Pursuing comprehensiveness, other platforms strip all data quality
assurance measures from the upload process to simplify contributing, for instance the
Catalogue of Life [4] and RefBank [27]. This incurs a large number of duplicate
records; be it variant representations of the same record or records that differ merely
by errors like misspellings.

A platform hosting a bibliography maintained by a community has to meet the
following conflicting requirements: (a) uploading references should incur little intellectual effort, (b) newly uploaded references should become available right away, and
(c) there should be few erroneous or duplicate references. Thus, the bibliography
platform has to check immediately if new references are duplicates of ones already
present and reconcile them if necessary. Furthermore, de-duplication should be
lightweight, i.e., consume as few resources as possible. This work proposes a

S.R. Urs, J.-C. Na, and G. Buchanan (Eds.): ICADL 2013, LNCS 8279, pp. 161–170, 2013.
© Springer International Publishing Switzerland 2013

de-duplication method tailored to bibliographic references to meet this combination of requirements.

Considerable research effort has gone into the clean-up of data sets: **Data de-duplication** [10], also known as **Entity Matching** [20], and **Record Linkage** [2] deal with the detection of duplicate records in large data sets, while **Data Cleansing** [13] aims at reconciling detected duplicates. Conceptually, entity matching compares all records in a data set pair-wise to find out which ones are duplicates of others. Its complexity thus is $O(n^2)$. To reduce computational cost, a blocking step groups the records into blocks prior to the matching. Blocks comprise records that might be duplicates of one another, and the matching step only compares records in the same block. There are three categories of blocking methods: disjoint, overlapping, and fuzzy. Disjoint methods assign each record to exactly one block, overlapping ones yield sorted blocks that overlap 'at the edges', and fuzzy methods assign records to several blocks. Draisbach [9] surveys different blocking strategies; their complexities vary from $O(n)$ to $O(n \log n)$. Blocking is more effective the smaller the blocks are because this reduces the number of comparisons in the matching step. To meet above requirements, this paper devises an effective blocking method for bibliographic references; its complexity is $O(n)$.

Entity matching in general has received considerable attention recently; cf. Köpcke [20]. The frameworks surveyed there also report results for bibliography data. However, the largest bibliographic data set evaluated consists of roughly 67,000 references to less than 6,000 works, with the best reported accuracy at only 89%.

Duplicate detection and reconciliation immediately after the arrival of new references further requires a blocking method that works incrementally. Re-computing the entire blocking every time would incur prohibitive effort. Reducing the workload by resorting to periodic cleanup leaves un-reconciled records in the data set most of the time and is not user-friendly.

To facilitate automated de-duplication in community contributed bibliographies, this paper proposes **RefConcile**, a technique tailored to both contemporary and legacy bibliographic references. The rationale is that a technique designed for this type of data can provide the accuracy and performance required, unlike generic approaches. To build RefConcile, we first thoroughly investigate bibliographic references and their peculiarities: For instance, identifying the last name of an author is far from trivial depending on the representation of author names; this may incur ambiguities. Based on our findings, we then propose a blocking method specifically tailored to bibliography data and the requirements outlined above. Regarding the six blocking methods surveyed in [9], our proposal is between key-based blocking and canopy clustering. This is because we use very fuzzy blocking keys for indexing to efficiently compute an ad hoc canopy around a newly added reference. Third, we propose a vote based reconciliation technique that works attribute by attribute.

Our evaluation on RefBank data demonstrates that RefConcile outperforms generic entity matching approaches with bibliographic data: The data set consists of about 150,000 bibliographic references, with about 20% duplicates. RefConcile detects such references with 95.6% f-measure at 99.7% precision. It takes less than one second per newly added reference.

## 2        Bibliographic References

This section describes bibliographic references and their individual attributes in detail, with a focus on how attribute values may vary in different representations of the same reference. Note that RefConcile works with atomized references. Reference parsing is a related, but distinct problem, and there are separate algorithms for solving it [5, 11, 26]. Thus, RefConcile handles different reference styles only with regard to their specific representation of individual attributes, especially author names (see below); ordering and intermediate punctuation of attributes is not an issue. Further, this section discusses the most commonly found errors in bibliographic references. Finally, this section introduces similarity measures commonly used in duplicate detection and related search tasks.

### 2.1      Attributes of References

To better understand the peculiarities of bibliographic references and their attributes, we have investigated a sample of several thousand references from the RefBank data set. This section describes our findings.

**Author names** are challenging for duplicate detection because the representation of a person name can vary considerably. Several problem patterns have been identified [26], namely double last names, leading and middle initials, noble titles, affixes indicating generation, and infixes like *van*. Reference style also plays an important role, with first and last name occurring in multiple orders and with various punctuation schemes, even within the same reference. Further, infixes and affixes may or may not be given, and if they are, their position and punctuation can vary considerably. The (fictional) author name *Alexis Ulysses van Thor*, for instance, can be given as anything from *van Thor, A.U. van* and *Thor AU* to *A. Ulysses van Thor*. Additional variation arises from names transliterated to Latin script, e.g., from Cyrillic. The last names *Iakowlew*, *Jakowlev*, and *Yakovlew*, for instance, may all refer to the same person. Further, sometimes only the first author of a referenced work is given, with *et al.* standing in for all others; we also found instances with the authors missing altogether.

The **title** of the referenced work does not vary as much. Safe for very few errors, the words are always in the same order, if with varying capitalization. However, long titles may sometimes be truncated, and individual words can be misspelled.

The **name of the journal** an article was published in is challenging for duplicate detection. Long journal names in particular tend to be reworked heavily: stop words may be omitted, and other words abbreviated to different degrees, down to their initial letter in extreme cases. The journal *Transactions of the Royal Entomological Society of London*, for instance, may be shortened to *T. Roy. Ent. Soc. Lond.* The order of the words remains the same, however. The use and degree of abbreviations is often motivated by spatial constraints in the bibliography of a publication. ISSN provides a list of suggested abbreviations [15]. However, it does not cover all abbreviations that occur in practice. The variation in abbreviated names has also spawned many web sites, such as those offered by CalTech [3] and the University of Leeds [29], which catalogue the variations to help with clarification. However, both web sites only list one suggested abbreviation per journal, with further ones hidden behind a login in [3].

The **publisher** of a referenced book or book chapter can also take a multitude of forms, especially when used in conjunction with the location(s) of the publisher, as the order of these two elements can vary. In addition, the representation of the name itself can vary considerably: The publisher name *Pensoft Publishers, Sofia, Moscow*, for instance, can be given as *Moscow: Pensoft Publishers*, or even simply as *Pensoft*.

Numeric attributes, like the **year of publication**, the **volume or issue number** in references to journal articles, and the **pagination**, exhibit little variation. However, the latter two may be lacking in some references. Thus, duplicate detection has to cope with their presence or absence.

## 2.2     Common Errors

Many duplicate references originate from slight variations in spelling. One reason for such differences is the varying transliteration schemes used for author names, as explained above. A more common reason for differences, however, are typographical errors. Davies [6] found that such errors are not equally frequent throughout a bibliographic reference: (1) misspellings are more likely to occur in the middle or at the end of a word rather than at the beginning; in particular, the first letter of a word is nearly always correct; (2) misspellings are most likely to occur in author names, somewhat less likely in titles, and least likely in journal and publisher names. We exploit these findings in the design of our blocking technique.

## 2.3     String Similarity Measures

This section describes measures for assessing the similarity (or difference) between two strings, with **similarity = 1 – distance**.

The **Levenshtein Distance** [22] (also referred to as the edit distance) between two strings is the number of single-character edits needed to change one word into the other using *insertion*, *deletion*, and *substitution*. If the two strings are equal, the Levenshtein distance is 0. The cost to compute it between two strings of lengths m and n is $O(m \times n)$. This makes it impractical to compute between full references, but it is well applicable to individual terms within a reference.

The **Jaro-Winkler Distance** [17, 30] measures similarity of strings: 0 indicates no similarity, and 1 is an exact match. The Jaro-Winkler distance is derived from earlier work [16] addressing the problem of person name variations, such as McDonald and MacDonald, in census taking. As such it is well suited to matching author names, as well as short strings in general.

**Term Frequency - Inverse Document Frequency (TF-IDF** for short) [18] indicates the significance of a word within an individual document that is part of a collection of documents. Its normal use is as a weighting factor in information retrieval and text mining, indicating how significant a given word is when used to select individual documents from the collection. Likewise, it is suited to weighting words in titles.

**N-grams** are the basis of several string similarity measures that are widely used in information retrieval, most commonly with n=3. Generating the n-gram representations of two strings is of linear effort, and comparison works in constant time (dependent on $n^3$). However, it is still relatively expensive in comparison to computing the Levenshtein distance when strings are short. In addition, n-gram based similarity measures abstract from the order of the n-grams, which can be detrimental to accuracy.

# 3    Related Work

Data de-duplication in general is closely related to the problems of Data Cleansing [13], Record Linkage [2], Entity Matching [20, 21], and clustering [7]. This section reviews respective techniques and assesses their applicability to the specific problem of keeping a community-contributed collection of bibliographic references clean.

The term **Data Cleansing** [13] refers to identification and cleanup of duplicate records in a data set. The closely related terms **Record Linkage** [2] and **Entity Matching** [20, 21] refer to the same activity when merging several data sets. Commonly, this works in two steps: blocking and matching. The latter often is computationally expensive especially if the former is not effective. Subsequent reconciliation may require input from human experts in the general case.

Köpcke et al. [20, 21] provide extensive surveys of entity matching techniques and respective frameworks. However, all approaches discussed there are generic, i.e., designed for entity matching in general. Exploiting domain-specific knowledge is orthogonal to the issues studied there. Generic approaches must learn all features in the text being analyzed. Yet phenomena like abbreviations and changes to the order and separating punctuation of first and last name are hard to infer. We speculate that this pursuit of generic entity matching is why the result quality of these frameworks on bibliographic data drops as data sets grow larger. According to [20], it decreases from 99% f-measure with 5,000 records to 89% with 67,000 records.

Draisbach [9] provides an overview of blocking techniques: **Sorted neighborhoods** do not appear to be well-suited to our setting: They are sensitive to changes to the order of the parts of author names and to abbreviations, let alone to omitted leading stop words. In addition, the size of the neighborhood would have to be very large for common author names like *Smith*. **Bigram indexing** is ineffective in our setting, as long strings like titles just yield too many combinations, and it is likely inefficient for the same reason. **Canopy clustering** in its generic form is computationally too expensive for our setting: If the fraction of duplicates in the dataset is low, its complexity approximates $O(n^2)$ with tight thresholds; if thresholds are relaxed, canopies grow impractically large. However, the incremental blocking method we propose can be seen as the efficient index-based computation of an ad hoc canopy around a newly added reference. **Blocking keys** are easy to use incrementally and, if constructed properly, are both efficient and effective. However, their construction is not trivial in our setting. This is because the construction has to cope with abbreviations and with different orderings of author name parts in situations where the last name may be ambiguous. On the other hand, the index entries we propose to use to efficiently compute canopies can be seen as fuzzy blocking keys.

Blocking is closely related to clustering, and incremental blocking is related to incremental clustering techniques. Much work has gone into clustering stream data [8, 12, 23, 31, 32]. However, all these approaches use rather rigorous pruning techniques to reduce memory consumption. This is not applicable in our setting, as blocking needs to retain all records, not only a few representatives ones.

# 4    Reference Reconciliation – The RefConcile Algorithm

This section describes the RefConcile technique in detail, in particular its custom tailored blocking mechanism, its matching technique, and how it reconciles references found to be duplicates.

## 4.1    Blocking

The purpose of blocking is to reduce the number of pair-wise reference comparisons in the matching step as far as possible, in our setting the number of comparisons to a newly added reference. Blocking in general is somewhat similar to hashing: it distributes records across multiple bins (called blocks), and subsequent matching works inside individual bins. With fuzzy blocking methods, records can also be assigned to multiple bins instead of one. To be effective, there should be many bins with few records in each. On the other hand, blocking should not assign any actual duplicates to different bins, as matching then cannot recognize them. Furthermore, blocking ideally has to be independent of the number of references already in the data set.

To meet these constraints, RefConcile uses fuzzy blocking keys [9] composed from all attributes of the bibliographic references. The keys are fuzzy in a sense that their individual parts consist of sets or ranges rather than single values. Two keys are considered equal if all the sets have a non-empty intersection and all the ranges overlap. If an attribute is not present in a reference, the corresponding part of the blocking key is a wildcard set or range that has a non-empty intersection with each non-wildcard set, or a wildcard range that overlaps with every non-wildcard range, respectively.

The rationale behind this approach can be demonstrated with an example: consider the following two representations of the fictional author name from Section 2.1: *Thor AU* and *Ulysses THOR*. However, it is possible that the first representation actually refers to a different author, someone with the first name *Thor* and the last name *AU*. The part of the blocking key that represents the author name has to reflect these possible alternatives. We use sets in alphabetical order as an easy form of normalization, thereby abstracting different name part orders. Hence, for *Thor AU*, the key would be be *{A, T}*, and for *Ulysses THOR, {T, U}*. RefConcile treats the individual attributes as follows:

-    **Author names:** First, discard all letter blocks that do not contain any capital letters and then all fully capitalized ones that do not contain a vowel, as they are probably blocks of initials. The remaining letter blocks are probably the author's last name. Construct a set containing the first capital letter from each block, normalized to alphabetical order, conflating the letters I, J, and Y, as well as V and W, to allow for differences in transliteration. Because all but the first author can be substituted with "et al.", RefConcile uses only the first author. Note that, while the order of the individual parts of a name can vary, author names as a whole exhibit little variation, especially the first few authors [6].
-    **Title:** Discard all stop words, as well as single letters. Construct a set containing the first letter of each remaining word. In addition, create a range for the number of remaining words, plus and minus one third.
-    **Year of publication:** Create a range covering the given year plus and minus one.

-   **Journal name:** Discard all stop words. Construct a set containing the first capital letter from each remaining word.
-   **Publisher name / location:** Discard all stop words. Construct a set containing the first capital letter from each remaining word.
-   **Volume / issue numbers:** Create a range covering the given volume or issue number plus and minus one.
-   **Pagination:** Use the given page range.

In addition to the attributes, RefConcile includes the **type of work** a reference refers to in the blocking key, distinguishing the following reference types: *journal article*, *journal volume*, *book chapter*, *book*, *proceedings paper*, *proceedings volume*, and *online resource*. The type of work is determined based on which attributes are present.

To optimize runtime, we propose persisting the blocking keys in a database. Modern relational database engines keep the computational effort for retrieving a block of references largely independent of the number of references in the data set.

## 4.2    Matching

RefConcile's matching step uses a decision tree to classify reference pairs as duplicates or non-duplicates, plus several hand crafted kill rules. The latter are motivated by phenomena we observed during our investigation of the RefBank data set. For instance, they prevent matching references to individual volumes of multi-part works. Such references tend to differ only in the part number, which often is included in the title. Conceptually, the kill rules are nodes we manually added to the otherwise learned decision tree. To train the decision tree, we labeled a sampled set of training examples, computed all the similarity measures described in Section 2.1 for each pair of references, and then used Weka [14] for the learning. In live deployment, however, it would be inefficient to compute all the pair-wise similarity measures for all references in a block, or even only for each pair comprising the newly added reference that triggers the matching. We therefore hard-coded the learned decision tree and implemented it to compute the similarity measures on the fly, i.e., right before their first use. If a decision is reached far up the tree, this saves computation of similarity values that would have been used only further down the tree. Furthermore, to avoid overfitting to the training set, we slightly relaxed the decision thresholds.

## 4.3    Duplicate Reconciliation

Once a group of duplicate bibliographic references has been recognized, RefConcile links them together and selects a common representative for the group.

If there are three or more duplicates in the group, this works by selecting the attribute values that are most frequent across the duplicate group, individually for each attribute. This yields a reconciled value for each attribute. The rationale is that the common representative reference should have the most agreed-upon value for each attribute, and that typographical errors are sufficiently random not to become the majority value. If there is a reference in the group all of whose attributes have the reconciled values, it becomes the representative. If there is no such reference,

RefConcile generates it by inserting the reconciled values into a template, and then adds it to the data set. While this adds a further duplicate record, it is the only way of providing a representative reference. Example 2 illustrates this.

Suppose RefConcile found the following threesome of duplicates (errors bold):

Thor, AU, Cond, SE (2012) Bibliographi**al** duplicates. Journal of TPDL **9**: 8-1**6**

Thor, AU, Cor**ld**, SE. Bibliographic duplicates. Journal of T**B**DL 8: 8-15, 201**3**

Tho**p**, AU, Cond, SE. Bibliographic duplicates. Journal of TPDL 8 (2012): **9**-15

The element wise majority vote yields the correct reference:

Thor, AU, Cond, SE. Bibliographic duplicates. Journal of TPDL 8 (2012): 8-15

**Example 2.** Reconciling three references that all contain minor errors

For groups of two duplicates, majority voting is not applicable. As a heuristic, RefConcile then selects the more recently added reference as the representative. The rationale is that the more recent duplicate might well be a correction of the other one.

## 5    Evaluation

This section reports on a thorough evaluation of the RefConcile algorithm based on the RefBank data set, a real-world community contributed collection of bibliographic references. We can only address the most interesting aspects here for lack of space.

**The RefBank Data Set.** RefBank is an open, multi-node platform collecting bibliographic references from various sources, including community contribution. Apart from storing the same reference string (in a character-by-character sense) only once, RefBank does not implement any duplicate detection or reconciliation measures. The data set grows constantly, as new references are added. At the time of our experiments, the data set comprised over 160,000 individual references. An atomized version was available for about 150,000 of them, and they are our test set.

**Experimental Setup.** To simulate a continuously growing reference data set, we start our experiments with an empty data set and then add the references one by one. Each addition of a reference prompts RefConcile to search for duplicates, and to reconcile any ones found. The experiments were conducted on a 4 x 2.0MHz 64-bit machine with 8GB of main memory running Ubuntu Linux 2.6.22, PostgreSQL 9.1, and a JVM 1.6 from Sun/Oracle.

**Experimental Results.** Table 1 displays our results. The high precision of 99.7% indicates that RefConcile rarely ever wrongfully labels a pair of references a duplicate. The recall of 91.9% means that RefConcile correctly finds 9 out of 10 duplicate relations. This corresponds to 95.6% in f-measure.

Even with around 150.000 references in the database, the fuzzy blocking returns only 9.14 candidate duplicates per reference on average. This means that the matching has fewer than 10 possible duplicates to deal with, underlining the scalability of RefConcile. Implemented on top of a relational database, the incremental blocking takes only 5.9 microseconds for each pair wise reference comparison. Matching takes an average 6.4 milliseconds for each pair of references.

**Table 1.** Evaluation results

| Precision / Recall / F-measure | 99.7% / 91.9% / **95.6%** |
|---|---|
| Avg. Number of Candidates | 9.14 |
| Avg. Time for Candidate Retrieval | 5.9 μs / reference, 47.8 ms / candidate found |
| Avg. Time for Candidate Assessment | 6.4 ms / candidate, 216.8 ms / duplicate found |

To assess the quality of automated references reconciliation, we manually inspected the generated cluster representatives, We found that only some 5-10% contained errors. This is in line with our expectations.

# 6     Conclusions

Relying on community contribution is popular to compile comprehensive bibliographies. Experience with ZooBank [24] shows that embedding duplicate detection procedures in the data input process that require intellectual input alienates users. To foster contribution, other platforms completely waive respective measures. This in turn affects data quality.

To ensure data quality automatically as contributors add new references, we have proposed a duplicate detection and reconciliation technique named RefConcile. Our evaluation on a real-world data set shows that it works well in practice: It finds and reconciles duplicate references highly accurately, and it scales very well.

**Acknowledgements.** This research has received funding from the Seventh Framework Programme of the European Union (FP7/2007-2013) under grant agreement no 261532 (ViBRANT – Virtual Biodiversity Research and Access Network for Taxonomy). The RefConcile algorithm is in productive use as part of RefBank[1], the platform of ViBRANT to build its Bibliography of Life.

# References

1. Beall, J.: Measuring duplicate metadata records in library databases. Library Hi Tech News 27, 10–12 (2012), doi:10.1108/07419051011110595
2. Blakely, T., Salmond, C.: Probabilistic record linkage and a method to calculate the positive predictive value. Int. J. Epidem. 31, 1246–1252 (2002), doi:10.1093/ije/31.6.1246
3. CalTech, http://library.3.edu/reference/abbreviations/
4. Catalogue of Life, http://www.catalogueoflife.org/
5. Cortez, E., da Silva, A.S., et al.: Fluxcim: flexible unsupervised extraction of citation metadata. In: Proceedings of JCDL 2007, Vancouver, BC, Canada (2007)
6. Davies, K.: Reference accuracy in library and information science journals. Aslib Proceedings 64(4), 373–387 (2012)
7. Defays, D.: An efficient algorithm for a complete link method. The Computer Journal (British Computer Society) 20(4), 364–366 (1977)

---

[1] RefBank: http://plazi.cs.umb.edu/RefBank/

8. Domingos, P., Hulten, G.: A general method for scaling up machine learning algorithms and its application to clustering. In: Proc. Intern. Workshop on Machine Learning (2001)
9. Draisbach, U., Naumann, F.: A comparison and generalization of blocking and windowing algorithms for duplicate detection. In: Proc. QDB Workshop at VLDB (2009)
10. Geer, D.: Reducing the storage burden via data deduplication. Computer 41, 15–17 (2008)
11. Giles, C.L., Councill, I., Kan, M.-Y.: ParsCit: an open-source CRF reference string parsing package. In: Proceedings of LREC 2008, Marrakech, Morocco (2008)
12. Guha, S., Mishra, N., Motwani, R., O'Callaghan, L.: Clustering data streams. In: Proc. Symp. on Foundations of Computer Science 2000, pp. 359–366 (2000)
13. Han, J., Kamber, M.: Data Mining: Concepts and Techniques. Morgan Kaufmann (2001) ISBN 1-55860-489-8
14. Holmes, G., Donkin, A., Witten, I.H.: Weka: A machine learning workbench. In: Proc. AUS NZ Conf. Intel. Inf. Syst., Brisbane, Australia (1994)
15. ISSN: http://www.issn.org/2-22661-LTWA-online.php
16. Jaro, M.A.: Advances in record linkage methodology as applied to the 1985 census of Tampa Florida. Journal of the American Statistical Society 84(406), 414–420 (1989)
17. Jaro, M.A.: Probabilistic linkage of large public health data file. Statistics in Medicine 14(5-7), 491–498 (1995), doi:10.1002/sim.4780140510
18. Jones, K.S.: A statistical interpretation of term specificity and its application in retrieval. Journal of Documentation 28(1), 11–21 (1972), doi:10.1108/eb026526
19. Köpcke, H., Rahm, E.: Training selection for tuning entity matching. In: Proc. Workshop on Quality in Databases and Management of Uncertain Data, pp. 3–12 (2008)
20. Köpcke, H., Rahm, E.: Frameworks for entity matching: A comparison. Data & Knowledge Engineering 69(2), 197–210 (2010), doi:10.1016/j.datak.2009.10.003
21. Köpcke, H., Thor, A., Rahm, E.: Evaluation of entity resolution approaches on real-world match problems. Proceedings of VLDB Endowment 3, 484–493 (2010)
22. Levenshtein, V.I.: Binary codes capable of correcting deletions, insertions, and reversals. Soviet Physics Proceedings 10, 707–710 (1966)
23. O'Callaghan, L., et al.: Streaming-data algorithms for high-quality clustering. In: Proc. Inntern. Conf. on Data Engineering (2002)
24. Polaszek, A.: A universal register for animal names. Nature 437(477), 477 (2005), doi:10.1038/437477a
25. PubMed Central, http://www.ncbi.nlm.nih.gov/pmc/
26. Sautter, G., Böhm, K.: Improved Bibliographic Reference Parsing Based on Repeated Patterns. In: Zaphiris, P., Buchanan, G., Rasmussen, E., Loizides, F. (eds.) TPDL 2012. LNCS, vol. 7489, pp. 370–382. Springer, Heidelberg (2012)
27. Sautter, G., King, D., Morse, D.: Towards a universal bibliography – the RefBank approach. In: Proc. TDWG 2012, Beijing, China (2012)
28. Thor, A., Rahm, E.: MOMA – a mapping-based object matching system. In: Proc. 3rd Bien. Conf. Innov. Data Syst. Research (CIDR 2007), pp. 247–258 (2007)
29. University of Leeds, http://www.efm.leeds.ac.uk/~mark/ISIabbr/
30. Winkler, W.E.: String Comparator Metrics and Enhanced Decision Rules in the Fellegi-Sunter Model of Record Linkage. In: Proc. Sect. Surv. Res. Methods (ASA), pp. 354–359 (1990)
31. Cao, F., Ester, M., Qian, W., Zhou, A.: Density-based clustering over an evolving data stream with noise. In: Proc. Intern. Conf. Data Mining, pp. 328–339 (2006)
32. Wang, H., Yu, Y., Wang, Q., Wan, Y.: A density-based clustering structure mining algorithm for data streams. In: Proc. Intern. Workshop Big Data, pp. 69–76 (2012)

# Automatic Extraction of Event Information from Newspaper Articles and Web Pages

Hidetsugu Nanba, Ryuta Saito, Aya Ishino, and Toshiyuki Takezawa

Hiroshima City University, Graduate School of Information Sciences,
3-4-1, Ozukahigashi, Asaminamiku, Hiroshima 731-3194 Japan

**Abstract.** In this paper, we propose a method for extracting travel-related event information, such as an event name or a schedule from automatically identified newspaper articles, in which particular events are mentioned. We analyze news corpora using our method, extracting venue names from them. We then find web pages that refer to event schedules for these venues. To confirm the effectiveness of our method, we conducted several experiments. From the experimental results, we obtained a precision of 91.5% and a recall of 75.9% for the automatic extraction of event information from news articles, and a precision of 90.8% and a recall of 52.8% for the automatic identification of event-related web pages.

**Keywords:** newspaper article, web page, event, travel.

## 1 Introduction

Information about events that are scheduled to take place at the travel destination is crucial when planning a trip. Travel guidebooks and portal sites provided by tour companies and government tourist offices are useful for checking on well-known events, such as festivals. However, it is costly and time consuming to compile information about the full range of events for all tourist spots manually and to keep this data up-to-date. We have therefore investigated the automatic compilation of event information.

We use newspaper articles and web pages as information sources for the extraction of event information. In general, we can obtain information about popular or traditional events through newspaper articles. However, only a small percentage of the full range of travel-related events appears in newspaper articles. Therefore, we propose a method to collect travel-related event information from both newspaper articles and web pages. Generally, public venues, such as museums or exhibition halls, have their own web sites, which contain web pages that give schedules for events at these venues (we call them "event web pages"). We therefore extract venue names, where public events often occur from news corpora, and then identify event web pages using this list. Using this procedure, we can expect to obtain much travel-related event information rapidly.

The remainder of this paper is organized as follows. Section 2 describes related work. Section 3 describes our method. To investigate the effectiveness of our

S.R. Urs, J.-C. Na, and G. Buchanan (Eds.): ICADL 2013, LNCS 8279, pp. 171–175, 2013.
© Springer International Publishing Switzerland 2013

method, we conducted experiments, with Section 4 reporting the results. We present some conclusions in Section 5.

## 2   Related Work

In previous work on extracting event information from texts, Schneider [2] and Issertial et al. [1] proposed a method for extracting academic event information, such as schedules, conference locations, and conference names using "Call for Papers" documents as information sources. In our work, we use news corpora and web pages as our information sources.

## 3   Construction of the Event-Retrieval System

We obtain the event information in two steps: (1) extraction of event information from newspaper articles and (2) identification of event web pages from the web. We describe these two steps in Sections 3.1 and 3.2, respectively.

### 3.1   Extraction of Event Information from Newspaper Articles

We use information extraction based on machine learning to extract event information from event news articles. First, we define the tags used:

- **EVENT** tag includes an event name;
- **DATE** tag includes a schedule for an event;
- **ADDRESS** tag includes an address of a venue;
- **LOCATION** tag includes a venue name.

We formulate the identification of the class of each word in a given sentence by using machine learning. We opted for the CRF machine-learning method, where the features and tags used are as follows: (1) $k$ features occur before a target word and (2) $k$ features follow a target word. We use the value $k = 3$, which was determined via a pilot study. We use the following features for machine learning. (We use MeCab as a Japanese morphological analysis tool to identify the part of speech):

- a word;
- its part of speech;
- whether the word is a quotation mark;
- whether the word is frequently used in the event names, such as "live", "festival", or "fair";
- whether the word is frequently used in the names of venues, such as "gallery", "stage", "building", or "hot spring";
- whether the word is a numerical descriptor;
- whether the word is frequently used in the address, such as "prefecture" or "city";
- whether the word is frequently used in schedules, such as "date", "schedule", or "tomorrow".

## 3.2   Identification of Event Web Pages

For the identification of event web pages, we first search web pages using pairs comprising a venue name[1] and the word "ibento" (event) as the query. We next identify event web pages using cue words and unnecessary words as features for machine learning. Examples of the use cue phrases and unnecessary words are:

- whether the web page includes cue words, such as "schedule", "date", "participation fee", "event", "information", or "fair";
- whether the web page includes unnecessary words, such as "youtube", "blog", "twitter", "livedoor", "facebook", "wikipedia", or "mapple";
- whether the web page's URL includes cue words, such as "event" or "schedule";
- whether the URL includes unnecessary words, such as "youtube" or "facebook";
- whether the web page includes a table.

# 4   Experiments

We conducted two experiments to test (1) the extraction of event information from news articles, and (2) the identification of event web pages.

## 4.1   Extraction of Event Information from News Articles

Data Sets and Experimental Settings

We used 416 event newspaper articles with four kinds of tags, namely EVENT, DATA, ADDRESS, and LOCATION, annotated manually.

Machine Learning and Evaluation Measures

We employed CRF as our machine learning technique, and performed a four-fold cross-validation test. As a baseline method, we used words and their parts of speech as features for machine learning. As evaluation measures, we again used recall, precision, and F-measure.

Experimental Results

We show the experimental results in Table 1. To compare with the performance of our method, we calculated scores of recall, precision, and F-measure, when extracting the whole articles as event news articles.

As shown in the table, our method improved the recall score by more than 0.1 without impairing the precision score. However, our method was unable to extract event information in 24.1% of cases, caused mainly by the lack of linguistic clues. Table 2 shows examples of errors when our method failed. In the EVENT error, "HARA Asao ten" (Hara Asao exhibit) should have been extracted, but our method failed, because no cue words, such as quotation marks or particles (topic marker), except for "ten" (exhibit) appear in this context. In the ADDRESS error, there are no linguistic clues around the location name "Umeda", which should have been extracted as an address.

---

[1] We obtained 30,000 venue names from news corpora automatically using the method of Section 3.1.

**Table 1.** Evaluation results for the extraction of event information from news articles

|  | Baseline | | | Our method | | |
|---|---|---|---|---|---|---|
|  | Precision | Recall | F-measure | Precision | Recall | F-measure |
| EVENT | 0.899 | 0.510 | 0.651 | 0.912 | 0.673 | 0.774 |
| DATE | 0.965 | 0.799 | 0.874 | 0.968 | 0.855 | 0.908 |
| ADDRESS | 0.910 | 0.769 | 0.833 | 0.908 | 0.816 | 0.860 |
| LOCATION | 0.896 | 0.547 | 0.679 | 0.873 | 0.693 | 0.773 |
| Average | 0.918 | 0.656 | 0.765 | 0.915 | 0.759 | 0.830 |

**Table 2.** Examples of errors in the extraction of event information from event articles

| EVENT error | kajin, HARA Asao ten deha... |
|---|---|
|  | (at the poet HARA Asao exhibit...) |
| ADDRESS error | 2/1 made, Daimaru * Umeda no 11 F |
|  | (on the 11th floor of Daimaru (department store) * Umeda, |
|  | until Feb. 1.) |

## 4.2   Identification of Event Web Pages

### Data Sets and Experimental Settings

We used 1,022 web pages containing the word "ibento" (event) for our experiment. Of these, 264 web pages were identified manually as event web pages.

### Machine Learning and Evaluation Measures

We performed a four-fold cross-validation test, again using TinySVM software as the machine-learning package. We again used recall, precision, and F-measure as evaluation measures.

### Experimental Results

We show the experimental results in Table 3. As baseline results to compare with those of our method, we calculated scores for recall, precision, and F-measure, when extracting all pages as event web pages.

Our method achieved the high precision score of 0.824, while the recall score remained at 0.522. In many of the event web pages that our method could not identify, event schedules were written in a tabular form. Although our method does check for web page containing tables, as one of the features for machine learning, these pages did not contain additional linguistic cues, which our method requires for proper identification.

**Table 3.** Evaluation results for identification of event web pages

| Methods | Precision | Recall | F-measure |
|---|---|---|---|
| Baseline | 0.258 | 1.000 | 0.410 |
| Our method | 0.824 | 0.522 | 0.639 |

# 5   Conclusions

We have proposed a method for extracting event information from both news-paper articles and event web pages. In the extraction of event information from news articles, we obtained a precision of 91.5% and a recall of 75.9%. For the identification of event web pages, we obtained a precision of 90.8% and a recall of 52.8%. Our method outperformed a baseline method, thereby confirming the effectiveness of our method.

# References

1. Issertial, L., Tsuji, H.: Information Extraction and Ontology Model for a 'Call for Paper' Manager. In: Proceedings of iiWAS 2011, pp. 539–542 (2011)
2. Schneider, K.-M.: An Evaluation of Layout Features for Information Extraction from Calls for Papers. In: LWA 2005, pp. 111–115 (2005)

# PuntTable: A Flexible Repository System for Digital Library

Chao Lan[1,2], Tianyu Meng[3], Yong Zhang[2], and Chunxiao Xing[2]

[1] Department of Computer Science and Technology
[2] Research Institute of Information Technology
Tsinghua University, Beijing 100084, China
[3] Department of Computer Science
Iowa State University, Ames, IA, USA
lanc11@mails.tsinghua.edu.cn, tmeng@iastate.edu
{zhangyong05,xingcx}@tsinghua.edu.cn

**Abstract.** Digital libraries (DLs) provide various contents and services which become increasingly comprehensive and customizable. This has placed growing pressure on the repository systems of DLs. Common repository tools, such as Fedora and DSpace, have been widely deployed in DL systems. However, those repository tools often use traditional relational database management systems plus file systems as the storage layer, which cannot provide additional functionality. Complex services, such as user-generated content, recommendations, social networks services, etc. generate complex and heavy workloads on structured, semi-structured, and unstructured data. Those common repositories are not designed to handle such workloads, so the pressures are transferred to upper application layers. In this paper, we analyze the data structures and workloads of services provided by modern DLs and propose a data-storage strategy model. Based on this model, we describe the development of PuntTable, a flexible repository system for DLs. By integrating various data stores and making it extensible and flexible, PuntTable can easily support complex content and services. We deploy PuntTable to the Digital Library on History of Science & Technology in China, and evaluate the data-storage strategy and PuntTable.

**Keywords:** Digital Library, Repository System, Architecture, Storage Service.

Digital libraries (DLs) have been continuously developed since the early 90s. The driving force for this development lies in the increased demand for digital content and growing use of associated digital services. In terms of content, DLs have evolved from managing simple documents, images, and audio and video files to managing huge volumes of complex objects described by complex content models [1]. From the service point of view, DLs have grown from providing basic services such as content preservation, management, browsing, searching, and discovery to providing more advanced services, including automated methods for content, annotation, recommendation system in digital, trends analysis and support, user

S.R. Urs, J.-C. Na, and G. Buchanan (Eds.): ICADL 2013, LNCS 8279, pp. 176–177, 2013.

generated content support, and social network analysis and support. All of these requirements are driving the digital library systems (DLSs) that support DLs to become larger and more complex.

Compared to the rapid growth in the volume of content, as well as the variety and complexity of services, the development of repository tools has been relatively slow. The requirements of content and services to be supported now are far more complicated than when the common repository tools were developed. Currently, systems typically describe the metadata according to some specifications and store this information in the filesystem with the content data. Such a design simplifies the implementation of the repository, but adds additional burden to the upper layers that provide services relaying the structural information of the metadata. The upper layers must decipher the metadata by writing a custom parser to determine the structures before using them. Such issues become serious when the sources of content in modern DLs are distributed and the metadata are heterogeneous, especially when supporting user-generated content (UGC). The situation becomes even more complex when the repository is shared by multiple applications, where each application must respect common parsing systems. When the structure of the metadata changes, or new structures are added, all of the upper layers must be revised to accommodate the changes. In addition, new services provided by DLs, such as the social network analysis, trend analysis and recommendation, add additional online analytical processing (OLAP) workloads, which are typically read-intensive. The common repository tools are not optimized for such workloads, and systems must be manually modified to improve the support for such services. If the repository were to provide optimization for such workloads, it would better support services for both users and administrators.

We summarize and compare the properties of row-oriented, column-oriented, and NoSQL databases. Then we analyze the workloads of modern DLs and propose a data-storage model that selects different data storage schemes for different workloads. We go on to propose a new data middleware called PuntTable, which is a flexible digital object repository designed to provide optimized data management to support the different workloads of various content and services required by modern DLs. We apply PuntTable to the Digital Library on History of Science & Technology in China (DLHSTC) DL to solve issues related to the integrated management of heterogeneous data. We conducted three case studies to test it under various workloads.

**Acknowledgement.** This work is supported by the History of Science & Technology in China (DLHSTC), China Academic Library & Information System (CALIS) project.

# Reference

1. Gonçalves, M.A., Fox, E.A., Watson, L.T., Kipp, N.A.: Streams, structures, spaces, scenarios, societies (5s): A formal model for digital libraries. ACM Trans. Inf. Syst. 22(2), 270–312 (2004)

# Scholarly Communication through Social Networks: A Study

Samar Iqbal Bakhshi[1] and Sridhar Gutam[2]

[1] National Law University, New Delhi 110078
samar26s@gmail.com
[2] Central Institute for Subtropical Horticulture, Lucknow 226101
gutam2000@gmail.com

**Abstract.** This paper attempts to look at how the scholarly communications are taking place through the various social media and community networks across the disciplines. Now the social and community networks had become an essential part of our lives and they have now grown beyond from a channel of communication with family and friends to a professional and scholarly communication channels. The most popular scholarly networks have now millions of academic and research articles. The technological features of these networks enable interoperability, openness and thus can be shared with other networks using various sharing applications. This paper presents an insight of the scholarly communications through social networks.

**Keywords:** Social Networking, Community Networks, Scholarly Communication, ResearchGate, Facebook, Social Network Analysis.

## 1 Introduction

There is a sea change in the landscape of academic and research interactions and innovative ways of scholarly communications is taking place. Blogs, Wikis, social networking sites etc. are emerging as new platforms for this purpose. Now the scholars (~30-34 lakhs) are using social networks like ResearchGate for their research and communications and to establish linkages with each other. An overview of these scholarly networks is presented in Research Front by Deepthi Varughese and Biji C L (2013). Apart from these, Facebook and Twitter are also playing an important role in the digital scholarship. At this backdrop, a desktop study was carried out to discover the social network communities and their engagement with the digital networks.

## 2 Methodology

Available data from the ResearchGate community was gathered, Facebook was searched for discipline wise groups and monitoring of blogs and twitter was carried out using Melwater's IceRocket and Twazzup in the month of during June-July 2013.

S.R. Urs, J.-C. Na, and G. Buchanan (Eds.): ICADL 2013, LNCS 8279, pp. 178–179, 2013.
© Springer International Publishing Switzerland 2013

# 3     Results and Discussion

The discipline wise data about membership and publications on ResearchGate shows that out of the 24 major disciplines, the highest membership and publications were in the Biology followed by Medicine, Chemistry and Engineering. The same were searched for mentions in blog posts, TPH and Facebook groups (Table 1). The results revealed that though the Biology was having highest membership and publications, the hashtag/keyword 'Biology' was mentioned very less in the blog posts and in tweets. However, on Facebook, all the four popular disciplines were having equal number of groups. The study of Gruzd et. al. (2012) revealed that social media is gaining importance and more researchers are now using it to keep updated in their research areas and they like to comment on blogs.

**Table 1.** Discipline mentions in Blog Posts and Tweets Per Hour (TPH)   between 12:00 PM and 1:00 PM (IST) on 3.07.2013

| Discipline | Membership in ResearchGate | Publications in ResearchGate | Blog Mention | TPH | Facebook Groups |
|---|---|---|---|---|---|
| Medicine | 729,350 | 7,973,228 | 58,215 | 1100 | 90 |
| Biology | 607,436 | 9,183,359 | 15,794 | 365 | 99 |
| Chemistry | 268,882 | 3,894,792 | 23,124 | 392 | 101 |
| Engineering | 285,220 | 2,883,917 | 47,942 | 361 | 103 |

# 4     Conclusion

Academicians and researchers are embracing various social networks for communication and also for sharing their research outputs. Therefore, Indian publishers also must integrate social media tools into their publishing channels. The study reveals that most of the scholarly communication is now happening via social networks. A full detailed study with all the disciplines would provide good insights of scholarly communications in the social networks and its impact.

# References

1. Deepthi, V., Biji, C L.: Social Media in Research and Academics. Research Front. CSI Communications (June 2013), http://www.csi-india.org/c/document_library/get_file?uuid=ef6caa61-dc45-4ff0-a5b2-820989d44a08&groupId=10157 (retrieved on July 5, 2013)
2. Gruzd, A., Goertzen, M., Mai, P.: Survey Results Highlights: Trends in Scholarly Communication and Knowledge Dissemination in the Age of Social Media. Social Media Lab Report (Dalhousie University, Halifax, NS, Canada) (2012)

# The Evolution of Scholarly Digital Library Needs in an International Environment: Social Reference Management Systems and Qatar

Hamed Alhoori[1], Carole Thompson[2], Richard Furuta[1], John Impagliazzo[3], Edward A. Fox[4], Mohammed Samaka[5], and Somaya Al-Maadeed[5]

[1] Dept. of Computer Science and Engineering, Texas A&M University, College Station, USA
{alhoori,furuta}@tamu.edu
[2] Consultant (formerly with Texas A&M University, Qatar)
carolethompson1@gmail.com
[3] Dept. of Computer Science, Emeritus, Hofstra University, Hempstead, New York, USA
john.impagliazzo@hofstra.edu
[4] Dept. of Computer Science, Virginia Tech, Blacksburg, Virginia, USA
fox@vt.edu
[5] Dept. of Computer Science and Engineering, Qatar University, Doha, Qatar
{samaka.m,s_alali}@qu.edu.qa

**Abstract.** Qatar has become an active research producer of data, publications, and other scholarly works. We studied the evolving scholarly activities and needs of researchers in this relatively new research environment, and compared them with previous findings from a well-established environment in the United States. The initial findings shed some light on the similarities and differences in information seeking behavior and information needs. We also highlighted some requirements and solutions appropriate for future international digital libraries and social reference management systems.

**Keywords:** Scholarly communication, Digital libraries, Information seeking, Information needs, Social media, Academic social networks, User studies.

Social media tools have been widely used in academia and research environments to support the scholarly needs of researchers. Social network sites are becoming tailored to scientists' needs. Over the past decade, social reference management systems such as CiteULike, Zotero, and Mendeley have emerged and evolved, and currently millions of researchers are using them.

A number of researchers have conducted studies to learn about other researchers' scholarly activities and their needs. Most of these studies were limited to a single university campus, a language, or a culture. Moreover, they did not investigate the effects of academic social media sites. Accordingly, Alhoori and Furuta [1] conducted a study in the United States to understand better the scholarly activities of researchers and found that academic social media sites have a significant effect on researchers.

With the proliferation of publications in Qatar along with numerous social media tools, researchers' scholarly activities and needs have little clarity. This study aims to

S.R. Urs, J.-C. Na, and G. Buchanan (Eds.): ICADL 2013, LNCS 8279, pp. 180–181, 2013.
© Springer International Publishing Switzerland 2013

fill the gap by providing a better understanding of dynamic international scholarly needs and by contrasting similarities and differences in the United States and Qatar. We conducted in-depth semi-structured interviews with twenty-one faculty members from Qatar University. We found a number of similarities between the researchers from the United States and Qatar who participated. Both groups of researchers used similar scholarly resources, used more than one way to save articles, have taken notes, and collaborated with other researchers; they also used social media tools to save and share research outcomes. Researchers studied in both sites were looking for advanced research tools that could assist them in collecting, summarizing, and analyzing results from scholarly articles. A number of participants from both studies avoided organizing their articles despite the fact that they usually do not succeed in finding articles they have previously read.

Current academic digital libraries and social reference management systems base themselves on a "one size fits all" approach, even though there are special needs for different disciplines and researchers. In the United States study, 44% of social reference management systems users search for articles within those systems, while none of the Qatar participants search within such systems. None of the participants in Qatar used tags to organize their collections, while 13% of the United States study participants used tags. Publication overload (trying to keep abreast with many publications) affected 64% of the faculty in the United States study while it affected only 19% in the Qatar study. One explanation could be that most participants from Qatar focused on selected journals and conferences while researchers in United States had access to more publications and more multidisciplinary areas. To reduce publication overload, researchers in both sites used recommender systems.

In the future, the project team plans to conduct a quantitative study on a wider group of researchers in Qatar and to investigate the special scholarly needs with regard to different disciplines. The team will use SeerSuite [2] to build different collections. The project team also will explore the use of an academic social media platform with Arabic content. The plan is to investigate ways in which social media could build and affect research cultures in new scholarly environments.

**Acknowledgements.** This work was supported in part by the grant NPRP 4–029–1–007 for the project titled "Establishing a Qatari Arabic-English Digital Library Institute," which is funded by the Qatar National Research Fund (QNRF). The authors also thank the remaining project team members C. Lee Giles, Tarek Kanan, Robert Laws, Susan Lukesh, Asad Nafees, and Myrna Tabet for their support in advancing the project.

# References

1. Alhoori, H., Furuta, R.: Understanding the Dynamic Scholarly Research Needs and Behavior as Applied to Social Reference Management. In: Gradmann, S., Borri, F., Meghini, C., Schuldt, H. (eds.) TPDL 2011. LNCS, vol. 6966, pp. 169–178. Springer, Heidelberg (2011)
2. Teregowda, P.B., Khabsa, M., Councill, I.G., Fernández, R.J.P., Zheng, S., Giles, C.L.: Seer: Developing a scalable and reliable application framework for building digital libraries by crawling the web. In: USENIX Conference on Web Application Development (2010)

# Implementation of Social Technologies in Community Networks: From Digital Curation Perspective

Bhojaraju Gunjal[1], Ramesha[2], and Panorea Gaitanou[3]

[1] Department of Library and Information Studies, University of Mysore, Manasagangotri,
Mysore – 570006, India
Bhojaraju.G@gmail.com
[2] Dept. of Library and Information Science, Bangalore University, Jnana Bharathi Campus,
Bangalore – 560056, India
bbramesha@gmail.com
[3] Department of Archive and Library Sciences, Ionian University, Ioannou Theotoki
72, 49100 Corfu, Greece
rgaitanou@gmail.com

**Abstract.** This article gives a brief introduction to the digital curation (DC) concept emphasizing on its role to the Knowledge Management (KM) and Library community users.

**Keywords:** Social technologies, Digital curation, Social Networks, Knowledge Management, Library Management.

## 1 Introduction

The term "digital curation" (DC) was first used in 2001 as a title for a seminar on digital archives, libraries and eScience in which various communities came together to discuss the urgent challenges of improving the long-term management of, and preservation of access to, digital information [1]. Digital curation (DC) is the selection, preservation, maintenance, collection and archiving of digital assets. It establishes, maintains and adds value to repositories of digital data for present and future use. This is often accomplished by archivists, librarians, scientists, historians, and scholars [2]. Some of the most used DC tools are explained in this article.

## 2 Digital Curation: Advantages and Disadvantages

The process of DC presents several advantages: it helps to curate content of similar interest at one place; it can enhance usage among community networks of similar groups; long term preservation of selected digital material is provided; Moreover, as mentioned in [3] reliable re-use of digital material is only possible if materials are curated in such a way that their authenticity and integrity are retained. On the other hand, we can also refer to few disadvantages: user education is very important so that digital material is carefully selected and curated; induction for both curators and

S.R. Urs, J.-C. Na, and G. Buchanan (Eds.): ICADL 2013, LNCS 8279, pp. 182–183, 2013.
© Springer International Publishing Switzerland 2013

end-users is needed for effective use; Moreover, ensuring that digital data remain accessible and reusable over time requires the implementation of proactive, scalable and sustainable preservation strategies that have to be carefully examined and designed.

# 3   Application of DC in Libraries and Knowledge Management Domain

The changing role of libraries to deal with research data and to cope-up with the digital curation activities in libraries has been discussed by several authors in both scholarly and professional literature as explained in [1]. The impact of Social Networking on KM can be seen with a broad look at all the components of KM. All these components - People, Process and Technology along with content are greatly influenced by Social Networking. Social Networking itself is the process whereby technology allows people to collaborate, and so does KM [4].

# 4   Conclusion

Digital curation tools can be used for long term preservation of content and help to reduce the digital obsolescence. With the proper use of social technologies, organization can yield productivity and collaborate effectively among communities. Its applications among library or KM communities can benefit the organization to a large extent. They can surely change the culture of knowledge sharing among the communities by building social aspects.

# References

1. Kim, J., Warga, E., Moen, W.E.: Competencies Required for Digital Curation. The International Journal of Digital Curation 8(1), 66–83 (2013), doi:10.2218/ijdc.v8i1.242
2. Digital curation: From Wikipedia, the free encyclopedia,
   https://en.wikipedia.org/wiki/Digital_curation
   (accessed on June 18, 2013)
3. Pennock, M.: Digital Curation: A Life-Cycle Approach to Managing and Preserving Usable Digital Information. Library & Archives Journal, 1 (2007)
4. Gunjal, B., Gaitanou, P., Yasin, S.: Social Networks and Knowledge Management: An explorative study in Library. In: Boughzala, I., Dudezert, A. (eds.) Knowledge Management 2.0: Organizational Models and Enterprise Strategies, pp. 64–83. IGI Global (2012), doi:10.4018/978-1-61350-195-5.ch004

# Every User His Visualization? User Performance and Preferences of Different Hierarchical Layouts

Tanja Merčun and Maja Žumer

University of Ljubljana, Ljubljana, Slovenia
{tanja.mercun,maja.zumer}@ff.uni-lj.si

**Abstract.** Lately, more studies have started to look into adapting information visualization to individual users. This paper adds to those studies by analysing whether gender, field of study, and experience influenced user performance and preference in four different hierarchical layouts. The results show that, generally, the three factors did not show significant differences between layouts, but also revealed some interesting indications for further studies.

**Keywords:** information visualization, hierarchical technique, usability, users.

## 1 Introduction

Visualization systems have traditionally used a one-size-fits-all approach [1], but with recent interest in user-adaptive visualizations, it is becoming increasingly important to better understand relations between individual's characteristics and the various information visualization techniques [2]. So far we have seen some studies inspecting the effects of cognitive factors, gender, and prior knowledge on visualization effectiveness and perception (overview in [3]). Our work wishes to add to this knowledge and the question whether different techniques or layouts are needed for different types of users by analysing the effect of gender, field of study, and experience on user performance and preferences in four different hierarchical layouts.

## 2 Methodology

Developing a bibliographic information system prototype, 4 different hierarchical information visualization layouts were implemented: radial tree, circlepack (circular treemap), hierarchical indented list, and sunburst. A larger usability study was carried out between December 2011 and January 2012 and a part of the final analysis also investigated possible differences between the four layouts from the viewpoint of participant's characteristics (gender, field of study, and experience in searching fiction). The formal experiment altogether included 120 volunteers from eleven faculties at the University of Ljubljana. Each participant worked with three prototype designs, randomly chosen between 4 hierarchical layouts and a baseline prototype. Each test took about 45 minutes and was recorded and analysed using Morae software. To examine

S.R. Urs, J.-C. Na, and G. Buchanan (Eds.): ICADL 2013, LNCS 8279, pp. 184–185, 2013.
© Springer International Publishing Switzerland 2013

users' performance, each task was timed and evaluated by the observer on several measures: completion success, optimal use of visualization, and observed ease of use. Participant's views on different prototype designs were collected using reaction cards and ranking from least to most favourite design.

## 3    Results and Conclusions

Men and women displayed similar performance and preferences for all four visualizations, the only difference appeared within sunburst layout, where men completed tasks more successfully ($p=.002$) and have also ranked the sunburst layout significantly better. Considering the overall performance by broad study areas "engineering & science" and "humanities, social science & education", the average performance scores and prototype rank again showed no significant differences between the two groups. However, reaction cards (the average number of positive and negative words chosen to describe the layout) indicated that "science & engineering" students were less critical of the radial layout while "humanities & social science" students were more inclined towards hierarchical and circlepack layout. There were also no significant differences between less and more experienced participants within any of the four performance categories. However, it is interesting to observe that according to prototype rankings, more experienced testers favoured the hierarchy design over sunburst ($p=.03$), while participants with less experience strongly preferred the sunburst design ($p=.002$) and have also ranked radial prototype significantly better ($p=.003$) in comparison to the more experienced testers.

Looking at our data we can say that in general, gender, field of study as well as experience did not play a significant role in performance and preference between the four layouts. There are, however, some indications that less experienced searchers, males, and "science & engineering" students (the three factors are to some degree connected) were more inclined towards the two radial designs (radial tree and sunburst), while females, more experienced searchers and humanities & social science students preferred using a more traditional hierarchical layout. To draw final conclusions, however, a more systematic study would be needed to investigate these factors.

## References

1. Steichen, B., Carenini, G., Conati, C.: User-Adaptive Information Visualization – Using Eye Gaze Data to Infer Visualization Tasks and Cognitive Abilities. In: Proceedings of IUI 2013, pp. 317–328. ACM, New York (2013)
2. Toker, D., Conati, C., Carenini, G., Haraty, M.: Towards Adaptive Information Visualization: On the Influence of User Characteristics. In: Masthoff, J., Mobasher, B., Desmarais, M.C., Nkambou, R. (eds.) UMAP 2012. LNCS, vol. 7379, pp. 274–285. Springer, Heidelberg (2012)
3. Chen, C.: Information Visualization: Beyond the Horizon, ch. 6. Empirical Studies of Information Visualization. Springer, Heidelberg (2006)

# Hold, Touch and Read It: Border Interactions in Mobile Reading Environment

Zhenkun Zhou and Jiangqin Wu

College of Computer Science and Technology, Zhejiang University
Hangzhou 310027, China

**Abstract.** With the popularity of mobile devices, more and more people read on their phones or tablets in fragmented time. Screen sizes, handedness and other habit factors make the user interface (UI) and interactions far from satisfying every reader. In this study, we present a capacitive sensor based prototype and some novel interactions. The palm grasp style and finger touch gestures are used to infer user reading intent. The user study shows our system can provide efficient recognition and good usability.

**Keywords:** Mobile reading, Tangible interaction, Human factors.

## 1   Introduction

By sensing user palm and fingers on device borders, the grasp style and finger gestures could be detected and recognized. Some novel interactions are implemented, including implicitly adjusting the UI layout, restoring reading context according to user identify, as well as other finger gesture applications.

## 2   Methodology

### 2.1   Prototype

As shown in Fig.1, a capacitive sensor based prototype consists of a plastic back case, an Arduino circuit board and 40 wire-connected double-layer cooper tape sensors. There are 17 sensors on both left and right borders, and 6 on the top (in survey the bottom border was found seldom used). Through a sensor's capacitive variation, we can infer whether it is being touched. With this data,two types of input can be inferred:

- Touch gesture, i.e. finger touches and swipes.
- Grasp pattern, i.e. handedness (single or both hands, left or right hand) and the thumb interaction area (see Fig.1c).

### 2.2   Interactions

With the prototype, some tangible interactions are designed and implemented.

S.R. Urs, J.-C. Na, and G. Buchanan (Eds.): ICADL 2013, LNCS 8279, pp. 186–187, 2013.

**Fig. 1.** a) 40 capacitive sensors (34 on left and right borders, 6 on the top) and wires in the plastic back case senses user grasp and touches. b) The back view of prototype, and an Arduion Mega 2560 circuit board. c) Grasp styles are detected. The red area shows the thumb cover area (see clear color image). d) The user identity is recognized and corresponding reading context could be restored automatically via holding style. The red bars shows the 'touched' sensors.

**UI Optimization.** People with different handedness habits may like to adjust the UI layout to meet their preferences. In survey, users would tend to use only one hand to hold and interact with devices, which requires the main widgets covered by in their thumbs active area. Recognizing the location and length of palm touches could help to achieve this (see Fig.1c).

**Finger Gestures.** Touching and swiping are the most common user input forms on smart phones. There exist 'mistaken touch' problem, because of 'fat fingers', small interactive widgets, self occlusion and rich embedded interactive contents. Through sensor touched status, a template based 2D gesture recognizer adopts a four parameter model to express the gesture and 'translates' the finger actions into commands.

**Wake Up by Grasp.** The screen is one of the core power consumption components. By detecting whether the device is grasped, the app could switch between 'sleep' and 'wake-up' status, in order to save energy and extend its battery life.

**Reading Context Restoring.** Tablet devices may be shared among several people, for example in a family. The various of holding habits (i.e. one or both hands, the holding position) could be used to recognize different users and restore their corresponding reading context automatically. In detail, a classifier calculates the style similarity based on the weighted Manhattan distance and tell current user identity.

## 3   Conclusion

We proposed our prototype and some interactions. The prototype is able to be minimized and used widely in many common devices. A user study involving 15 partici-pants shows it could provide better usability and reading experience. The ongoing study will collect more data from more participants to evaluate system performance in large-term usage.

# SIARD Archive Browser – The Components*

Arif Ur Rahman[1,2], Gabriel David[1,2], and Cristina Ribeiro[1,2]

[1] Departamento de Engenharia Informática–Faculdade de Engenharia,
Universidade do Porto
[2] INESC TEC
Rua Dr. Roberto Frias, 4200-465 Porto, Portugal
{badwanpk,gtd,mcr}@fe.up.pt

**Abstract.** The Software-Independent Archival of Relational Databases (SIARD) project developed a tool known as the "SIARD Suite" for preserving relational databases. The tool converts a relational database to a XML format. This paper presents the components of the SIARD Archive Browser which is a simple to use and platform-independent tool for browsing a SIARD Archive. This may be helpful for users interested in using the software. Moreover, it may be useful for people who want to re-use the code and develop software for browsing a SIARD archive with more functionality.

**Keywords:** SIARD, database dissemination.

## 1 Browser Components

The SIARD Archive Browser[1] is a free, platform-independent and easy to use tool developed in Java. It offers functionality including viewing table data, sorting a table by a column, searching a specific value in a table and joining tables (left join) [1].

The architecture of the SIARD Archive Browser is presented in Figure 1. The SIARD archive is generated by the SIARD Suite. It contains the archived data and metadata. The browser has a very simple user interface for users to retrieve data. The control component includes different parsers for retrieving data from the archive based on some criteria. Users interact with the user interface, the control component mediates the input, converts it to commands for retrieving data from the SIARD archive and processes data before displaying it on screen.

The control component has sub-components which interact with each other to process the data. The sub-components include the following.

- Path: This component manages the file paths in the archive. Different file paths are set including the metadata file path and the table files paths when a user opens an archive for browsing.

---

* This work is supported by FCT grant reference number SFRH/BD/45731/2008.
[1] SIARD Archive Browser can be downloaded from http://goo.gl/RWCUI

S.R. Urs, J.-C. Na, and G. Buchanan (Eds.): ICADL 2013, LNCS 8279, pp. 188–189, 2013.

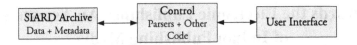

**Fig. 1.** Basic Architecture

- Parsing Metadata File: The `metadata.xml` file is parsed using the XML DOM parser. There are two reasons for using the DOM parser for parsing this file. Firstly, the size of this file is small and it does not require a lot of memory. Secondly, the browsing process requires the extraction of pieces of metadata which can be done easily using the DOM parser.
- Parsing a Table for Displaying: Users may choose to access a table and search the data in it. A SAX XML parser is used for loading all the data in a table which requires lesser memory for the operation than to DOM parser.
- Parsing a table to identify the single matching row: When a base table is displayed on screen, a user may click on any of the foreign keys in the table. Clicking a value in a foreign key column displays the single matching row in the referenced table. A SAX XML parser is used for this functionality which parses the referenced table till the matching row is found.
- Parsing a table to identify all referenced rows: When a table referenced by the base table is displayed on screen, a user may click on the key column used as a reference in the base table. The SAX XML parser for this functionality parses all the base table. The matching rows are identified and displayed on screen.
- Joining tables: The software supports joining (left join) the base table with the tables it references. The result includes all the rows from the base table joining them with the tables it references, one at a time.

These components may be re-used in other software with more functionality for disseminating a SIARD archive. For example they may be re-used to develop a software for browsing SIARD archives stored in a DSpace² repository.

## 2   Future Work

This is a work in progress and in the future support for browsing large objects in an archive will be included. Furthermore, the functionality of joining tables in which users may include some criteria (SQL 'where' clause) will be included.

## Reference

1. Rahman, A.U., David, G., Ribeiro, C.: SIARD Archive Browser. In: Zaphiris, P., Buchanan, G., Rasmussen, E., Loizides, F. (eds.) TPDL 2012. LNCS, vol. 7489, pp. 496–499. Springer, Heidelberg (2012)

---

² http://www.dspace.org/

# Towards the Electronic Publishing: An Assessment of Indian Publishing Media

Vilas G. Jadhav

Gokhale Institute of Politics & Economics, Pune, Maharashtra, India
vilasjadhavg@gmail.com

**Abstract** .his paper describes the contribution of Indian publishing media in e-publishing. It outlines the range of publication such as subject, languages, Indian cities and publishing services into electronic publishing. Publishing portal of PublishersGlobal directory was extracted to find out the existing situation of leading publishers in electronic publishing in India. It is concluded that for e-publishing, publishers needs to make serious commitment to invest and develop the indigenous e-publishing market.

**Keywords:** Electronic Publishing, e-publishing, Indian Publishers.

## 1 Introduction

India has been generating a great deal of scholarly resources in all disciplines. The shift from paper to on-line resources has been a boom today. Publishing media are giving preferences to the on-line resources which are extremely popular and easily available all over the world. This study consists of publishing portals that are providing different type of online information service like e-journals, e-newspapers and e-book publishing companies for authors, illustrators, suppliers, service providers.

## 2 Objectives of the Study

The specific objectives of the present paper are:

1. To identify leading Indian publishers, societies, organizations who are actively involved in electronic publications.
2. To identify prominent subjects, sub-fields in where Indian publishers are more prominent in electronic publications.
3. To identify preferred languages in where the Indian publishers are more prominent in electronic publications.
4. To suggest the ways to encourage the e-publishing activities in commercial as well as non-commercial publishers in India.

## 3 Scope and Limitation

The study is limited to Indian publishers companies that are registered to PublishersGlobal directory up to February 2013.

S.R. Urs, J.-C. Na, and G. Buchanan (Eds.): ICADL 2013, LNCS 8279, pp. 190–192, 2013.

# 4     Methodology

A checklist had been designed and the same was used for collecting pertinent data from the website. In order to gather data PublisherGlobal site from http://www.publishersglobal.com/directory/india/ was accessed and confined the Indian publications industries in all discipline involved in electronic publishing.

# 5     Results and Discussion

## 5.1     Leading Publishers in E-Publishing

There are 246 different publishers who are listed PublisherGlobal portal who are involved in electronic publishing in India. Among these publishers Cambridge University Press India Pvt. Ltd. (CUPIPL) which is a joint venture subsidiary of Cambridge University Press is the leading publisher in India.

## 5.2     Prominent Subjects in E-Publishing

It is found that, Education (19%), Science and Technology (15%), Arts (12%), Business (12%), are the publisher who are more prevalent.

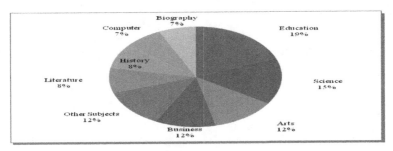

**Fig. 1.** Distribution of Publishers by Subject

## 5.3     Prominent Languages in E-publishing

In -publishing English is more preferred language. Hindi is second preferred language in e-publishing and other languages.

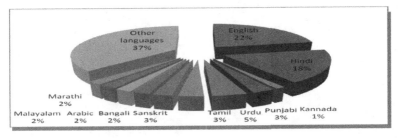

**Fig. 2.** Distribution of Languages in E-Publishing

### 5.4    Major Cities Involved in E-Publishing

New Delhi the capital of India is the hub of publishers where electronic publishing is mostly carried out.

**Fig. 3.** Distribution of Cities in E-Publishing

# 6    Conclusion and Recommendations

In conclusion, it seems that though India is much ahead in technology, but still e-publishing in developmental stage. Publishers need to make serious commitment to invest and develop the indigenous e-publishing market.

# Novel Measures for Reciprocal Behavior and Equivalence in Signed Networks

Muinulla Shariff[1], Mandar R. Mutalikdesai[2], Kourosh Malekafzali[1], Shoaib Najeeb Arayilakath[3], Vinay Sudhakaran[3], and Muneer Altaf[3]

[1] International School of Information Management, University of Mysore
[2] DataWeave Software Pvt. Ltd., Bangalore
mandar@dataweave.in
[3] Siemens Technology and Services Pvt. Ltd., Bangalore

**Abstract.** Signed Networks allow explicit show of trust/distrust relationships between actors. In this poster, we provide novel measures for analyzing the following phenomena in signed networks: (i) reciprocal behavior between pairs of actors in terms of trusting/distrusting each other, and (ii) equivalence of actors in terms of their patterns of trusting/distrusting other actors.

**Keywords:** signed social networks, reciprocal behavior, equivalence.

## 1 Introduction

A signed social network is characterized by the existence of two types of directed relationships between actors, viz. *trust* and *distrust*. In this poster, we attempt to model the following in a signed network: (i) reciprocal behavior between actors, and (ii) equivalence between actors.

The *reciprocity* of nodes in a network refers to their tendency to reciprocate the connections that they receive. While reciprocal behavior is well-studied in the domain of unsigned networks (c.f. [1]), this know-how is not sufficient for signed networks due to the presence of "positive" (i.e. trust) as well as "negative" (i.e. distrust) relationships in the network. We therefore propose novel measures for modeling reciprocal behavior in signed networks, namely *Positive Reciprocity, Negative Reciprocity, Positive Anti-reciprocity*, and *Negative Anti-reciprocity*. This work has applications in (i) the design of reliable messaging routes for information dissemination, (ii) inferring the interaction patterns of actors, which might give insights into phenomena like entrenchment, and (iii) detecting the formation of implicit communities.

Two nodes in a network are said to be *structurally equivalent* if they connect to the same set of nodes. Similarly, two nodes are said to be *regularly equivalent* if they connect to the same *classes* of nodes (c.f. [2]). However, in signed networks, a question arises as to the nature of the connection–trust or distrust. We therefore describe novel measures for structural equivalence and regular equivalence between actors in signed networks. We define both these types of equivalence

S.R. Urs, J.-C. Na, and G. Buchanan (Eds.): ICADL 2013, LNCS 8279, pp. 193–194, 2013.

separately for trust relationships and distrust relationships. Further, we define the notion of *Regular Anti-equivalence* to model a pair of nodes that display contrasting behaviors in trusting or distrusting other nodes. Applications of this work include: (i) efficient in-memory representation and storage compression of trust/distrust relationships for analytics, and (ii) inferring "similar" actors for targeted information dissemination.

## 2    Novel Measures for Reciprocity in Signed Networks

We define *Positive Reciprocity* as having occurred when a nodes trusts another node $A$, and receives trust from $A$ in return. *Negative Reciprocity* is said to have occurred when a node distrusts another node $A$, and receives distrust from $A$ in return. *Positive Anti-reciprocity* is said to have occurred when a node trusts another node $A$, but receives distrust from $A$ in return. *Negative Anti-reciprocity* is said to have occurred when a node distrusts another node $A$, but receives trust from $A$ in return. For measuring the extent of these four types of reciprocities in a signed network, we define the following four indexes for a given node $A$: (i) *Positive Reciprocity Index*, (ii) *Negative Reciprocity Index*, (iii) *Positive Anti-reciprocity Index*, and (iv) *Negative Anti-reciprocity Index*. These indexes are given by $PRI(A) = \frac{|I_T(A) \cap O_T(A)|}{|O_T(A)|}$, $NRI(A) = \frac{|I_D(A) \cap O_D(A)|}{|O_D(A)|}$, $PAI(A) = \frac{|I_D(A) \cap O_T(A)|}{|O_T(A)|}$, and $NAI(A) = \frac{|I_T(A) \cap O_D(A)|}{|O_D(A)|}$, respectively. Here, $I_T(A)$, $O_T(A)$, $I_D(A)$, and $O_D(A)$ stand for the set of nodes that: (i) trust $A$, (ii) $A$ trusts, (iii) distrust $A$, and (iv) $A$ distrusts, respectively.

## 3    Novel Measures for Equivalence in Signed Networks

We define two nodes to be *Structurally Trust Equivalent* if they trust the same set of nodes. Similarly, we define two nodes to be *Structurally Distrust Equivalent* if they distrust the same set of nodes. Given a set of classes into which all the nodes can be categorized, we define a *trust regularity vector* $\mathbf{t}_A$ for each node $A$ such that $|\mathbf{t}_A| = $ no. of classes defined, and $\mathbf{t}_A[i]$ represents the probability that $A$ trusts a node belonging to class $i$. Similarly, we define a *distrust regularity vector* $\mathbf{d}_A$ for each node $A$ to represent the probability distribution of $A$ distrusting nodes of various classes. We now define a *Regular Trust Equivalence Index* (RTEI) and a *Regular Distrust Equivalence Index* (RDEI) for a given pair of nodes $A$ and $B$ as: $RTEI(A, B) = $ Pearson_Correlation$(\mathbf{t}_A, \mathbf{t}_B)$, and $RDEI(A, B) = $ Pearson_Correlation$(\mathbf{d}_A, \mathbf{d}_B)$. If the RTEI/RDEI tends towards $+1$, we infer the extent to which $A$ and $B$ are regularly trust/distrust equivalent. If the RTEI/RDEI tends towards $-1$, we infer the extent of their regular trust/distrust *anti-equivalence*.

## References

1. Garlaschelli, D., Loffredo, M.: Patterns of link reciprocity in directed networks. Physical Review Letters 93(26), 268701 (2004)
2. Hanneman, R., Riddle, M.: Introduction to social network methods (2005)

# Designing and Engineering the Digital Library Ontology

Son Hoang Nguyen[1] and Gobinda G. Chowdhury [2]

[1] Library and Information Center, Vietnam National University, Hanoi
[2] Department of Mathematics & Information Sciences, Northumbria
University, Newcastle, UK
son.nh@vnu.edu.vn,
gobinda.chowdhury@northumbria.ac.uk

**Abstract.** The paper reported method for designing and engineering digital
library domain ontology. Based on the digital library knowledge map, Protégé
software was used for creating the main components of the digital library
ontology, viz. individuals, properties and classes, etc. that can be visually seen
as a knowledge map of digital library research

**Keywords:** Digital Library Ontology, Domain Mapping.

## 1 Introduction

In earlier research (Nguyen & Chowdhury, 2013), the core topics and subtopics of
digital library research were identified in order to build a knowledge map of the
digital library domain. The methodology comprised a four - step research process
and two knowledge organization methods (classification and thesaurus building). A
knowledge map covering 21 core topics and 1015 subtopics of digital library
research was created, providing a systematic overview of digital library research of
the last two decades (1990-2010). In this research, based on the digital library
knowledge map (Nguyen & Chowdhury, 2013, p. 1241–1243), Protégé software
was used for creating the main components of the digital library ontology, viz.
individuals, properties and classes, etc. for building the basic digital library ontology
that can be visually seen as a knowledge map of digital library domain. The
method for designing and engineering the digital library ontology is illustrated in
Figure 1.

| Knowledge Acquisition for the DL Domain: | Modelling the DL Ontology: |
|---|---|
| Applying the four - step research process to capture the DL domain and create the DL knowledge map ( with classification and thesaurus building methods) | Using Protégé to create the DL ontology (visualizing the DL domain) |

**Fig. 1.** Method for designing and engineering digital library domain ontology

S.R. Urs, J.-C. Na, and G. Buchanan (Eds.): ICADL 2013, LNCS 8279, pp. 195–196, 2013.
© Springer International Publishing Switzerland 2013

By using the Protégé, main components of the digital library ontology, viz. Individuals, Properties and Classes were created to build a basic digital library ontology playing as a framework for the full digital library ontology development.

## 2    Main Components of the Digital Library Ontology

**Individuals:** In the digital library ontology, individuals are 21 core topics and 1015 subtopics representing the basic and specific concepts at ground level of the domain. However, some other individuals (member lists), such as: member lists of topic Access (General), viz. *Authors (top 5 authors), Institutions (top 5 institutions), Publication number within (1990-2010) and First year of appearance of the topic* are added for showing some examples of Object Properties and Data Properties for the digital library ontology.

**Properties:** There are two main types of properties representing relationships, viz.

- **Object Properties:** In the digital library ontology, there are 2 Object Properties, viz. *HasPart* and *IsPartOf*   which link and show the relationships between individuals (topics) and 4 Object Properties, viz. *IsAuthorOf, IsInstitutionOf, IsPublicationNumber(1990-2010), IsTheFirstYearOfAppearanceOf* which link and show the relationships between individual members and topics

- **Data Properties:** In the digital library ontology, some datatype properties are used to describe the *NamesOfAuthors, NamesOfInstitutions* and the number *of Publications(1990-2010), FirstYearOfAppearance* of a topic (Individual).

**Classes:** The digital library ontology classes are interpreted as sets that contain individuals with common characteristics. They are described using formal (mathematical) descriptions that state precisely the requirements for membership of the class. The digital library ontology classes may be organised into a superclass-subclass hierarchy, which is also known as a taxonomy. Subclasses specialise (are subsumed by) their superclasses. The superclass-subclass relationships (subsumption relationships) can be computed automatically by a reasoner.

## 3    Conclusion

As a knowledgebase of digital library domain, the digital library ontology can be applied into following areas: a backbone for software agents and semantic web development within the digital library domain; a framework for knowledge management of digital library domain; a platform for managing and conducting digital library research and education.

## Reference

1. Nguyen, H.S., Chowdhury, G.: Interpreting The Knowledge Map Of Digital Library Research (1990-2010). Journal of The American Society for Information Science and Technology 64(6), 1235–1258 (2013), doi:10.1002/asi.22830

# Author Index